Praise for *Spectacle and Diversity:*
Transnational Media and Global Culture

"Lee Artz masterfully links the political economy of contemporary transnational entertainment media to our highly mediated and densely saturated global entertainment culture. Artz reveals that our US-centric categories are woefully inadequate. By looking at multiple regions, Artz addresses vast changes in global entertainment media's division of labor, labor practices, financial, distributive, and consumption patterns. Artz's work revives a 'cultural industry' approach but he shows us how neoliberalism's master frame suffuses the content of new cultural products. Artz's book is an indispensable critical theory of the present; it aligns global media with an emergent global ideology for capital accumulation."

Robert F. Carley, *Texas A&M University, USA*

"A very comprehensive, extremely well-researched evidence-based book for those who are interested to know transnational entertainment media's hidden political economic agenda. With systematically relevant interesting examples, Artz unpacks how TNMCs through film and television present world views, beliefs, and values which support transnational capitalism and blind consumerism. A must read book for all those who consider themselves media scholars and activists."

Bushra Hameedur Rahman, *University of the Punjab, Pakistan*

"There is no one better than Lee Artz to examine the state of global media. In this latest work, Artz provides detailed analysis of media corporations by using the framework of transnational capitalism to challenge our understanding of cultural imperialism. Original, insightful, revealing and necessary reading for anyone interested in globalization, media, culture and political economy."

Jerry Harris, *Director, Global Studies Association of North America*

"It is what it's not. This enigmatic catchphrase may be the dialectic key to understanding the critical perspective that stems from Artz's thorough analytical and empirical uncovering of transnational media corporations. His skilled and informed 'unpacking' of media containers reveals contemporary capitalist development—monopolies that concentrate their market power, political influence and cultural outreach—while our bodies, attention and expectations become the major source of an unprecedented and seemingly infinite, intangible accumulation of surplus value. Media rewrite domination as we click our bodies and souls to exhaustion and unlimited frustration. Whereas multinational corporations already surpassed the boundaries of national frontiers and labor exploitation, it is now capital as a spectacle of delusive diversity that continuously transforms itself into sameness and ludicrosity. Artz helps us understand why our stories 'are still being told by someone else.' That someone is actually the eternal return of the same ghostly spirit of greed, accumulation and mass mediation taken to the extreme of apparent immediacy and passive acceptance of what is, but should not be."

Gilson Schwartz, *University of São Paulo, Brazil*

SPECTACLE AND DIVERSITY

This book shows how transnational media operate in the contemporary world and what their impact is on film, television, and the larger global culture. Where a company is based geographically no longer determines its outreach or output. As media consolidate and partner across national and cultural boundaries, global culture evolves. The new transnational media industry is universal in its operation, function, and social impact. It reflects a shared transnational culture of consumerism, authoritarianism, cultural diversity, and spectacle. From "Wolf Warriors" and "Sanju" to "Valerian: City of 1000 Planets" and "Pokémon," new media combinations challenge old assumptions about cultural imperialism and reflect cross-boundary collaboration as well as boundary-breaking cultural interpretation. Intended for students of global studies and international communication at all levels, the book will appeal to a wide range of readers interested in the way transnational media work and how that shapes our culture.

Lee Artz (Ph.D., University of Iowa), a former machinist and union steelworker, is Professor of Media Studies and Director of the Center for Global Studies at Purdue University Northwest. Artz has published twelve books and fifty book chapters and journal articles on media practices, social change, and democratic communication. He speaks regularly on global media, popular culture, media hegemony, and the political economy of the media.

MEDIA&POWER

David L. Paletz, Series Editor

https://www.routledge.com/Media-and-Power/book-series/MP
Media and Power is a series that publishes work uniting media studies with studies of power. This innovative and original series features books that challenge, even transcend, conventional disciplinary boundaries, construing both media and power in the broadest possible terms. At the same time, books in the series are designed to fit into several different types of college courses in political science, public policy, communication, journalism, media, history, film, sociology, anthropology, and cultural studies. Intended for the scholarly, text, and trade markets, the series should attract authors and inspire and provoke readers.

Published Books

Presidential Road Show
Public Leadership in an Era of Party Polarization and Media Fragmentation
Diane J. Heith

Politics in Popular Movies
Rhetorical Takes on Horror, War, Thriller, and Sci-Fi Films
John S. Nelson

Presidents and the Media
The Communicator in Chief
Stephen E. Frantzich

Star Power:
American Democracy in the Age of the Celebrity Candidate
Lauren Wright

Politics, Journalism, and the Way Things Were
Martin Tolchin

The Political Voices of Generation Z
Laurie L. Rice and Kenneth W. Moffett

Fixing American Politics:
Solutions for the Media Age
Edited by: Roderick P. Hart

Spectacle and Diversity
Transnational Media and Global Culture
Lee Artz

SPECTACLE AND DIVERSITY

Transnational Media and Global Culture

Lee Artz

Routledge
Taylor & Francis Group

NEW YORK AND LONDON

Cover image: © Getty Images

First published 2022
by Routledge
605 Third Avenue, New York, NY 10158

and by Routledge
2 Park Square, Milton Park, Abingdon, Oxon, OX14 4RN

Routledge is an imprint of the Taylor & Francis Group, an informa business

Library of Congress Cataloging-in-Publication Data
Names: Artz, Lee, author.
Title: Spectacle and diversity : transnational media and global culture /
Lee Artz.
Identifiers: LCCN 2021031687 (print) | LCCN 2021031688 (ebook) | ISBN
9780367754198 (hardback) | ISBN 9780367754174 (paperback) | ISBN
9781003162452 (ebook)
Subjects: LCSH: Mass media and culture. | Culture and globalization. | Mass
media and globalization. | Communication, International. | Intercultural
communication.
Classification: LCC P94.6 A8253 2022 (print) | LCC P94.6 (ebook) | DDC
302.23--dc23/eng/20211014
LC record available at https://lccn.loc.gov/2021031687
LC ebook record available at https://lccn.loc.gov/2021031688

ISBN: 978-0-367-75419-8 (hbk)
ISBN: 978-0-367-75417-4 (pbk)
ISBN: 978-1-003-16245-2 (ebk)

DOI: 10.4324/9781003162452

Typeset in Bembo
by KnowledgeWorks Global Ltd.

CONTENTS

TABLES

INTRODUCTION

Transnational Media: The New Order

In one of the best known fantasy movies ever, *The Wizard of Oz* (1939), it turns out that the Wizard doesn't have incredible powers; he's just a carnival con-man. *Vertigo* (1958), *Infernal Affairs* (2002), *Captain America: Civil War* (2016), and many other movies present stories with twists and unexpected developments that render initial appearances misleading. In the so-called post-truth age, it turns out that what often passes as news is also just carnivalesque fantasy. Questions of reality, fantasy, abstraction, concreteness, and reification—to make a feature of something its whole essence—all impact our understanding of culture, values, and beliefs. How media appear on the surface and what they seem to represent culturally are not necessarily indicative of either their structures or practices. So where to begin?

Start with what is. Seems reasonable. Seems simple enough. When you understand the details, it's easier to make sense of the whole picture. But what if "what is" keeps changing? Currently, the changes in media structures and practices are acute, especially when we take in the whole world. Yet to understand media and its impact on our daily lives, we need to closely observe emerging trends, identify actual media structures and practices, and highlight the dominant content in news and entertainment—and avoid accepting easy descriptors of media as geographically, nationally, or culturally as sufficient.

So we begin with unpacking the media containers. Streaming is transforming the entertainment industry. Netflix, Hulu, Apple, Disney+, HBO Max and other commercial streaming services are restructuring film and television production as they adapt to new technologies, new forms of content creation, and most importantly, new distribution structures and practices. Netflix has reordered entertainment into a self-contained empire that controls everything from production to screening (Barnes, 2020). Yet, streaming alone

DOI: 10.4324/9781003162452-01

did not curtail theater attendance—world box office receipts topped a record $425 billion in 2019 and ticket sales in 2019 were highest among mobile users (Rubin, 2020). More significantly, during the coronavirus pandemic more than half the movie theaters in the US closed, with Regal Cinema, the second largest chain, near bankruptcy in 2020 (Ovide, 2020). Still, with online viewers numbering almost 700 million generating $60 billion in revenue (Rubin, 2020), media producers globally are intent on catching up with Netflix, which has over 200 million subscribers, 67 million in the US. Disney purchased 21st Century Fox, in part to expand its library for its new streaming service, and also to gain majority control of Hulu. Telecom giant ATT's Warner Bros. studio simultaneously released all of its 2021 films in theaters and on its new streaming service, HBO Max. Meanwhile in 2021, Bollywood—the $2.5 billion Hindi-language film industry—released 28 big budget films straight to streaming on Netflix, Amazon, and Disney's Hotstar. These releases are only a fraction of the 1800 films produced yearly in India, but the shift toward joint ventures by India filmmakers and global entertainment media is unmistakable; streaming media invested $520 million on India content in 2020 alone (Arora & Singh, 2020). With less control over distribution and with fewer big budget films available; theaters everywhere are likely to close. Is this the end of Hollywood, Bollywood, and big screen movies? Perhaps not. Box office revenues (most of which remit to distributors and theaters anyway) are not the only source of income for movies studios, which reap profits from DVDs, television broadcasts, streaming services, and phone apps (Epstein, 2012).

Whichever media distribution system dominates in the coming years, we can expect all commercial media will feature several common content themes. Whether animation, action adventure, telenovela, science fiction, fantasy, or dramatic comedy it is apparent that television programs, movie franchises, limited mini-series, and made-for-streaming productions emphasize spectacle, self-interested protagonists, a preference for hierarchy, a deference to authority, and fabricated cultural diversity. In the following chapters on regional transnationals, multiple examples illustrate and confirm the conformity of creative style and ideological content across transnational media entertainment. Because "the capitalist mode of production is the primary driving force of media corporations, strategic action, and of the media economy's structural transformations" (Knoche, 2019, p. 287), a global culture amenable to transnational capitalism and culturally diverse consumerism defines global entertainment in the 21st century. The presumed nationality of the media is less important than its ownership and function.

This book unpacks and describes the new structures, production practices, and dominant content of entertainment by TNMCs (transnational media corporations) starting with current conditions and trends to assemble explanations and concepts for a fuller understanding of the realities of global entertainment.

MEDIA MATTERS

Femi Odugbemi, founder of a film festival in Lagos, Nigeria and producer of television soap operas, explained the importance of cinema for a country emerging from colonialism. His remarks apply to media everywhere. This is an edited excerpt that replaced "cinema" with "media," to reflect our screened world:

> "Now: media are political. All media are political. The only way media works for you is if you are in charge. Every colony used media—whether in the documentary or the genre of drama—they used media to what? To alter behavior. They used media to explain that it was civilized use knives and forks to eat, as though the natives were not eating before they came. There was replacement therapy and media was the tool. If you knew a god before they came, media was able to give you a better god, and explain to you that your god was rubbish. If you dressed a certain way before they came, they were able to use media to assure you that what the queen approved as gentlemanly was a suit. Media allowed them to be able to show, to tell, to wow, to entertain—while indoctrinating, Unless you were in control of that your story was at risk. Your story was told by someone else."
>
> (Odugbemi, 2017, p. 13)

Media are still political. Our stories are still being told by someone else—the owners, producers, and distributors of transnational media joint ventures and partnerships that show, tell, and entertain us with self-interested stories, plots, and characters.

As with all investigations, if we are bound by preconceptions or ill-informed expectations, we run the risk of missing what is. Contemporary trends in global media do not neatly fit past theories or conditions. The truth of global media is more material, immediate, more concrete. This book finds that even as what is roils up in flux and constant change, there are still several noticeable trends shifting media norms and disrupting some of the standard explanations of media relations and practices. For example, many theories of globalization, cultural hybridity, and active audiences fail to explain the continued power of national governments and the increasing influence on culture and communication by consolidated commercial media organized cooperatively across national borders.

Some globalization theorists saw a digitally-connected world with unfettered democratic access to new media unconstrained by nation-states or cultural dominance (Friedman, 2006)—ignoring the stranglehold dominance of global corporations. Others envisioned audiences cutting and pasting pieces of dominant Western culture into pastiches of reconstructed cultural hybrids used for diverse and pleasurable purposes, undermining power and control (Fiske, 1989; Bahba, 1994; Lull, 2001; Lash & Lury, 2007). Some theories even suggested that technology might overcome social inequality, as if technology was key to resolving structural and relational obstacles (Castells, 1996).

In contrast, on the cusp of globalization some 50 years ago, other scholars and media activists observed that dominance by US corporate media influenced the cultures of many developing nations. In the 1970s, resistance to US and Western dominance in media entertainment and cultural production accompanied dependency theorist observations (Frank, 1967) and anti-colonial social movement demands for national autonomy. An international effort for democratizing media by more than 100 nations affiliated with the Non-Aligned Movement was codified in 1980 in the MacBride Report to UNESCO, "Many Voices, One World" (2004). Herb Schiller (1976), a leading proponent of the call for a New World Information Order, decried the "cultural imperialism" of dominant media that convinced or pressured elites in other nations to adopt the values and structures of dominating nations. For many scholars, cultural imperialism still appears in the global distribution and dominance of US entertainment.

While cultural imperialism accurately, albeit incompletely, described media relations among nations in the late 20th century, this book argues that capitalism has changed and developed new means for its accumulation of wealth, with parallel changes affecting the global production of news and entertainment. While the global media industry continues to produce and circulate images and information which influence popular beliefs and behaviors, there is diminishing evidence of US media overwhelming national or domestic media around the world.

Globally, partnerships among media from multiple nations are increasing, as capitalism's neoliberal project champions national deregulation, privatization, and the reduction of public interest. Revenue and profits from domestic markets alone cannot cover production costs even in the US. Thus, with declining theater attendance and increased competition from streaming services, the global market and transnational co-productions have become vital to film studios in Hollywood, Bollywood, London, Paris, Beijing, and elsewhere (Richeri, 2016, p. 314). Studio executives moved quickly to a menu of economic calculations "based on practical choices being made by actors throughout the system" of transnational media production, investment, and distribution—always alert to "subsidies and incentives, global producers nonetheless require a support infrastructure that includes production and post-production services" (Meyer, 2016, pp. 68, 69). The subsequent changing social relations of power, contradictory cultural practices and identities, and the urgent need for expanding markets have led commercial media everywhere to seek mergers, partnerships, and joint ventures to increase profits. Consequently, as Schiller (1991) concluded, cultural imperialism no longer adequately describes emerging global media relations, nor does it express clearly the new global developments of capitalism (pp. 14–15). Unpacking the various insights and applications of cultural imperialism reveals how its several components need to be updated for our new world order.

Media entertainment is often overlooked or dismissed as non-essential to the social order, as indicated by its short shrift in international political economy studies. In other cases such as film studies or media economics, global media entertainment is treated esthetically or generically as part of media business plans or as an indication of popular trends. But film and television are more than just entertainment, they present engaging stories and attractive images of world views, cultural values, and beliefs about gender, race, and social class. Entertainment carries advertising and more importantly consumerist messages. Media entertainment is part of a global culture industry seeking profits from sales of tickets, media products, and audiences to advertisers. In the 21st century, much media entertainment is produced and distributed through joint ventures and temporary or long-term partnerships among national media across borders and cultures. Media do not stand separate from the rest of society, nor do they exist apart from the transnational transformation of global capitalism. As the following chapters will demonstrate, regional transnational media indicate the shared class interests of national capitalist owners, investors, and subcontractors profiting from a new transnational division of cultural labor.

Media production includes thousands of "invisible" workers, such as camera operators, sound techs, lighting techs, film editors, set builders, prop makers, decorators, costume designers, CGI editors, post-production editors and technicians, "stunt artists, body doubles, junior artists/extras, makeup artists, lower end technicians, and spot boys" who "remain on the margins of big-budget production discourses" (Mazumdar, 2015, p. 26). These jobs number in the hundreds of thousands. For instance, the stage employees' union in the US/Canada alone numbers over 140,000 technicians with thousands more working non-union jobs. Even greater numbers of media workers contribute to productions in Europe, Latin America, and Asia. Transnational production journeys across borders relying on location workers who are left behind when the shoot is over, making life precarious for those who actually produce media. Transnational media travel to reduce costs of labor and location. Mindworks Global Media in New Delhi provides journalists and copyeditors for news media in Europe and the US, similar contractors provide film editors and post-production technicians for entertainment media expecting to save 35–40% (Lakshman, 2008). Governments increasingly offer tax incentives and contributions to attract TNMCs—which makes media labor contingent on unstable incentive structures. As national media and their governments work to lure transnational partners, countries work to replicate the infrastructure of Hollywood. So-called global media cities, like Mumbai, Paris, Hong Kong, Shanghai, Abu Dhabi, Toronto, and Tokyo build studios and site facilities financed by government resources and private investors hoping to cash in on TNMC productions. Public funds go to the TNMCs and their domestic partners, but no social security and scant resources are provided to media workers. "Celebratory accounts tend to emphasize the value of entrepreneurship, self-actualization, creativity, and freedom expected of a career in the media" with little recognition of the "self-exploitative, impermanent, and insecure nature" of much media employment (Deuze, 2014) and the creeping precarity of cultural work across media industries (Duffy, 2017). As transnational consolidation builds, the more interlocked firms will centralize creative control and outsource the actual production to contractors or independent studios across nations and cultures (Artz, 2016, p. 29).

Audiences only see the finished content on screen, much like tourists at Disneyland that never see park workers, maintenance crews, custodial staff, mechanics, cooks, or groundskeepers, or even the human actors inside the Disney character costumes (Van Maanen, 1999). Nor do we notice the human and environmental toll from mining the tungsten, tantalon, tin, gold, and cobalt needed for the hard technology of the digital revolution, as well as the assembly and waste work for their disposal—it is not all virtual. And just like Disneyland employees, media workers are regularly underpaid: 75% of stuntmen in India live below the poverty line (Mazumdar, 2015, p. 27). Along with scriptwriters, directors, show runners, and others "above the line," these workers fuel the media machine that churns out content commodities for film, television, and digital platforms—and the primary beneficiaries are transnational corporations.

Here is one brief example to illustrate transnational media relations. In 2011, the independent film, *Cloud Atlas* was released. The film starred Halle Berry, Tom Hanks, Susan Sarandon, and Hugh Grant and featured British, Korean, Chinese, and Ghanaian actors. *Cloud Atlas* was a joint effort by Australian, German, and American producers and distributed by Warner Bros. and Germany's X-Verleih. In addition to the multi-national cast, international locations from New Zealand to Germany and Britain, and the labor of hundreds of transitory and precarious creative and technical workers from many nations, the $100 million film was funded by Korean, Chinese, German, Singaporean, and other investors. Thoroughly transnational in production with no discernible national or cultural content, *Cloud Atlas* serves as a guidepost for transnational media; filmmakers "are turning to a globe-straddling independent finance system for their most expensive projects" (Kulish & Cieply, 2011).

Oscar winning films, *Slumdog Millionaire* (2008) a British-French-Indian film, *Hurt Locker* (2009) an American-French thriller, *The King's Speech*

(2011) the British-American-Australian historical drama, *The Artist* (2012), a London-Brussels-Paris-LA produced French comedy, *12 Years a Slave* (2016) an American-Canadian-British funded film starring a Nigerian actor, *The Shape of Water* (2017) by Mexican and Canadian co-producers, and *Green Book* (2018) a story of race relations in the US South produced by American-Indian-Chinese partners, were all transnational co-productions globally financed and distributed. *Una Mujer Fantastica* won the best foreign film for Chile in 2017, but was co-produced by Chilean, German, US, and Spanish studios. It would be difficult to determine the national culture of any of these films or of the film producers. Is *Hurt Locker* American cultural imperialism? Is *The Artist* French imperialism or *Green Book* an example of China's Alibaba and India's Reliance Media imposing its messages on US audiences? It seems that transnational production and distribution have arrived along with transnational culture unimposed by US media imperialism.

All of the largest film markets in the world—China, North America, Japan, India, and Korea—include large audiences for US movies, including many that are transnational in production and distribution, as well as a bounty of regionally co-produced films. This largely explains why most transnational movie studios have consciously displayed cultural diversity in recent films, featuring African-American, Hispanic, Asian, Arab, and African actors to demonstrate their commitment to social equality and to profit from larger audiences which are increasingly culturally diverse. *Business Today* found that the top 10 grossing movies in 2016, had opening weekend audiences that were 47% non-white, and films with a culturally diverse cast outperformed films without diverse casts, grossing almost three times as much (Benedict, 2018). Cultural diversity is becoming a defining characteristic of transnational media as they reach across borders—armored with explosions, chase scenes, lingering romantic glances, and other spectacular images.

The following chapters address the contrasting approaches to explaining and understanding global media. The first two chapters open with observations about contemporary capitalism and its social relations, then challenges the remnants of cultural imperialism and introduces some of the elements of transnationalism.

The subsequent chapters describe the leading transnational media in each geographic region, unpack their regional partnerships, note the shifting new international division of cultural labor, and present some of the prominent themes of film and television content to illustrate the new political economies of interlocked media and how their social relations construct meaning for mass dissemination.

Chapter Three, "From Public to Private to Transnational," briefly applies some of the concepts and premises laid out in this chapter. The chapter summarizes regulatory changes in India prompted by its national media lobby that sought global media partners. From dominance by the public broadcaster,

Doordarshan, to national deregulations that opened the Indian media market to foreign direct investment, mergers, and multi-year partnership, the commercialization and consolidation of media in India was dramatic and sudden. Within a decade from the mid-1990s, Reliance ADAG became a major media force globally, purchasing DreamWorks and then partnering with Stephen Spielberg's Amblin Entertainment. (Reliance Industries—the majority owner of TV 18, another transnational media—is the media division of the Mukesh Ambani's conglomerate that produces industrial, aerospace, construction and other commodities.) Both Reliance media groups benefitted from the Indian deregulations, forming partnerships with CBS and Bertlesmann, among others. Fox, Sony, and Disney also found national partnerships, with Disney eventually purchasing UTV, now the second largest TV network, while Reliance, Essel, and other Indian media corporations expanded their partnerships regionally to Malaysia, Indonesia, China. Reliance bought 50% of DreamWorks, an iconic US media giant, and has since partnered with Steven Spielberg, Participant One, and China's Alibaba in Amblin Entertainment, a global film leader. Recently, Reliance/DreamWorks has established joint ventures in the opening Chinese media market. In a nation of 1.3 billion, transnational media (Reliance, Amblin, Sony, Fox, others) continue to expand, shift alliances, collaborate, and compete with other national and TNMCs.

China has become the largest media market in the world with mass audiences and millions in profits. In Chapter Four, "Crouching Tigers: Transnational Media with Chinese Characteristics," the mediascape in China is found to be slowly but continually opening to foreign media partnerships. With an official limit of 36 foreign movies allowed in China yearly, there is an urgent need for TNMCs to find domestic partnerships and joint ventures—Sony, Warner Bros, and Disney are among the leading suitors. Likewise, Chinese national media as well as private media corporations like Dalian Wanda and Bona Films seek to expand their production and distribution to global audiences, Chinese media troll for TNMC collaboration, including seeking transnational regional partnerships with Korean, Indian and other media producers. Despite the recent conservatism of the Chinese government toward international investments, multiple private media, including Internet giant Alibaba, continue to find opportunities for joint ventures. In 2017, *Wolf Warriors 2*, became the highest grossing non-English film in history. *Wolf Warriors* is a multi-film franchise by China-based Bona Films and a bundle of partners including Wanda, Japan's Kadokawa, Singapore's Shaw, and other regional TNMCs. Wanda is a leading private Chinese TNMC that illustrates transnational media relations and practices through its ownership of familiar US companies, including a minority stake in AMC Theaters (the largest US chain) and Legendary Films (the producer of *Kong, Jurassic World, Pacific Rim*, and other high-grossing iconic global films

Chapter Five, "Latin America: From Telenovelas to Transnational Media," takes a more expansive approach to illustrating TNMC operations on the continent. Given there is no single primary TNMC in the region, the several media and their more global partnerships are presented to demonstrate that transnationalism is not primarily global, nor singularly dominant. At first glance, TNMC media in Latin America seem to demonstrate the cultural imperialism relations identified in the 20th century. However, new conditions require a more nuanced discussion of transnational trends which are occurring as US media seek larger audiences for their own products. A more complete assessment emerges when the operations of regional TNMCs are included: Globo (Brazil), Caracol (Argentina), and Televisa (Mexico), among others. Each of these smaller TNMCs have established partners across nations in the hemisphere, and several have expanded to Europe and the US. Brazil's Rede Globo, which has long been an exporter of telenovelas, now is a major TNMC (with national partners) in Spain, Poland, Italy, Croatia, and has a presence in other European markets. Transnational media relations and operations in Latin America give empirical heft to claims about shifting structures and adjustments by the commercial media industry as it seeks to further expand its reach, its audiences, and ultimately its profits from media commodities targeted to multiple cultures. This chapter concludes with an appraisal of telenovela themes represented by two recent popular mini-series.

Chapter Six, "The New Frontiers of Europe: Transnational Media Partners," describes and assesses the evolving transnationalism as the European Union grapples with national identities, multiple languages, and a common market. With its 1989 "Television Without Frontiers" Directive, the EU set two goals: free movement across national borders within the EU and a 50% EU broadcasting quota—which sought to both protect and create a European wide market and region for EU media companies. However, given the large expense and small linguistic markets for national media and the prevalence of English as the primary secondary language, by the 21st century, most nations had modified their investment and ownership regulations, opening the EU to foreign direct investment, which largely came from the US. Still, there was an inexorable move to transnational relations within and outside the EU. This chapter relates several examples of TNMC relations in Europe. One is the French company, Banijay/Endemol, which produces and distributes more than 700 television programs, including *Deal or No Deal*, *Big Brother*, and *Peaky Blinders*, among others. Other brief but illustrative examples of TNMC practices in Europe, including Vivendi/Canal+, Sky TV, Constantin Films, and Fremantle will be considered while recognizing the ongoing appearance of Hollywood movies in EU theaters.

The book concludes with Chapter Seven, "Hegemony: Consent and Desire for Transnational Entertainment." The closing chapter returns to the globalization of neoliberal capitalism (deregulation of public interests, privatization of public resources, and collaboration among companies across borders). The closing chapter discusses the turn to transnational production, including national deregulation allowing for foreign direct investment, joint ventures, partnerships, mergers, and equity partners seeking profits. The relations between the media structures of transnational partnerships and the content of transnational productions are highlighted to explain how content expresses values, norms, beliefs, and ideologies favorable to consumerism, social hierarchy, and deference to authority—practices necessary for both transnational media and for market dominance over social decisions. As closing examples, this chapter recounts the rise of Nollywood, the Nigerian video production industry and relates the rise of Naspers, a South Africa-based TNMC. Naspers has established production and distribution arrangements with national media across southern Africa through its video, cable, and digital operations. Profiting from their TNMC activities in Africa has provided Naspers with resources for joint ventures in Europe, including Russia and elsewhere. Media appear as not just institutions and corporations but as producers of global culture, which includes the culture of consumption, individualism, and consent to dominant authority. Finally, the appearance of cultural diversity in most TNMC film and television is explained as the outcome of the political economy of TNMCs which need enthusiastic audiences and fans. Themes of villains and superheroes and sensational special-effects are considered as part of the process of attracting paying audiences and reproducing the social relations of production necessary for the success of TNMC and neoliberal globalization.

References

Arora, P., & Singh, K. D. (2020, December 28). Bollywood starts shift to streaming. *New York Times B1*, B3.

Artz, L. (2016). Transnational media corporations and global division of cultural labor and consumption. *Les Enjeux de l'information et de la communication 17* (2), 25–38.

Bahba, H. K. (1994). *The location of culture*. New York: Routledge.

Barnes, B. (2020, November 29). Hollywood's end, the sequel. Now streaming. *New York Times*, B6–B7.

Benedict, C. (2018, June 4). The rise of racial diversity in Hollywood: Here to stay or fad? *Business Today*. https://journal.businesstoday.org/bt-online/2018/the-rise-of-racial-diversity-in-hollywood-here-to-stay-or-fad

Castells, M. (1996). *The rise of the network society, the information age: Economy, society and culture. Vol. I*. Malden, MA: Blackwell.

Deuze, M. (2014) Work in the media. *Media Industries Journal 1*(2). https://quod.lib.umich.edu/m/mij/15031809.0001.201/-work-in-the-media?rgn=main;view=fulltext

Duffy, B. E. (2017). *(Not) getting paid to do what you love: Gender, social media, and aspirational work*. New Haven, CT: Yale University Press.

Epstein, E. J. (2012). *The hollywood economist: The hidden financial reality behind the movies*. Brooklyn, NY: Melville House.

Fiske (1989). *Understanding popular culture*. New York: Routledge.

Frank, A. G. (1967). *Capitalism and the underdevelopment in Latin America: Studies of Chile and Brazil*. New York: Monthly Review Press.

Friedman, T. (2006). *The world is flat*. 2nd ed. New York: Farrar, Straus and Giroux.

Knoche, M. (2019). The crisis-ridden capitalist mode of production as driving force for restructurations and transformations in and of the media industry. *Triple C: Communication, Capitalism, and Critique 17*(2), 287–307.

Kulish, & Cieply, (2011, December 5). Around the world in one movie: Film financing's global future. *New York Times*. https://www.nytimes.com/2011/12/06/business/media/around-world-in-one-movie-film-financings-global-future.html

Lakshman, N. (2008, July 8). Copyediting? Ship the work out to India. *Business Week*. https://www.bloomberg.com/news/articles/2008-07-08/copyediting-ship-the-work-out-to-indiabusinessweek-business-news-stock-market-and-financial-advice

Lash, S., & Lury, C. (2007). *Global culture industry: The mediation of things*. Malden, MA: Polity Press.

Lull, J. (2001). *Culture in the communication age*. New York: Routledge.

MacBride, S. (2004). *Many voices, one world: Towards a new, more just, and more efficient world information and communication order*. Lanham, MD: Rowman & Littlefield.

Mazumdar, R. (2015). "Invisible work" in the Indian media industries. *Media Industries Journal 1*(3), 26–31.

Meyer, V. (2016). The production of extras is a precarious creative economy. In M. Curtin & K. Sanson (Eds.), *Precarious creativity: Global media, local labor* (63-74). Berkeley: University of California Press.

Odugbemi, F. (2017). Prologue. In E. Witt (Ed.), *Nollywood: The making of a film empire* (pp. 12–19). New York: Columbia Global Reports

Ovide, S. (2020, December 7). A revolution in movie-watching. *New York Times*, B3.

Richeri, G. (2016). Global film market, regional problems. *Global Media and China 1*(4), 312–330.

Rubin, R. (2020, March 11). Global entertainment industry surpasses $100 billion for first time ever. *Variety*. https://variety.com/2020/film/news/global-entertainment-industry-surpasses-100-billion-for-the-first-time-ever-1203529990/

Schiller, H. I. (1976). *Communication and cultural domination*. White Plains, NY: International Arts and Sciences Press.

Schiller, H. I. (1991). Not yet the post-imperialist era. *Critical Studies in Media Communication 8*(1), 13–28.

Van Maanen, J. (1999). The smile factory: Work at Disneyland. In P. J. P.J. Frost (Ed.), *Reframing organizational culture* (pp. 58–76). Thousand Oaks, CA: Sage Publications

1

GLOBAL ENTERTAINMENT

Not Yet the Democratic Age

We live in a capitalist world. Media are a primary part of that world with commercial media and culture produced by national and multinational capitalist industries. Thus, at least some rudimentary explanation of capitalism is necessary to understand media. Capitalism is an historical form of social relations in which wage labor produces commodities—goods and services sold for a profit. Profits are taken by capitalist owners by withholding a portion of the value produced by wage labor. Profits are realized when the commodities are sold. Although manufacturing jobs have disappeared from the US and Europe due to technology and the globalization of production, globally the number of workers has increased to three billion. Hundreds of millions of those workers create value with their labor, applying skills and technology to produce valuable commodities and services. Thousands of corporate owners, financial investors, and shareholders in media corporations and other industries capture part of that created value in the form of profits. This is the market system. We work. They profit. Those few who own the factories, machines, technology, land, and resources determine working conditions, wages, grabbing their wealth from the labor of millions.

Working for 40 years at Amazon in the US might net you a total of $500,000 over your entire lifetime. If you lived in Seattle, you'd spend most of that on rent, the rest on food. If you spend your lifetime working for Jeff Bezos, you'd live broke and die broke. Meanwhile, Bezos collects $150,000 *every minute* from the labor of 500,000 workers just like you. Add that to the cut he takes from thousands of small businesses, he has captured $200 billion so far. This is not just American capitalism. Carlos Slim, owner of Telmex telecom in Mexico, has accumulated $60 billion from the work of his 50,000 employees. Jack Ma, the owner of Alibaba—the Chinese version of

DOI: 10.4324/9781003162452-02

Amazon—has accumulated over $50 billion from his 100,000 Chinese workers. Pony Ma, owner of Tencent and WeChat, also has taken $50 billion from the labor of 70,000 employees. Altogether there are 389 billionaires in China taking their wealth from almost 800 million workers, while millions more are impoverished. Anil Ambani, owner of Reliance Media (partnered with DreamWorks and Amblin Entertainment) has reaped almost $40 billion from his many enterprises in India. Similar relations of work and wealth exist in France, Germany, Brazil, Turkey, everywhere—some are more dramatic and startling, some less obscene—but globally all are part of transnational capitalism (Forbes, 2020).

This book recognizes that we have entered a new stage of capitalism: transnational capitalism. Capitalists from nations large and small coordinate their partnerships, notably in media ventures, which share production, distribution, costs, and profits from wage labor in many nations. Capitalism did not get here by accident. Capitalism developed over several centuries; it was not birthed full grown. Banking, renting, merchant trade, and even production for profit—often called mercantile capitalism—developed as the dominant socio-economic system in the late 18th century. In the 19th century, industrial capitalism privately owned the primary means of mass production and employed wage labor to produce commodities for profit through sales in the market. Industrial capitalism developed largely, but not only, within nations.

Capitalism did not grow the same everywhere. It did not follow some theoretical template for development. Instead, material conditions and social relations for each nation presented different options and possibilities. Where working classes were organized and politically active, capitalism adopted more social reforms like public health care, accessible public education, and public regulations on growth—as in Sweden, Denmark, and other European nations. US capitalism had a different trajectory given its geographic expansion, indigenous genocide, race slavery, immigration, a restrictive two-party electoral system, and the political and cultural impact of those conditions on social class relations. Saudi capitalism morphed from an archaic feudal system into a family and clan-dominated global investor based on private profits from oil production. More recently, the Chinese state has become capitalist, albeit with some special characteristics given its socialist history, including very strong government control and significant government enterprises, including in media. Still, the government promotes capitalism, consumerism, and the market. A new class of Chinese capitalists has emerged, including thousands of millionaire corporate owners and investors. Notably, other capitalist formations grew from their specific material conditions and social and political battles. Until recently most European countries had a robust public media system; in the US and Latin American media began and remain largely a private, commercial industry; China has a mix of large state-owned media and vibrant private media corporations like Dalian Wanda and Alibaba.

As institutions of political power, national governments promote and defend dominant social classes and the social relations of power, while mediating the dominance over other social classes (Davidson, 2016, p. 191). Thus, as capitalist economies reached the material limits of production and consumption within European nations, leading industries consolidated and capitalism became monopolized by fewer large enterprises. Each national governments backed colonial expansion to secure more resources and new markets for their own corporations. In the 20th century colonial era—the time of monopoly capitalism and imperialism—national competition increased between states representing their national capitalist interests. Rivalries within Europe and over colonial conquests led to international conflicts that took more than 100 million lives. The victors continued to impose sanctions and military interventions against their former colonies. A crucial point here is that imperialism as a form of capitalism is more than empire, colonialism, or even military conquest. Imperialism is the monopoly stage of capitalism, the point at which consolidated national corporations shoved aside smaller enterprises to dominate production, trade, and the subsequent accumulation of wealth from their colonies. We will come back to imperialism when we further consider whether cultural imperialism sufficiently informs our understanding of media developments around the world. For now, imperialism can be understood as a significant stage in the growth of what has become a global socio-economic system. Capitalism grew from mercantilism (17th and 18th century), to industrialism (19th century), to imperialism and monopoly (20th century), to its latest iteration as 21st century transnationalism.

Capitalism

To understand how monopoly capitalism and imperialism have morphed into what will be explained as transnational capitalism, a few brief points about capitalist social relations are needed.

Capitalism organizes social relations so that resources and the means of production are privately owned for individual profit. Labor has always been needed to obtain natural resources by using tools to produce goods to be sold. Human labor itself has become a commodity, privately purchased and controlled. However, the capitalist employer is not "buying" the worker—although the restrictions on our civil liberties while at work might suggest as much. The capitalist is actually buying our labor time. Capitalism needs trained and educated workers. It needs to produce and reproduce workers, including providing them with time to sleep, eat, have some leisure time, and learn the norms of capitalist social relations. Under most conditions as a wage laborer, there is no choice but to submit to an employer in order to survive.

Capitalism turns human relations into market transactions. Capitalism reduces human abilities into factors of production for profit. Capitalism positions citizens as consumers. Notably, while corporations dictate the terms of employment, the capitalist class does not rule society directly. Decisions and actions defending capitalism are left to its political hirelings. Capitalism develops in tandem with national governments (Anderson, 2016, p. 140). Capitalism resides within state power—in economics, politics, culture, and civil society—while state power responds to capitalist influences, activities, and interests, such that a Princeton Study determined the US is no longer a democracy (James, 2014). Capitalists throughout history have relied on vigilantes, private security, organized violence, and other means to control labor. State enforcement of private property rights offers some semblance of political legitimacy to the defense of social relations of power, appearing as unbiased enforcement of laws incumbent on all. Just as corporations have dropped their programs for labor social welfare, including pensions, health insurance, and supplement wages, so too corporations have deferred enforcement and violence to the government. In most cases, state managers, politicians, bureaucrats will act in what they perceive to be the best interests of capital (which they understand as equivalent to the best interests of society).

In a capitalist world, you only get what you can buy. Food, housing, health, education, and recreation depend almost solely on your own resources. Under capitalism, everyone is formally recognized as free. We are not forced to work for someone else, but are "free" to sell our labor power to whomever we choose. Those who own a means of production can employ you for a wage and make a profit that in turn increases their capital. You are formally recognized as free, but if you do not own a means of production, you are effectively forced to labor for the sake of someone else's profit in order to live. Instead of religion, nobility, or nature, under capitalism it is the dominant social relations of production that justify the subordination of one person by another.

Social classes arise according to their relation to the production of wealth. Capitalists own land, factories, machines—but do not actually work. Workers own little other than their labor power, so they work the land and operate the machinery in factories they do not own. Small businesses own their means of production and often work in their own enterprises. Politicians and bureaucrats are part of a professional social class that neither owns the means of production of wealth, nor works as producers. Rather, this social class serves as managers for the capitalist class and its practices, maintaining control and leadership over the working class and small business capitalists. "Regardless of their class origins, state managers and capitalists are drawn together into a series of mutually supportive relationships" (Davidson, 2016, p. 213). The former need the resources provided by individual national capitals, from political contributions, taxation and loans, in order to tend to the needs of capitalism as a whole; the latter need policy initiatives to regulate demands of the working class and other social groups domestically and to advance the preferred goals of national capital in the global economy. Importantly, politicians must be able to negotiate the dominance of capital with the challenges posed by the working majority, maintain connections with those social classes and sectors, and on occasion offer reforms to appease public demands for more equity and social welfare. Media function to report, justify, and promote modest reforms intended to win consent from working and middle classes and bolster the social order.

Workers receive a wage for their labor, but not for the total value of their production. Goods and services produced are then sold in the market, but workers are paid less than the value produced. Capitalist profits come from keeping the surplus of the difference between the value of the commodity and the wages paid labor. In every stage of capitalism, profits have been made by selling commodities produced by underpaid labor to consumers. Of course, without sales, no product provides a profit.

How much time is needed to produce a commodity, a chair, a dress, a car? What is the socially necessary labor time to produce goods and services for an entire society? It depends largely on the available technology and means of production; as socially necessary labor time declines, the value of the commodities produced declines. Technology increases surplus value taken as profits, because technology-using labor produces more commodities in less time, keeping wage costs down. Thus, capitalists compete for technology, for work practices and processes that lower labor time, and constantly push for lower wages to lower the costs of production and raise profits. Herein, lies the inherent contradiction of capitalism.

The total wages allowed to workers are ultimately insufficient for purchasing all the goods produced for exchange. The problem of overproduction has always presented an insurmountable contradiction for capitalism. Workers create commodities for sale, but workers receive only part of the value of the goods produced—the surplus value is withheld as profit. In other words, in the aggregate, across society and now the globe, the total purchasing power of all consumers, based on wages received, is less than the value of the products produced. Overproduction is inevitable. This is not overproduction of what citizens need or even want, but overproduction of goods that can be profitably sold. Food is plentiful. Millions are hungry. Under capitalism, food is destroyed or wasted whenever and wherever people cannot afford the prices.

A cursory example may help to illustrate this social relation of production. If workers are paid $8 to build a chair sold for $10 (and the owner keeps $2) then workers collectively cannot afford to buy all the chairs they produce. If a worker is paid $40,000 year to produce 100s of cars sold for $50,000 that worker cannot afford to buy that car. Some might be able to buy a chair or car made more cheaply, but to make a chair or car more affordable means either other workers will be paid less (while the capitalist still profits), or the capitalist must find new means for lowering costs—through lowering wages, intensifying working conditions, or developing better technology. Because workers own little other than their labor, they must work for wages to survive. To continue to profit, capitalists must constantly find new methods of production to constantly expand to make more profit to invest in more technology and more efficient work methods. From the capitalist perspective, new markets for manufactured goods solves the profit problem. Even if workers in one locale cannot afford to buy those goods, as long as a capitalist can find consumers somewhere who can buy the commodities produced, profits will be secured. This brief illustration does not adequately describe capitalist productive relations, wage labor, profits, social class, or other important components. More extensive and accessible explanations of capitalism are available (e.g., Choonara, 2019; Hägglund, 2019; Mandel, 1968).

Since the 17th century, capitalist accumulation has been world-wide: gold, silver, slavery, looting the West Indies, and exploiting natural resources on every continent. The accumulation of wealth has meant an accumulation of poverty (Callinicos, 2009, p. 53), repeatedly enforced by violence (Linebaugh, 2014, p. 67). Capitalists have historically relied on coercion—including repression, occupation, sabotage, war, and thievery. And it's still true: Amazon owner Jeff Bezos was fined $61.7 million for stealing 100% of his drivers' tips for two and one half years (Debre, 2021).

A less violent solution was advanced in the early 20th century when banks and corporations offered consumers loans so they could buy goods they couldn't otherwise afford. Not only were capitalists able to sell more products, lenders also were able to profit from the interest collected on the loans provided. Yet the fix is always temporary and ultimately still hits the limit of wage incomes that not only provide for daily expenses, but also cover the costs of previous purchases and interest payments. You may get a loan to buy a car, but payments come from your otherwise limited resources based on wages. Unless wages increase, loans will only create debt and postpone the crises. As economist Wolff (2020) notes, capitalism creates an overproduction crisis every decade or so (e.g., 2000, 2008, and 2019).

Even if some skilled individuals and professionals receive higher wages and have more purchasing power, more commodities are produced than are needed or wanted by those higher income consumers. For individual families who own a house, car, washer, dryer, refrigerator, stove, and furniture, more production of those items will not automatically result in more consumption. Hence, to sell more commodities to those who can afford them (or afford with credit), capitalists produce appliances that are intended to wear out, become obsolete, and need replacement, assuring a recurring market for some commodities. Capitalists also rely on media advertising to persuade consumers that they want or need new things that have more features or capabilities. For example, while all mobile devices are essentially the same in function, consumers are persuaded each year that new features are desirable: 270 million

American adults own 275 million cell phones, with another 125 million sold in 2020 (Statista, 2020).

Given the continued growth of labor productivity—the value of goods produced per worker per hour—domestic national overproduction is inevitable because as working citizens we collectively produce more commodities than our collective wages can afford. In fact, by the late 1960s, in all advanced capitalist countries, production exceeded the needs or financial capabilities of their citizens. Gross overproduction needed an outlet, so European and US corporations looked to producers and consumers in other nations to secure profits from commodity production.

Capitalism has always politically functioned through its control of state power. Although capitalism did not develop out of nation-states and it has no intrinsic interest in governments per se, capitalist governments do protect private property and function to advance the interests of corporations, as attested by the US government's $1 trillion assistance to business in March 2020 (Rasmus, 2020) and millions more in December. Capitalist governments are quite varied in their structures and operations—from Britain, France, and Sweden's parliamentary and welfare states, to the two-party, private industry state in the US, to the authoritarian Communist party defense of capitalism in China.

Throughout the 20th century colonialism was resisted and disrupted by the colonized. As Asian, African, and Latin American peoples successfully built movements for independence, colonial powers adjusted to neo-imperialism: they accepted formal independence of their subject nations while maintaining economic control over production and natural resources by establishing agreements with local comprador elites (Nkrumah, 1965). In all capitalist nation-states from Europe and the US to the colonial and post-colonial world, capitalists dominated governments, the economy, and civil society. Capitalists owned industry, funded and controlled political parties, and dominated public civic institutions from the Chamber of Commerce and public education to public and private media. The capitalist class recruited, employed, and trained professionals in each sector: politicians to establish and enforce laws protecting private property and corporate profits; managers to organize and oversee labor; and journalists, publicists, teachers, pastors, and directors of non-profits (such as the Boy Scouts, YMCA, youth sports, 4H Clubs, and the junior chamber of commerce Jay-Cees).

In other words, capitalists lead not primarily through conspiracy, deceit, or constant violence, but by hegemonic influence—winning consent from allies and acquiescence from opponents, while silencing or coercing any alternatives (Gramsci, 2000). Hegemony provides apparent benefits for politicians, managers, and civic leaders that adopt and internalize the values of individualism, the free market, and deference to institutional authority. Leading capitalists (rich from the labor of millions) also turned to politically organized philanthropy to further direct and induce supportive norms and practices across society and its cultures. Carnegie, Rockefeller, Ford and now Bill Gates, Mark Zuckerburg, and Warren Buffet contribute millions to charitable programs that reinforce the social relations of corporate power and wealth. Globally other corporate rich have used philanthropy to promote their own pet programs: Azim Premji (India), Al Rajh (Saudi), Li Ka-Shing (China), Carlos Slim (Mexico), and Dietmar Hopp (Germany), among others (Martin & Loudenback, 2015). Likewise, in each nation, the news and entertainment media have been essential to normalizing existing dominant social norms of the free market, consumerism, and austerity.

The increase in human atomization and alienation prompts capitalist social and cultural leaders to seek consent from the working class and others for their own exploitation and dehumanization, through entertainment, consumerism, and modest economic or political benefits. Self-gratification, self-realization, and self-fulfillment through commodities predominate as offerings in contemporary consumerist culture. Even a "happiness industry" has developed to encourage all to take individual responsibility for their own life conditions (Cabanas & Illouz, 2019). In parallel efforts, politicians, media, and educators encourage nationalism and patriotism as "psychic compensation" to the general population. Ironically but effectively, nationalism can be mobilized under a banner of making the nation more competitive—even as national capitalists strike transnational partnerships with capitalist enterprises in other nations.

Yet, while capitalist nations successfully socialized citizens to nationalist, consumerist, and individualist norms and the rule of the market, contradictions remained. Global labor productivity continually outpaced national consumption—even with consumer loans, planned obsolescence, advertising, corporate mergers, continued neo-colonial exploitation, military interventions and occupations, and a rising US-based global entertainment industry. As the post-WWII boom sputtered by the 1970s, corporations needing to increase profits sought to have public services privatized at home and abroad as they outsourced production to low-wage nations, introduced labor-saving technologies, launched concerted attacks on unions, and built capitalist partnerships in other nations to open borders to foreign trade and direct investment which included shared corporate management.

Neoliberalism

Given that capitalism covered the globe by the late 20th century, in the industrial core of Europe, North America, and Japan, the capitalist classes had little choice but to find more robust methods for attaining wealth from the rest of humanity: increased accumulation through dispossession of public resources and increased consolidation of global production. By the 1980s, capitalists and their government representatives in most Western nations implemented policies favorable to unfettered corporate production, investment, and profits. As the cycle of economic growth slowed, capitalism reorganized through financialization aided by the digitalization of communication and finance (Harvey, 2005). Enacted "neoliberal" reforms by national governments removed limits on foreign investment, deregulated protections of the public interest, privatized national resources and public services, and invited international mergers, acquisitions, and partnerships that prioritized corporate profits over citizen rights (Artz, 2015, pp. 18–45).

NEOLIBERALISM

Neoliberalism refers to market-oriented reform policies such as eliminating national regulations on prices and trade, reducing government support for public services, privatizing public ownership of programs and resources, and instituting austerity in public expenditures. Neoliberal reforms benefit corporations, investors, and their managers while increasing social inequality. Following WWII, capitalists and their governments created the International Monetary Fund (IMF) and the World Bank. Since the 1980s, the IMF and World Bank enforced neoliberal practices. International loans were contingent on Structural Adjustment Programs that required developing countries to balance their national budgets by cutting social services, deregulating trade and investment, and privatizing public programs. Margaret Thatcher in the UK and Ronald Reagan in the US were proponents of neoliberal reforms, while Chile under the Pinochet dictatorship is a severe example of the social consequences of neoliberal privatization. Ideologically, neoliberalism advocates extreme individual self-interest based on unregulated open markets and unhindered by public responsibility.

Media were directly affected in each nation that initiated neoliberal reforms. From India to Europe and Latin America, neoliberal governments gutted public media and facilitated private broadcasting and advertising. New profit-oriented channels produced diverse and spectacular entertainment content that encouraged self-interest and consumerism.

Under the leadership of the IMF, the World Bank, the World Economic Forum, the G-20 and other policy groups, along with multiple bilateral trade agreements, neoliberalism was codified as an international capitalist project. Neoliberalism was born in practice and philosophy, as capitalist classes sought continued expansion—"aimed at nothing less than extending the values and relations of markets into a model for broader organization of politics and society" (Robinson, 2004, p. 4). Public interests and public services became targets for privatization and profit. Mergers and acquisitions domestically and internationally created new economies of scale and profit. Capitalists in almost every nation (from Korea, India, and Russia to Greece, Nigeria, and Bolivia) prodded and persuaded their respective nation-states to privatize public transportation, utilities, media, natural resources, and even the human genome. In deference to the regime of the IMF and World Bank, national governments accepted and even invited foreign corporate investment, joint production, and co-management.

Neoliberalism is more than the economic practices of expansion and market dominance that have restructured capitalism. Neoliberalism also advances individualism and consumerism in philosophy and ideology. Thus, media and entertainment are essential to political and economic power. Media—as purveyors of signs, symbols, and stories—assist in constructing consent for dominant social relations, practices, and explanations. Not surprisingly, movies, television programs, and news frames—from every nation—center on self-interest. Echoing the proclamations of the World Economic Forum and politicians of every stripe, global entertainment settings and tropes suggest that "we are all independent, autonomous actors meeting in the marketplace, making our destinies and in the process making society" (Aschoff, 2015, p. 87).

Neoliberalism now informs and organizes global social relations among nations. The Hong Kong People's Forum notes that China has "evolved into a global engine promoting a neo-liberal agenda" while the Worker's Party in Brazil reports that nation's push for privatization, austerity, and anti-labor legislation (Bonde, 2017). Globally, deregulation, privatization, foreign partnerships, and free trade agreements according to neoliberal reforms were touted as freer, more open, more democratic, and more beneficial for all—even as extreme poverty increased to 150 million in 2021 (World Vision, 2021). Yet, ironically, short of war or economic decline like the 2008 global recession and the 2019 pandemic, this expansion of the capitalist market is already reproducing the problem of overproduction on a global scale. The vaunted rise of the BRICS (Brazil, Russia, India, China, and South Africa) capitalist alliance in 2009 has already encountered overproduction, over-indebtedness, and austerity, as transnational capitalism in each country has reached excess capacity for profit (Bonde, 2017).

Under these neoliberal capitalist relations of production, global overproduction will return because even after war, recession, and economic crises, neoliberal reforms to expand transnational commodity production inevitably exceed the purchasing power of the wages of those producing the commodities. Outsourcing, off-shoring, and technological improvements drive down the cost of labor and hence appear to make commodities more "affordable," but as workers lose jobs or take less pay to be competitive, even less expensive commodities cannot permanently offset the decreased purchasing power resulting from lower wages and fewer workers.

Neoliberalism represents the self-interested efforts of the transnational capitalist class (TNCC) united in vision and practice as it transitions to a new stage of capitalism that seeks corporate partnerships for accumulation through dispossession of public resources. Wars between developed countries armed with nuclear weapons are an undesirable option. Even wars of occupation and intervention have proven costly and politically untenable, as the US learned from its war in Vietnam. Limited occupations and interventions by France, Britain, and the US will recur (as in the Falklands, Mali, Nicaragua, Iraq, Afghanistan, and Venezuela) but with modest economic and political success and with the constant danger of instigating domestic social unrest.

Despite the appearance of nationalism in several countries (e.g., Hungary, Brazil, India, and the US during the Trump years), the most powerful capitalists in every nation concur that neoliberal agreements are preferable. In India, Prime Minister Narendra Modi foments Hindi-nationalism but initiates neoliberal privatization of farming for national and international investors (Parth, 2021). Capitalism uses existing or created beliefs and values (including religion, race, ethnicity, gender) to justify inequality and misdirect anti-capitalist sentiment and challenges to other causes and identities. Nationalist ideology seeks to bind the working class and others to a territorial identity expressed as patriotism, while the capitalist seeks the freedom to exploit and profit unconstrained by national borders or cultures.

Arguments by Davidson (2016) and Callinicos (2009) that capitalists foment national conflict for their own interests seem forced. Historically, capitalist industries in provinces or states within nations did not organize conflict between states and provinces within a nation, but competed and consolidated nonetheless. There is little evidence that cities or regions took up arms to defend "their" capitalists. Why don't capitalists who compete with others within a nation not engage in military conflict, but competition with those outside the nation inevitably result in war? What is it about the scale of protection that requires nation-states to militarily battle other nation-states fronting for their own capitalist interests?

In fact, now, most capitalist industries are already implementing non-national collaborative norms: Fiat-Chrysler merged with Puegeot (an Italian-US-French partnership); GM has eight joint ventures including Wuling in China; Toyota has a joint venture with Kirloskar Group in India; Bayer merged with Monsanto in a giant German-US agro-pharmaceutical; Chinese companies have invested more than $1.4 billion in US biotech firms; Renault-Nissan is a Franco-Japanese auto industry; DreamWorks, Alibaba, and Spielberg formed Amblin Entertainment (an Indian, Chinese, Canadian, American media company); multiple Nigerian film producers have partnered with South Africa's Naspers/Mnet Africa Magic which is aired in 53 African countries, broadcasts on Sky TV in Britain, and in 2021 Nigeria's largest distributor, FilmOne, signed a deal with Disney.

What is the logic or tendency of such verifiable transnational class relations? Investment, partnerships, joint ventures, and cooperation in rules and regulations do not exhibit primarily competitive impulses. Undoubtedly,

GM shareholders would benefit from the demise of Wuling in China, but also irrefutably GM prefers profiting immediately from joint ventures from Wuling as opposed to some questionable military conflict intended to improve its competitive advantage for selling cars in Beijing.

Moreover, transnationalism cannot be reduced to a US economic strategy for dominance. Globally, corporations from every nation are seeking partners, investors, and joint ventures to expand their production, limit risk, and increase profits. In 2020, the largest free trade agreement in history, the Regional Comprehensive Economic Partnership (RCEP) was signed by 15 Asia-Pacific nations, including Australia, Brunei, Cambodia, China, Indonesia, Japan, Laos, Malaysia, Myanmar, New Zealand, the Philippines, Singapore, South Korea, Thailand, and Vietnam—but no US or EU. RCEP encompasses 30% of global GDP and more than 2.2 billion people. In 2021, the US was poised to rejoin the Trans Pacific Partnership trade agreement linking many of those same nations with Canada and the US. In short, by the early 21st century, transnational capitalism was healthy and rapidly growing.

Capitalist investment, production, distribution, and profit-sharing now regularly cross national and cultural boundaries. Although distinct national cultures may still exist in some nations, consumerism characterizes even the most diverse from India and Turkey to Brazil. Consumerism in China has taken off. With household consumption at $6 billion annually, China is the second largest consumer market in the world. In Nigeria, where two-thirds of the population lives on less than two dollars a day, its popular culture exhibits pronounced consumerist lifestyles (Haynes, 2018, pp. 9–11). Whatever their traditional social relations, practices, and cultural rituals, wage labor for corporate profits prevails in most countries and regions—establishing capitalist relations of power as a daily means of survival.

Importantly, mergers and partnerships are increasingly orchestrated by domestic capitalist interests that collaborate with foreign partners promoting public deregulation, market norms, and consumer lifestyles. Meanwhile, media render all social problems as stories and dramas of individual protagonists. The "structural deficits, contradictions and paradoxes" of social inequality appear as "psychological features and individual responsibilities" (Cabanas & Illouz, 2019, p. 51). Predictably, the marketing of personal happiness is prominent in neoliberal societies—and a prevalent theme in global entertainment—because it rekindles and legitimizes individualism in an apparently non-ideological way, "presenting a discourse that conceives one's life as separate from community and which sees the inner self as the cause and root of all behaviours" (Cabanas & Illouz, 2019, p. 53). With this view, public interests do not exist. Work, education, health, housing, and the quality of life are all individual responsibilities and choices. As will be shown in the following chapters, in all nations, national media and transnational media feature individualism as the prime motivation for storylines and the path to happiness and success.

Mexican, Brazilian, Turkish, and Egyptian telenovelas and dramas are individualist genre. India's masala films emphasize individual interest extended to the family unit. Even "Ne Zha" (2019), China's highest-grossing animated film at $725 million, revised an ancient story of redemption to present one "full of individualism" (In Zhejiang, 2019).

In other words, the new global structures of transnational production and distribution have altered daily life and culture—for most citizens consumption and consumer goods have become a means for expressing cultural and personal identity—providing limited respite from alienating work. Globalization is an inadequate catch-all term that does not fully consider the social relations that characterize this new transnational stage of capitalism. As noted earlier, capitalist industrial and financial corporations have always looked to the world market for resources and consumers, which privileged Western interests and cultural norms, but transnationalism is a new phenomenon.

Cultural Imperialism

Attempts to reconcile cultural imperialism with globalization theories are multiple but inoperative at both a theoretical and practical level. Demont-Heinrich (2011) presents an admirable example. In his list of disagreements between cultural imperialism and globalization of culture, he numbers structure and agency, production and consumption, cultural flows, social levels of personal and cultural identity, hierarchy, inequality, and power. Demont-Heinrich omits social class, social relations of existing political economies, and the centrality of capitalism to all nation-states in the contemporary world. Demont-Heinrich quotes Schiller (1991) who locates capitalism as central to any assessment of media structures and practices. But, then Demont-Heinrich applauds Sparks (2007), who obscures the class relations of capitalism. Thus, Demont-Heinrich and Sparks adopt a geographic center-periphery vocabulary, decrying the US-based "global consciousness" (p. 145). It is not that either Demont-Heinrich or Sparks dismiss capitalist social relations as determinants of cultural production, rather they assert that the relations of production "offer little insight into processes determining which cultural significations" are produced—which is what Boyd-Barrett (2005) astutely criticized about elusive postmodern concepts (p. 22).

Demont-Heinrich proposes that cultural imperialism is primarily an "optic" for concentrating on domination and production which imposes a dominant ideology, whereas globalization is an "optic" focused on cultural resistance and consumption (p. 4). In this valiant effort to dialectically inflect cultural imperialism with globalization of culture, Heinrich ends up with two cloudy lenses that further blur recognition of the material conditions of both production and consumption. He criticizes studies of geographically based cultural flows that find culture is "highly-fluid, malleable, and fundamentally hybrid" in its localization of polysemic variety, noting that culture is the hegemonic outcome of global, political, and cultural power configurations (p. 5). Yet, even that apparent insight lacks the material prerequisite indicating the actual social relations of power—based on contemporary adjustments to the capitalist accumulation of wealth from labor. Cultural hegemony (with its broad consensus supporting transnational capitalist leadership) is not primarily geographic; it is the normative outcome of a social, economic, and cultural leadership developed by intellectuals in service to capitalism and its social relations of production by wage labor (Artz & Murphy, 2000; Gramsci, 2000).

Zhao (2008) offers a useful corrective to the "essentialist notion of Chinese culture and a nation state-centered frame of analysis" that loses "any discussion about the domestic class, regional, gender, and ethnic politics of 'Chinese culture'" (p. 140). She notes that focusing on the simple imbalance of media imports and exports "underplays the active role of various domestic agents in China's reintegration" into capitalist social relations, while "equating the penetration of transnational corporations with cultural assimilation and homogenization" provides a static view of cultural practices and obscures how national media owners reorganize formats for their own profitable purposes (pp. 140–141).

The investigations informing this book attempt to uncover the conditions of media production, distribution, and consumption without stumbling into preconceived essentialized categories of nation and culture. Of course, from the historical materialist perspective guiding this book, a full political economy of media and culture must identify who owns, who decides, who writes, casts, films, edits, and how those production practices are organized to create media content, as well as how and by whom media products are marketed. It also would explain who owns the screens, regulates the screenings, promotes the products, and the economic and structural relations distributors have with content producers. A complete assessment must include the conditions and locations of reception, the costs and access to receiving, the social forms of presentation and reception, the cultural conditions informing interpretations of meanings, and the social context and cultural–political significance of media use. Some of these components appear (albeit incompletely) in chapters that follow.

In contrast, Demont-Heinrich's (2011) description of MTV as "homogenous" localization (p. 7), does not tell us much about Indian media conglomerate Sun TV's thriller–romance "Run" co-produced with British transnational ad giant WPP. We need more than cultural imperialism to unpack the "localized" production decisions, corporate relations, series ideological content, and any political or social significance of the series for Tamil culture in India. Categorizing "Run" as British cultural imperialism seems insufficient for explaining and understanding the transnational corporate relations between Sun TV, WPP, and co-producer Vikatan Televistas. It does not reveal much about the cultural impact of this and similar series on daily life or world views. "Run" was produced in Chennai, Hong Kong, and Bangkok as a rich girl meets poor boy story appropriate for the rising entrepreneurial Tamil middle class. The consumerist message so important to transnational corporations (TNCs) is dominated by the apparent cultural raw materials of Tamil India at the decision and behest of Indian-based transnational media. No British, no US, not even Western domination is manifest.

Western cultural influence is likewise tangential in Essel's Zee Studio production, "Secret Superstar" (2017), a musical drama about a heroine of gender equity in India. Although Disney co-produced Aamir Khan's Hindi story of female wrestlers, "Dangal" (2016) which with a $330 million box office became the highest grossing Indian film ever, the movie is based on an Indian true story emphasizing competition and individual success. In other words, the Hindi and Tamil cultural iconography becomes fodder for the promotion of India capitalism—not for Western corporate profits or influence per se. Appeals to egalitarianism that provides citizens with opportunities to create their own identities, practices, and forms of expression do not reside in cultural iconography, but depend entirely on citizens having direct access to media production and dissemination. The "reality of inequities in global cultural relations" (Demont-Heinrich, 2011, p. 8) are not geographic but socio-economic. Power is not an abstraction—it is obtained through the social relations of ownership and control over the means of producing and sharing—in this instance, media content.

Here, we might pause and consider how cultural imperialism might be applied within a nation or country. Salih (2020) makes an interesting argument that Turkish dominance over the Kurdish minority should be understood as internal cultural imperialism, because the Turkish government's goal is subjugation and possible eradication of non-Turkish cultures. Extending Salih's approach elsewhere would find internal cultural imperialism at work in France's treatment of Algerian immigrants and white supremacist domination and repression of African-Americans in the US. White artists appropriated black music. Black cultural production was marginalized or coopted by the white culture industry. Of course, cultural imperialism could apply if culture, ethnicity, and nationality are essentialized, reified without regard for capitalist social relations. If every instance of control, media dominance, and public relations falls into the cultural imperialism rubric, we lose the ability to discern the actual material conditions that organize our world. The hegemonic pull of racism and nationalism benefits the owners and overseers of the economy and political structures, but reducing capitalist social relations to cultural imperialism misidentifies those class relations as geography and distracts from possibilities for democratic social change.

The dialectic claimed for "middle ground" between cultural imperialism and the globalization of culture (Demont-Heinrich, 2011; Kraidy & Murphy, 2008; Mirrlees, 2013; Rogers, 2006) simply synthesizes two flawed approaches. Hybridization, transculturation, glocalization, cultural flow, or other such concepts do little to unpack cultural dominance until and unless one incorporates transnational capitalism with its new social relations of power assembled and enforced by actual corporate ownership and nation-state regulation. What is the purpose of finding middle ground? Perspectives and theories should arise from conditions investigated, not simply from previous theoretical claims.

The truth of our condition is concrete, whether it fits existing and previous perspectives is of little importance—unless those perspectives disorient and disarm those seeking strategies to secure equality and justice (as post-modern theories did in the Nicaraguan revolution against dictatorship, Artz, 1997). Findings and discoveries and "understanding the real contours of the world economy" (Callinicos, 2009, p. 198) should inform our theories and understandings. Reality has changed. In the early 21st century, the conditions informing cultural imperialism perspectives are receding. Rising TNC relations and practices organize media production in most geographic regions, according to the interests and goals of transnational investors, producers, advertisers, and neoliberal political leaders. Empirical evidence from multiple cases presented in the following chapters illustrates the constraining and constructing conditions of transnational ownership, creative and technical labor, production practices, content (including form, theme, and ideology), distribution, and profit-taking across borders and cultures. The concern for equality expressed by cultural imperialism perspectives can best be addressed now through "redistribution, confiscation, and levelling" of media access and control by non-capitalist social classes and movements (Linebaugh, 2014, p. 136).

Transnationalism

TNCs differ from international and multinational corporations by their relations of production. An *international* corporation does business across national borders by selling products produced by workers in one nation to consumers in another (e.g., Comcast's Universal exports *Fast and Furious* films to China). *Multinational* corporations owned and based in one nation operate subsidiaries in another nation. The subsidiary has workers producing commodities in and for the domestic national market. Ownership, control, and profits of the subsidiary are retained by the multinational parent (e.g., Disney produces television programs for its wholly owned UTV India, while production decisions and profits remain with Disney US). In both instances, the capitalist class structure provides profits to national capitalist owners based on the skills and technical expertise of thousands of cultural workers at home and in the foreign country. Still, the relative benefit that international and multinational corporations receive from the labor of their domestic and international working classes was deemed by shareholders as insufficient for maximizing profits. Sales of commodities from centralized production neither always keep pace with costs or meet the interests of culturally diverse consumers, nor could prevailing wages at home and abroad sustain consumer driven demand. Even where labor organizations won improved benefits in wages and working conditions, global overproduction plagued multinationals in auto, pharmaceutical, home appliance, and even food and clothing. Because capitalism needs unending growth, corporations sought increased labor productivity with decreased labor benefits at home (through Reagan and Thatcher-era attacks on labor and the introduction of labor-saving technologies), off-shore production in countries with lower wages, and most importantly in the increased expansion of global markets for an already overabundance of commodities.

International and multinational production no longer sufficed as "best practice" for visionary corporate leaders at Toyota, Honda, Vivendi, and Sony (van Tulder & van der Zwart, 2005). Advanced technology increased labor productivity that was temporarily sufficient to fund millions of service professionals, meeting the material needs of all with the labor of some. In early 21st century, manufacturing workers accounted for less than 20% of employment in the largest industrial nations (West & Lansang, 2018), producing appliances, cars, food, and all other material needs for the world. Rational thought would suggest that sharing the productive benefits of technology would improve life for all humanity, but capitalism insists that the majority of wealth will be appropriated by a very few. A plurality may be comfortable in advanced capitalist countries, but millions suffer on the margins of society: average pay for the bottom half of the world's workers is less than $10 per day (Kollewe, 2019). Almost two billion people, about one-fourth of the world's population, live on $3.20 a day (World Bank, 2020), while eight capitalists own more wealth than half of the world's population (Oxfam International, 2017).

Still, in the 21st century, large corporations continued to search for new technologies, delivery systems, and relations of production to lower wages and increase consumption. New digital technology and willing national politicians promoted consumerism and corporate profits by facilitating consolidation and deregulating protections of public interests. Free market reforms allowed nationally based multinational corporations to partner with their corporate industry peers in other nations. Across all industries, corporations agreed on collaborative cross-border relations of production—further establishing the social relations of production based on wage labor, commodities, and corporate profits, all with increased government protection and decreased corporate taxes. This can be understood as transnationalism.

Transnationalism is an awkward term; one that has no agreed on definition. In film studies, for instance, transnationalism appears elusive, stuck between the global and international, the "intermediate and open term transnational acknowledges the persistent agency of the state, in a varying but fundamentally legitimizing relationship to the scale of the nation. At the same time, the prefix 'trans-' implies relations of unevenness and mobility… to accommodate the scale of below-global/above-national" (Durovicová, 2010, p. x). While legitimate, this description still provides no categorical definition to identify conditions and relations.

Hjort (2009) offered a more categorical description of transnationalism that included elements related to levels of production, distribution, reception, and the cinematic works themselves, especially related to co-production and distribution by media from multiple nations. Hjort also noted that transnationality is not necessarily apparent in a film's content. Thus, he presents a transnational typology, privileging epiphanic, affinitive, and milieu-building as collaborations among smaller nations to maintain and defend their artistic and productive integrity, in contrast to opportunistic, cosmopolitan, and globalizing transnationalisms which are driven by economic considerations in service to a global elite.

Nonetheless, whatever the creative intent of television producers and film-makers from around the world, the practices and relations built over the last decade or so strongly indicate that neoliberal transnationalism has become hegemonic—surviving and consolidating media in every country have opted for market-based production, distribution, and narrative content. Of course in almost every instance a remnant of auteur film festival productions remain, but they do not reach mass audiences and thus have slight contribution to the emergence of the new global culture marked by consumerism, self-interest, and deference to hierarchical authority.

At some time or other most national cinemas are not coterminous with their nation-states. Thus, any bounded, highly territorialized concept must be over-come. In other words, reference to a national culture cannot function as an essentialist, unitary, all-encompassing category of analysis. Media, news, and entertainment should be understood as relational—a set of processes rather than an essence. In the 21st century, those processes are transnational in scope and action.

In the global search for increased capitalist collaboration, TNCs formed. The United Nations Conference on Trade and Development (UNCTAD, 2016) defines transnational companies as those with owners and investors in multiple countries jointly managing the operation. In other words, TNCs are capitalist partnerships jointly owned by multiple companies from two or more nations producing goods within several nations and distributing these "local" commodities in each of the several nations, while sharing the profits among the multiple national owners. For example, Reliance India buys 50% of the US studio DreamWorks and enters into a joint venture with Chinese filmmakers to produce movies for all three markets (Szalvai, 2012). "We are not multi-national, we are multi-local" (Iwabuchi, 2002, p. 90) insist TNCs such as Sony, Coca-Cola, Mercedes, and McDonalds.

Certainly, mergers and acquisitions, joint ventures, and foreign direct invest-ments (FDI–investments by one company in a company based in another coun-try) have blurred the national identity of many TNCs that enlist local labor to make local products. In 2008, the UNCTAD identified over 78,000 transna-tional companies (UNCTAD, 2008). The Swiss Federal Institute of Technology in Zurich searched a database listing 37 million companies and investors world-wide, and pulled out the leading 43,060 TNCs and the shared ownerships linking them. Researchers constructed a model of which companies controlled others through shareholding networks, coupled with each company's operating revenues, to map the structure of economic power. They found a core of 1318 corporations that collectively own through their transnational shares the majority of the world's large blue chip and manufacturing firms representing 60% of all global revenues (Adl-Tabatabai, 2017). Whether 1300 or 43,000, these TNCs lead a radically different capitalist system than one dominant post-WWII. The TNCC shares investment, production, distribution, risk, and profits from the labor of millions producing commodities consumed by millions more.

To repeat: these cooperatively constructed structures and social relations of production are no longer nationally based. As might be expected, the largest TNCs have home bases in the most developed capitalist countries. Although these capitalist owners do not represent a "coherent, homogeneous collective" group that has transcended national states, they do function through "highly variegated and regionalized formations" with tensions and contradictions (Carroll, 2017). This developing TNCC has collectively instituted social relations of production with value chains of commodities, cooperatively exploiting and profiting from labor across nations, simultaneously exerting their collective political influence on several nation-state governments. This is crucial for understanding media's structural transformation which is the result of "purposeful and strategic restructuring activity" (Knoche, 2019, p. 288). For all industry, including media, transnationalism has become the latest stage of capitalism (Appleyard, Field, & Cobb, 2006).

INTERNATIONAL, MULTINATIONAL, TRANSNATIONAL

Globalization as a catch-all term obscures more than it enlightens. Many other descriptive terms suggest agreement and understanding, but can also disguise primary differences. The following definitions have no consensus, but provide working definitions and differences important for understanding contemporary media forms and practices.

International corporations sell commodities, goods, and services produced by workers in their own national factories to consumers in other nations. International corporations trade across borders, but do not own or partner with corporations in other countries. Disney is operating internationally when it distributes its US-produced films to theaters in other nations. Disney's global expansion, especially to Latin American, informed the critique of cultural imperialism.

Multinational corporations produce and sell commodities, goods, and services produced by workers in their own national factories and in factories owned by the same corporation as a subsidiary in another nation or nations. Multinational corporations operate their subsidiaries to produce goods and services for consumers in the country of the subsidiary. Multinational corporations trade across borders and their subsidiaries produce in other countries, but they do not have partnerships or joint ventures with companies in other countries. Disney is operating multinationally when its Disney Star channel in India or Disney Spain produces and broadcasts television programs in those countries. Acquisitions and mergers dominated by Disney bolstered the claims of cultural imperialism in the 1980s and 1990s.

TNCs are jointly owned by two or more companies from two or more nations. Transnational media corporations (TNMCs) may exist through short-term joint ventures to produce a single film, or transnational media may be more permanent partnerships with majority and minority shares of a joint company owned by two or more companies from two or more countries. Disney is a TNMC as 26% owner of Canada's Vice Media; as co-producer of the Indian hit, *Dangal* (2016), with Aamir Khan; and as one-third owner of Argentine film studio, Patgonik.

Many regional TNMCs in Europe and Latin America do not have the same international reach as Disney and very few have multinational subsidiaries in other countries. The need to survive and economically benefit from co-productions, partnerships, and joint ventures propel national film and television producers toward transnational relations between two or more companies from two or more different countries. As transnational media become more dominant and the national identities and cultural values become more diffuse, cultural imperialism loses both its effect and descriptive value. Transnational media continues to replace cultural dominance by any one country or its cultural norms. Consumerism, individualism, and self-interest are promoted by capitalist classes everywhere, as apparent even in China. Market values have multicultural inflections, but no longer belong exclusively to the US or Europe. Transnationalism has become hegemonic with the consent of media and their diverse audiences.

As with all social change, the transnational process has not proceeded without interruptions or setbacks. The COVID pandemic immediately and materially affected global neoliberal restructuring. UNCTAD (2020) reported $36 trillion in total global FDI before 2019, but predicted new transnational annual investments falling by 30% to only $1.5 trillion due to pandemic lockdowns. Simultaneously, neoliberalism expanded in 54 countries with new reforms that opened national economies (especially in Asia) to increased foreign investment and partnerships. Given the constraints on production and trade caused by COVID, UNCTAD foresaw the increased use of robotics and digitalization, even as many industries would geographically regroup due to supply chain constraints related to the pandemic. Expansion shifted from cross-continental partnerships to increased regionalization of joint production and investment. The new stage of capitalism took a side step to *regional* transnational partnerships. These are especially prominent among TNMCs as described in the following chapters.

Whether regionally focused or linked cross-continent, TNCs have no national home per se and certainly no national allegiance. Their only allegiance is to capitalist class owners and shareholders from the two or more nations seeking profits from commodities produced and sold in multiple nations. As Thomas Middelhoff, chairman of Bertlesmann, clearly explained when his German company took over US-based Random House in 1998, "There are no German and American companies. There are only successful and unsuccessful companies" (in Robinson & Harris, 2000, p. 35). Transnational capitalists (TNC) do not seek to override or dismantle national or cultural boundaries. In fact, they depend on the national and cultural characteristics suggested and supported by their class partners for operation in each country. Transnational capital does not undertake the imposition of some elusive national norms on subordinate cultures, rather it "seeks to accumulate profit on a global scale... [with] no particular interest in destroying or sustaining local cultures apart from the drive for increased profitability" (Sklair, 2001, p. 256).

Scholars in international political economy have assessed and described the rise of transnationalism organized by an emerging TNCC (Robinson, 2004,; Sklair, 2001; van der Pijl, 1998). The efforts of this well-organized TNCC have resulted in capitalism conquering and establishing a complete world system. Capitalism has not only effectively overcome all indigenous precapitalist formations, with transnationalism it has also completed the commodification of every meaningful instance of social life, including public institutions, social welfare responsibilities, and nation-centric cultural practices with privatized, for-profit operations around the world.

Transnational capitalism—partnerships and joint ventures crossing national boundaries—now control most natural resources such as land and water as well as social necessities such as education, health care and global culture, including entertainment, sport, and leisure (Robinson, 2004). In fact, by the end of the 20th century, transnational production exceeded the amount of national import–export trade (Miller, et al, 2005, p. 113). Objections to transnational theories echo some of the same critiques of globalization, but miss the materialist, class-based analysis, and overlook the empirical evidence provided. A transnational political economy does not replace or overcome the state as globalists like Hardt and Negri (2000) argued. Nation-states have not been replaced under transnationalism. To transform global production and distribution, capitalists favoring global integration lobby and direct their national governments to deregulate investment, labor rights, and public protections. Transnational capitalism still needs the consent of governments and the governed who are still organized within nations, borders, languages, laws, unions, armies, and cultures.

Transnationalism recognizes that because capitalism controls the economy, the rest of the nation-state, its politics and culture, will also be heavily influenced. The leading social class relies on the state for regulations, laws, and enforcement protecting capitalist interests, as well as the education, socialization, and assimilation of civil society. Within each nation, the TNCC confronts national capitalists who still defend national protectionism. Religion, education, entertainment, and popular culture are sites of battle for dominant social relations of power. Across the world, capitalists fund public–private initiatives laden with the values and ideology of neoliberal privatization. Gates, Soros, Ambani, and Jack Ma, Democrats, Republicans, and the Chinese Communist Party advance neoliberal reforms with joint ventures and partnerships. Ironically, even as each support neoliberal reforms to open international markets, they continue to rhetorically and publicly advocate increased international competition to strengthen their own nation.

None of this means capitalist competition has disappeared, but competition has saddled up and mounted joint ventures and partnerships to carry the restructuring of global production and consumption. This is especially true for transnational media because "the trading of creative content, capital, and talent bridges the physical gaps between urban clusters of film production companies across the globe" (Hoyler & Watson, 2019, p. 944). TNCs continue to extract surplus value from wage labor, seek national tariffs and subsidies, look for advantages over competing firms, develop labor-saving technology, campaign against labor unions, encounter disruptions in their production chains, failures in marketing plans, and face overproduction. Moreover, competition among firms does not preclude collaboration between capitalists in mergers, partnerships, and co-productions that are transnational, establishing new social relations of production that encompass and reorganize industries, their suppliers, managers, and working classes across national borders.

A vital component of the restructuring of capitalism, and the topic of this book, is the role of TNMCs and their commercial–entertainment–consumerist structures, practices, and communication content (Artz, 2015; Rantanen, 2005). Control of media has always been central to political and cultural power. To ensure that the dominant ideas of a society are the ideas promoted by rulers: priests, nobles, publishers, government bureaucrats—and now corporate media directors and publicists—dominate media production, news, entertainment, language, vocabulary, signs, symbols, and images. After the Chinese invented paper in the 13th century, emperors tightly controlled printing and banned the first printing press invented by Koreans. From the Roman, Greek, and Ottoman empires to feudal monarchs and the Catholic hierarchy to modern dictatorships and the PR agencies of contemporary liberal democracies, dominant social classes and their government bureaucrats have sought to control public access to communication, and recently including most recently the closing of Internet access (Stauffer, 2020). Dominant social strata have sought control and regulation over language (Anderson, 2016, pp. 43–46), communication, and media to better socialize and persuade citizens of the values and norms of the dominant national social order—albeit not always successfully. Today, authoritarian leaders in Hungary, India, China, and elsewhere censor news and close digital platforms to curtail citizen access to communication.

Media also comprise a global capitalist industry. As major capitalist enterprises that produce and distribute both goods and ideological messages, media are thoroughly embedded in neoliberalism and transnational capitalism. Media are corporations owned and operated by investors, banks, private equity firms, insurance companies, fast food and consumer products companies, and other transnational corporate interests. Most major media have boards with extensive interlocks with additional corporations as well as other media firms. Twelve of the largest companies in the world are media corporations, including Alibaba, Google, Tencent, Samsung, Disney, ATT/Time Warner, and Facebook. Not surprisingly, media corporations are integral to the global restructuring of capitalism and its drive for increased profits. As political economist Garnham (1987) observed, reproduction of movies and music is marginal compared to the costs of production, so commercial media have a particular compulsion to maximize sales and expand audiences to enhance profits globally through distribution contracts, streaming services, satellite, cable, and pay-TV, or direct television rebroadcasts. Thus, in addition to promoting consumerism in content and behavior to diverse national markets, media also lead the neoliberal push for deregulation of global markets.

As for-profit businesses, commercial media produce and distribute commodities for sale and profit: magazines, newspapers, movies, audiences, cable and streaming services, and ancillary products connected to media content. Importantly, each of these commodities are more than just products sold for profit; each carry symbolic meanings, political messages, and cultural values. In other words, media produce and distribute news, information, and entertaining stories that reflect and promote existing social beliefs and behaviors useful for reproducing dominant relations. In short, media function as an essential component for existing relations of power.

Capitalist media, globally and nationally, clamor for the need for more competitive regulations, production practices, and flexible working conditions—including technological improvements—presumably so *their* nation might win the global contest for jobs, profits, dominance. Thus, commercial media urge national governments to increase foreign investment and partnerships, deregulate and privatize public media, and further commercialize media production and distribution to mass audiences while curtailing labor rights and reducing wages (Artz & Kamalipour, 2003). At the same time, media owners reach "partial cooperation in the interest of all owners of capital (for example regarding waged workers, consumers, and the state)" (Knoche, 2019, p. 295). As transnational partnerships are formed, the social relations of production and distribution practices evolve, organizing multiple production sites employing wage labor or short-term contractors, expanding the social and cultural effects of media within diverse nations. Given the changing practices and relations among national and global media, including the function and effect of US media monopolies, some of the claims of previously valid theories must be reconsidered and revised accordingly. Cultural imperialism, as an accurate description of international relations for more than 40 years, no longer applies to the conditions of contemporary media relations and practices, rather transnational relations dominate across cultures. As Curtin (2016) concludes, media "operate according to distinctive cultural presumptions and professional protocols… Dubai is a crossroads for transnational television in the Arab world and its an interface between Arab and global media. Likewise, Mumbai is the media capital of South Asia as is Miami for Hispanic media. Moreover, each of these hubs makes use of service centers within its respective sphere of operations. Telemundo in Miami contracts with producers in Bogota, Buenos Aires, and Mexico City. Mumbai is networked to media resources in Chennai, Hyderabad, and the United Arab Emirates" (p. 70). In short, profit seeking TNMCs have grown tentacled networks across national borders and cultural identities.

References

Adl-Tabatabai, S. (2017, August 25). Swiss government study confirms 147 corporations 'Run The World.' *Shiftfrequency.com*. https://www.shiftfrequency.com/147-companies-run-world/

Anderson, B. (2016). *Imagined communities: Reflections on the origin and spread of nationalism*. New York: Verso.

Appleyard, D. R., Field, A. J. Jr., & Cobb, L. (2006). *International economics*. 5th Ed. New York: McGraw Hill.

Artz, L. (1997). Social power and the inflation of discourse: The failure of popular hegemony in Nicaragua. *Latin American Perspectives 24*(1), 92–113.

Artz, L. (2015). *Global entertainment media: A critical introduction*. New York: Wiley Blackwell.

Artz, L., & Kamalipour, Y. (2003). *The globalization of corporate media hegemony*. Albany, NY: State University of New York Press.

Artz, L., & Murphy, B. O. (2000). *Cultural hegemony in the United States*. Thousand Oaks, CA: Sage.

Aschoff, N. (2015). *The new prophets of capital*. New York: Verso.

Bonde, P. (2017, August 31). BRICS Xiamen summit: Capitalist "deglobalization" could crack the bloc even if internal geopolitical strife eases. *Links: Journal of Socialist Renewal*. http://links.org.au/brics-xiamen-summit-capitalist-deglobalisation-internal-geopolitical-strife

Boyd-Barrett, O. (2005). Cyberspace, globalization, and empire. *Global Media & Communication 2*(1), 21–41.

Cabanas, E., & Illouz, E. (2019). *Manufacturing happy citizens: How the science and industry of happiness control our lives*. Medford, MA: Polity Press.

Callinicos, A. (2009). *Imperialism and global political economy*. Malden, MA: Polity Press.

Carroll, W. K. (2017). Rethinking the transnational capitalist class. *Alternative Routes*. http://www.alternateroutes.ca/index.php/ar/article/view/22452

Choonara, J. (2019). *A reader's guide to Marx's capital*. Chicago: Haymarket Books.

Curtin, M. (2016). What makes them willing collaborators? The global context of Chinese motion picture co-productions. *Media International Australia 159*(1), 63–72.

Davidson, N. (2016). *Nation-states: Consciousness and competition*. Chicago: Haymarket Books.

Debre, E. (2021, February 2). Amazon will pay $61.7 million for stealing Flex driver's tips. *Slate*. https://slate.com/news-and-politics/2021/02/amazon-ftc-pay-flex-drivers-stolen-tips.html

Debre, E. (2021, February 2). Amazon will pay $61.7 million for stealing Flex driver's tips. *Slate*. https://slate.com/news-and-politics/2021/02/amazon-ftc-pay-flex-drivers-stolen-tips.html

Demont-Heinrich, C. (2011). Cultural imperialism versus globalization of culture: Riding the structure-agency dialectic in global communication and media studies. *Sociology Compass 5*(8): 666–678.

Durovicová, N. (2010). Preface. In N. Durovicová, & K. E. Newman (Eds.), *World cinemas, transnational perspectives* (pp. ix–xv). New York: Routledge.

Forbes. (2020). *World's billionaire list: The richest in 2020*. https://www.forbes.com/billionaires/

Garnham, N. (1987). Concepts of culture: Public policy and the cultural industries. *Cultural Studies 1*(1), 23–37.

Gramsci, A. (2000). *The Antonio Gramsci reader: Selected writings, 1916–1935*. D. Forgacs, (Ed.). New York: New York University Press.

Hägglund, M. (2019). *This life: Secular faith and spiritual freedom*. New York: Pantheon.

Hardt, M., & Negri, A. (2000). *Empire*. Cambridge, MA: Harvard University Press.

Harvey, D. (2005). *The new imperialism*. Oxford: Oxford University Press.

Haynes, J. (2018). Keeping up: The corporatization of Nollywood's economy and paradigms for studying African screen media. *Africa Today 64*(4), 3–29.

Hjort, M. (2009). On the plurality of cinematic transnationalism. In N. Durovicová, & K. E. Newman (Eds.), *World cinemas, transnational perspectives* (pp. 12–33). New York: Routledge.

Hoyler, M., & Watson, A. (2019). Framing city networks through temporary projects: (Trans)national film production beyond "Global hollywood. *Urban Studies 56*(5), 943–959.

In Zhejiang. (2019, August 5). *Refuse to accept the fate: Ne Zha and Chinese animations*. https://inzj.zjol.com.cn/News/201908/t20190805_10732195.shtml

Iwabuchi, K. (2002). *Recentering globalization: Popular culture and Japanese transnationalism*. Durham, NC: Duke University Press.

James, B. (2014, April 18). Princeton study: US no longer an actual democracy. Talkingpointsmemo.com. https://talkingpointsmemo.com/livewire/princeton-experts-say-us-no-longer-democracy

Knoche, M. (2019). The crisis-ridden capitalist mode of production as driving force for restructurations and transformations in and of the media industry: Explanatory theoretical elements of a critique of the political economy of the media. *TripleC: Communication, Capitalism & Critique 17*(2), 287–307.

Kollewe, J. (2019, July 4). Nearly half of global wages received by top 10%, survey finds. *Guardian.* https://www.theguardian.com/inequality/2019/jul/04/just-1-in-10-workers-earn-half-of-all-global-wages-survey-finds

Kraidy, M., & Murphy, P. (2008). Shifting gears: Towards a theory of translocalism in global communication studies. *Communication Theory 18*, 335–355.

Linebaugh, P. (2014). *Stop, thief!: The commons, enclosures, and resistance.* Oakland, CA: PM Press.

Mandel, E. (1968). *An introduction to Marxist economic theory. Vol 1.* New York: Monthly Review Press.

Martin, E., & Loudenback, T. (2015, December 2). The 20 most generous people in the world. *The Independent.* https://www.independent.co.uk/news/people/20-most-generous-people-world-a6757046.html

Miller, T., Govil, N., McMurria, J., Wang, T., & Maxwell, R. (2008). *Global Hollywood 2.* 2nd Ed. London: British Film Institute.

Mirrlees, T. (2013). *Global entertainment media: Between cultural imperialism and cultural globalization.* New York: Routledge.

Nkrumah, K. (1965). *Neo-colonialism: The last stage of imperialism.* London: Thomas Nelson & Sons.

Oxfam International. (2017). Just 8 men own the same wealth as half the world. https://www.oxfam.org/en/press-releases/just-8-men-own-same-wealth-half-world

Parth, M. N. (2021, January 5). India's farm crisis. *Counterpunch.* https://www.counterpunch.org/2021/01/05/indias-farm-crisis-farming-is-our-religion-we-love-to-feed-people/

Rantanen, T. (2005). *The media and globalization.* Thousand Oaks, CA: Sage.

Rasmus, J. (2020, March 25). US Senate's final stimulus bill: Why it won't be enough. *Counterpunch.* https://www.counterpunch.org/2020/03/25/us-senates-final-stimulus-bill-why-it-wont-be-enough/

Robinson, W. I. (2004). *A theory of global capitalism: Production, class, and state in a transnational world.* Baltimore, MD: Johns Hopkins University Press.

Robinson, W. I., & Harris, J. (2000). Towards a global ruling class? Globalization and the transnational capitalist class. *Science & Society 64*(1), 11–54.

Rogers, R. (2006). From cultural exchange to transculturation: A review and reconceptualization of cultural appropriation. *Media, Culture, & Society 19*, 47–66.

Salih, M. (2020). Internal cultural imperialism: The case of the Kurds in Turkey. *International Communication Gazette.* https://doi.org/10.1177/1748048520928666

Schiller, H. I. (1991). Not yet the post-imperialist era. *Critical Studies in Media Communication 8*, 13–18.

Sklair, L. (2001). *The transnational capitalist class.* New York: Wiley.

Sparks, C. (2007). What's wrong with globalization? *Global Media & Communication 3*(2), 133–155.

Statista. (2020). *Number of smartphones sold to end users worldwide from 2007-2021.* Statista.com. https://www.statista.com/statistics/263437/global-smartphone-sales-to-end-users-since-2007/

Stauffer, B. (2020). Shutting down the Internet to shut up critics. *Human Rights Watch.* https://www.hrw.org/world-report/2020/country-chapters/global-5

Szalvai, E. (2012). Power and culture in media internationalization: The unusual case of a minority media conglomerate. *Revista de Negocios Internacionales 4*(1), 28–56.

UNCTAD (United Nations Conference on Trade and Development). (2008). Largest transnational corporations pursued further expansion abroad in 2007, report says. *World Investment Report.* https://unctad.org/fr/node/21156

UNCTAD. (2016). *Development and globalization: Facts and figures.* https://stats.unctad.org/Dgff2016/DGFF2016.pdf

UNCTAD (2020). *World investment report: International production beyond the pandemic.* New York: United Nations Publications. https://unctad.org/system/files/official-document/wir2020_en.pdf

van der Pijl, K. (1998). *Transnational classes and international relations.* New York: Routledge.

van Tulder, R., & van der Zwart, A. (2005). *International business-society management: Leading corporate responsibility and globalization.* New York: Routledge.

West, D. M., & Lansang, C. (2018, July 10). Global manufacturing scorecard: How the US compares to 18 other nations. *Brookings.edu.* https://www.brookings.edu/research/global-manufacturing-scorecard-how-the-us-compares-to-18-other-nations/

Wolff, R. D. (2020, June 10). There's a crisis in US capitalism. *Counterpunch.* https://www.counterpunch.org/2020/06/10/theres-a-crisis-in-us-capitalism/

World Bank (2020). *Poverty overview.* https://www.worldbank.org/en/topic/poverty/overview

World Vision (2021). *Facts, FAQs, and how to help.* https://www.worldvision.org/sponsorship-news-stories/global-poverty-facts

Zhao, Y. (2008). *Communication in China: Political economy, power, and conflict.* Lanham, MD: Rowman & Littlefield.

2

CULTURAL IMPERIALISM AND TRANSNATIONAL MEDIA

Cultural imperialism emphasizes the cultural imposition of the values and practices of an imperialist nation onto a subordinate nation. *Imperialism*—understood as the stage of capitalism where concentration and consolidation created monopoly capitalism linked with finance and government—led to inter-national conflict. The decline of capitalist competition from mergers, bankruptcies, and industrial monopolies within nations led to a battle between nations over new territories for resources and markets for accumulation of wealth. National monopolies bolstered by the military might of their national governments sought colonies for their "national" corporations. Imperialist and colonial powers conquered less powerful nations and fought among themselves to partition the world. Ultimately, rabid battles for colonial power led to imperialist wars.

The post-war era found former imperialist powers facing national liberation struggles and the rise of the Soviet Union and "socialist" China. Competing capitalist nations, seeking to protect the interests of their national corporations, accepted formal independence for their former colonies while maintaining neo-colonial economic control and political influence (Nkrumah, 1965). In this new non-imperialist, post-colonial world, most industrially-developed capitalist nations constructed extensive unequal relations with the national elites of developing nations, providing aid, loans, investments, media technology, scholarships, and commodities including film and television programs that exuded the norms and models of social and political behaviors amenable to capitalism and consumerism—including individualism, self-interest, market dominance, and bureaucratic authority.

As noted earlier, recognizing that US and European corporations often extended their economic dominance and cultural influence without resorting

DOI: 10.4324/9781003162452-03

to military force, Herb Schiller (1976), Armand Mattelart (1976), Jeremy Tunstall (1977), Oliver Boyd-Barrett (1977), and many others observed that US power in Latin America and elsewhere could be seen as a form of "cultural imperialism"—meaning US dominance was maintained in part by entertainment media, music, business practices, and religious and educational activities in developing countries. Unfortunately, packing late 20th century capitalist dominance into pre-world war nation-state terminology handicapped reception of the accurate insights and valid concerns about cultural imposition in the developing world.

Multiple authors have defended the continuing usefulness of the concept imperialism (Wood, 2003; Harvey, 2005; Patnaik & Patnaik, 2017) massaging the definition, emphasizing US dominance and military power (Panitch & Gindin, 2004; Callinicos, 2009), or asserting that nations "inevitably" must resort to military conflict (Davidson, 2016). In such cases, war appears as nations seek to maintain "credibility" like the US in Vietnam (Callinicos, 2009, p. 182) or "the competitive process spills into political violence" like the US occupation of Iraq (Davidson, 2016, pp. 234, 245). Overall, the authors missed the actual underlying materialist interests of the capitalist class and its need to prevent socialist relations (in Vietnam) or to overturn nationalized control of production (in Iraq).

While the nation-state has been and remains politically essential for the capitalist mode of production (Davidson, 2016, p. 236), as noted above, the form and function of diverse capitalist states has varied historically and geographically—depending on the social relations of power within each nation. The battle over government power in Venezuela, Bolivia, Greece, Tunisia, and elsewhere is between forces politically vying for governmental control because that power can be used to defend or disrupt the economic control of capitalism. The socialist-led governments of Bolivia and Venezuela as well as the left populist-infused Syriza government in Greece (and even the 2010–2012 Arab Spring) threatened to mobilize working classes and allies to restructure ownership and control over production. Those states remained capitalist while the governments were in turmoil. Those governments and others pressured by anti-capitalist social movements cannot be abstractly reduced to capitalist nation-states with state managers (whose transnational deniers assert will inevitably engage in inter-state military conflict because it is inherent to capitalism).

In other words, US and EU opposition to Venezuela, Bolivia, Chiapas, Yemen, and the Tuareg independence movement in Mali is driven not by capitalist competition, but by the possibility of alternative non-capitalist social relations that remove the possibility of capitalists profiting from wage labor. Evidence is marshalled by Callinicos (2009) comparing the GDP of developed nations with those of the South to illustrate an imperialist imbalance, but empirically "capitalism has no geographic boundaries" and regional transnational partnerships thrive (Rugman, 2005, p. 264).

21st century monopoly capitalism has forged significant transnational and regional cooperating nation-state partnerships for all industries. Over the last 40 years the EU has established transnational agreements between 27 nations on tariffs, currency, customs, cultural exchange, and unrestricted market relations. Likewise, for 30 years, Mercosur, the common market of 12 Latin American nations, has signed agreements on trade and culture. Mercosur is now the fifth largest economic block. There are other international agreements among states that accept and defend capitalist class interests and actions. While nationalist rhetoric may be used to culturally and ideologically win hegemonic consent within nations, that does not indicate that capitalists are verging on national military conflicts with competitors. While US, UK, France, Saudi, and other countries continue to use military force for economic control in the Middle East and Africa, in particular, such actions are not inter-imperialist conflicts. Instead, the actions are targeted at popular movements or governments unable or unwilling to join the new global order of neoliberal capitalism. Existing geopolitics finds that most national governments have moved away from inter-imperialist actions, while moving to facilitate and enforce market-based transnational relations on recalcitrant nations.

One way to avoid the difficulty in evoking imperialism is using it to describe multiple conditions. Noting that the concept was never "limited only to forms of imperialism that depended on annexation of territory" (Boyd-Barrett & Mirrlees, 2020, p. 1)—effectively reframes the term as one of US media *influence* on media systems and cultures of other countries. Imperialism is reduced to soft power. Once the concept is opened further to recognize "little" media imperialisms (e.g., Britain, France, Russia, China, Brazil, India, and South Korea), the template could be applied to "any period or phase" in the history of an "empire" whatever its history, size, or impact (p. 1). Conceivably, that should allow consideration of an internal cultural imperialism against African-Americans in the US, in Guatemala against indigenous nations, or in India against the Sikhs. Boyd-Barrett and Mirrlees recognize the material conditions and political economies that determine the functions, effects, and pathways forward. Nevertheless maintaining "imperialism," "media imperialism" or "cultural imperialism" as the rubric subsumes the actually existing forms of capitalist development within an ahistorical frame of influence and dominance.

Surely mercantile, industrial, monopoly, and colonial capitalism constructed different social relations with ramifications for culture and society that cannot be expressed as simply influence or class dominance? Analyses of media production must attend to the social relations of power that determine decision-making, content-producing, and profit-taking practices. Colonialism and neo-colonialism created and enforced different forms of dominance that politically and culturally organized society, materially offering possibilities for resisting and removing dominance.

In addition to US economic power, military coercion, and official public diplomacy, researchers observed that US commercial media materially and ideologically overwhelmed local cultures on behalf of US economic and political interests. While such observations about US media activities have been clear and verified, the values and norms of the local cultures that were overwhelmed have not been so clearly delineated.

Mattelart (1976) provided a detailed report on US media and government propaganda efforts. Moody (2017) and Mirrlees (2019b) documented recent evidence of US government and corporate media collaboration. Such findings by cultural imperialism adherents have been valuable, especially in illustrating US and European media production and distribution. However, support for their theoretical framing of cultural imposition has been more tenuous: evidence of US media dominance on television and in theaters does not necessarily demonstrate the loss of a more democratic or representative culture. In fact, Mattelart (1976) explained *national* culture was "elaborated and administrated by the national dominant class" that guaranteed the national elite's dependence on the US, while reproducing their national "class hegemony" and keeping themselves in power (p. 161). Mattelart noted that domestic elites may even "nationalize" US models to reproduce superstructural conditions favorable to the US *and* to the national capitalist class. Thus, there is little cultural value left in the "national culture" of the global South for working classes and the public to defend.

Imperialism as a tool for explaining capitalism in the 21st century has become unhelpful because it does not express the actual workings of transnational capitalism which are constructing social relations with capitalist classes across borders to better profit from working class labor across borders. Competition remains, national conflicts reappear, but class collaboration has grown more pronounced among the TNCC (transnational capitalist class) (van der Pijl, 1998; Sklair, 2001; Adl-Tabatabai, 2017; Phillips, 2018). Dominance remains but it is class dominance, not national dominance. Transnational capitalism has not collapsed the nation-state or flattened the earth, nor has transnationalism formed a global government. Instead, transnational capitalists share practices organized by capitalists from multiple nations, codified in global and bilateral treaties, agreements, policies, and infrastructures (e.g., IMF (International Monetary Fund), World Bank, Trans Pacific Partnership, NAFTA (North American Free Trade Agreement), RCEP (Regional Comprehensive Economic Project), BRICS (Brazil, Russia, India, China, and South Africa), and others). They collaborate to open markets, increase cross border investment, squeeze the working class, displace the peasantry, accumulate wealth through the national dispossession of publicly-owned national and social resources, and provide advertising and entertainment that promotes consumerism to increase sales and reap profits. Capitalist competition for profit is not just about dominating other firms, but more about which firms can extract the most surplus value from labor—pushing corporations to collaborate on both the exploitation of labor and the expansion of consumer markets.

Transnationalism may be preferred by industry owners, their managers, and politicians, but despite media efforts not all citizens accept the neoliberal practices undermining the public interest. Coercion and even armed intervention are often necessary, but transnational capitalism has no global military force. Instead, governments acting on behalf of national and transnational capitalists use violence in their own neo-colonial regions and participate in global conflicts challenging capitalism or its norms. NATO is one such alliance, which acts on behalf of the North American-European capitalist alliance. French forces responded to threats in Mali, British troops have been sent to the Middle East, Asia, and Latin America to protect corporate control. The US military functions as a force protecting TNCs. In each instance, commercial media have justified military actions as necessary responses to threats against civilization. Often a small humanitarian "coalition of the willing" is identified as participants with benefits. The US war on Iraq is a prime example. The US occupation was not to secure *only* US oil interests. Dutch BP, Russian Gazprom, French Total, Turkish TPAO, Japanese Japex, and Italian, Egyptian, Chinese, and Korean oil firms gained access to Iraq's oil and gas fields after the US invasion and occupation (Iraq Business News, 2020).

Despite its continued military superiority, US military interventions and occupations can no longer be deemed strictly "imperialist" in any definitional sense or with any accuracy as conquest and direct control. In fact, in several cases, US interventionist attempts have faltered: Iraq, Afghanistan, Bolivia, Iran, China, Ukraine, and other 21st century fiascos. Moreover, US militarism and America's economic interests have diverged. Apart from a few military contractors, US businesses have not followed the flag into the ruins of Iraq or other US military excursions. Military might has not secured economic advantages for US corporations. Today, Iraq's largest trading partner is China, Afghanistan's is Pakistan, Somalia's is the UAE (United Arab Emirates), and Libya's is the European Union. It seems military imperialism has lost its advantage.

As Venezuela's foreign minister, Jorge Arreaza said after seven years of US sanctions, sabotage, and intervention, the "United States cannot impose its programs on our continent... colonialism is out of date in this region" (Prashad, 2020). The vibrant example of citizen control over public and community media in Venezuela also demonstrates that remnants of "cultural imperialism" can best be extinguished by transforming and democratizing the political economy of media production.

Global politics and global policing are among the many questions that remain for observers of cultural imperialism. Notably the largest and most active transnational enterprises are initiated by corporations based in the US and Europe which draw from their existing financial and production power and expertise. The IMF, World Bank, and World Economic Forum are led and controlled by Western government and corporate interests (Danaher, 2001; Artz, 2015). Strong incentives attract diverse national governments to adopt neoliberal reforms allowing for more FDI (Foreign Direct Investment) and Transnational media corporation (TNMC) mergers. These conditions suggest several crucial questions for cultural imperialism approaches: Does media size and audience influence establish domination? What cultural practices and values do dominating media promote? What are the domestic cultural practices and values constrained by dominating foreign media practices and content? Are domestic media partners (and their governments) primarily representatives of dominating media? Do national media represent national cultures? More importantly, which domestic media and cultural producers represent and advance democratic values and cultural practices?

These challenges are not meant to question media effects on audiences, as empirically elusive as they might be. Enough evidence exists from audience consumer behavior following major media events to indicate that media content informs significant public beliefs and behaviors. The legitimacy of cultivation theory has been adequately demonstrated over decades of research, although the behavioral effects did not always increase conformity or acceptance of the media's ideological content (Gerbner, Gross, Morgan, & Signorielli, 1994). Recurring evidence of direct media effects also amply shows that media influence consumer behaviors: the Archery Trade Association found that the *Hunger Games* (2012, 2013, 2015) films by Lionsgate increased participation in the sport by 3 million (Meade, 2017): although Disney's *Finding Nemo* (2003) and *Finding Dory* (2016) promoted conservation, sales of endangered clown fish and blue tang fish increased by as much as 40% (Andrews, 2016); and in a few weeks after the 2020 Netflix hit *The Queen's Gambit* aired, chess set sales increased 125% (Fazio, 2020). Clearly, media content often affects viewer perceptions, even if subsequent behaviors veer from the manifest messages. It is not irrational or deterministic to posit that US film and television programs inform and persuade viewers in other nations. A more significant question might be: what cultural values and practices are presented that challenge or replace the existing cultural values of viewers? Or for that matter, what are the distinct cultural values of the nations subjected to media imposition?

Culture

Culture, cultural values, and cultural practices cannot always be clearly defined—for either the dominant nation or for the nation subjected to media domination. UNESCO (2001) defined culture as including the whole complex of distinctive, spiritual, material, intellectual, and emotional features that characterize a society or social group, as well as traditions and beliefs. So undoubtedly, culture is socially learned—including in contemporary times through the media. Yet, identifying distinct features of a particular culture remains elusive. Indeed, many attempts to categorize are generalizations about family values, conservative beliefs, and sociability that could substantially equate Polish, Brazilian, Indian, and Tibetan culture—each of which have distinctive cuisine and fashion. Yet, cuisine and style seem quaint expressions to define cultures. Surely there are historic explanations for contemporary design and diet, but these do not necessarily indicate significant cultural differences. These observations are not intended to obfuscate or undermine the value of cultural imperialism perspectives, but they do ask for clarification of definitional, descriptive, and responsive parameters. If we cannot clearly identify and recognize different cultures, how can the imposition of one over another be known? Or if cultures are reduced to cuisine or music preference or fashion, there would seem to be less urgent concern. Again, this is not to argue there are no cultural differences; it does ask for the source and significance of cultural difference.

Unfortunately, many otherwise robust defenses of cultural imperialism provide scant explanations of what specific cultural practices are being constrained within the receiving nation. For example, Paul Moody (2017) thoroughly documents US embassy support for Hollywood's economic interests. He quotes Herb Schiller's (1976) cogent summary of US media and government efforts to attract, pressure, and bribe elites in developing countries to promote the values and structures of the US. Moody applauds Colin Sparks' (2012) updated definition as "the use of state power in the international cultural sphere" (p. 293), but he gives no description of what those cultural values, structures or spheres are, nor does he indicate what are the values and structures of the neo-colonial client states. In fact, both Sparks and Moody insist that cultural imperialism does not need to have any particular impact upon their audiences (Sparks, 2012, p. 293) or any claims of influence by specific films or filmmakers (Moody, 2017, p. 2915). Quite strange. If cultural imperialism has no verifiable impact on audiences or nations, why the insistence that dominant-subordinate cultural relations matter and how would one even know?

Lydia and Damilola (2020) present similar arguments for cultural imperialism approaches in addressing contemporary media practices in Nigeria. In particular, the authors are concerned with the decline of popular interest in the norms and values of Nigerian society, rudimentarily summarized as the loss of traditional religion, non-traditional increased freedoms for women, and the acculturation to Western ways. Yet, neither Western nor Nigerian culture are described. Should 60% illiteracy be defended as traditional culture? Lydia and Damilola explain culture as "a way of life… deliberately fashioned to guide all aspects of a people's life" (p. 95), but they stop short of explaining actual Nigerian daily life. The British colonization of Africa artificially created nations for administrative purposes, but Nigeria remains culturally and ethnically divided between several dominant groups, including Yoruba, Igbo, and Hausa with more than 370 other indigenous cultures, many with their own language and traditions. Perhaps the only time Nigerians overcame their ethnic differences was in their common struggle against their colonial rulers (Countries, n.d.). Lydia and Damilola do not mention that since formal independence in 1960, ethnic conflicts over resources and political power have repeatedly become violent. They recount the history of the Arabic North of Nigeria and outline Portuguese and British imperialism's effect on the South, including slavery and then exploitation of raw materials, both accompanied by Christian evangelists—all historical and material evidence of imperialism and its cultural impositions in the 19th century. The authors then assert but do not provide evidence of cultural and consumerist effects on Nigerian commercial media, including in indigenous films that dominate the media market. The authors provide no description of any indigenous or contemporary cultures among the Nigerian population. We do not know what cultural values or practices have been overwhelmed by cultural imposition. Christianity and English were forcibly introduced in the 19th century, but we do not know the values and practices being imposed today. In fact, if cultural differences were even cursorily identified, it would most likely indicate the national imposition of the Yoruba or Igbo culture rather than British or American.

A more contemporary rendering of cultural imperialism by Tanner Mirrlees (2019a) reports on the global reach of Canadian television. Citing several instances of Canadian fears of American influence that suggested Canada was the "world's most dependent 'developed' country" in the words of Dallas Smythe (1981, p. 232), Mirrlees notes that the preponderance of US media giants places Canada in the global media periphery. He acknowledges the collaboration of Canadian media and the Canadian government to protect Canadian culture. This cogent overview exhibits one of the difficulties with cultural imperialism and much of media studies—geography becomes reified—attributing a national essence to commercial media as representative of an entire nation and people, disregarding social class and social relations of power. There are no shared interests between media owners and average citizens. Mirrlees observes that Canada's big five media conglomerates have gotten bigger and "exert much more power over the structure of Canada's TV sector than US companies do," even noting that all companies in Canada's TV sector are "market oriented and pursue profit" such that Canada is home to "powerful cultural industries, big media conglomerates and a flourishing TV sector" (p. 13). So, does or will Canadian-owned media protect Canadian culture? Should Canadians who fear becoming Americanized support Canadian media monopolies and advocate the export of Canadian culture?

The other glaring question is: what exactly is Canadian culture? The Mounties? The metric system? Hockey? Displacing indigenous nations? Perhaps the content and form of globally popular TV series produced by

Canadian media express the cultural identity of Canada? *DeGrassi* was an ostensibly Canadian teen drama aired for 14 seasons on Canadian TV, in the US on Nickelodeon and PBS, and also in Australia and South Africa. *DeGrassi* featured a changing ensemble of youth in a fictional school facing dramatic teen-aged challenges, such as bullying, teen pregnancy, mental health, and other teen-aged issues. Nothing about the series, besides the location, exudes Canadian identity. *Schitt's Creek*, an immensely popular Canadian comedy, recounted the travails of a previously rich family that has to adjust to small town life. Not only does the series feature American actors, the story itself follows the typical plot of how a displaced privileged elite cope as average citizens. Again, besides some well-known Canadian actors and the locale, it is unclear what makes this uniquely Canadian—even the production and distribution of the program was a transnational venture by the Canadian Broadcast Company and US and British media.

Finally, Mirrlees references *Cardinal*, a four season Canadian crime drama based on Giles Blunt's novels (at least one of which was set in New York). The lead character is an American actor. Besides the presence of the Royal Canadian Mounted Police, Canadian landmarks, and some laconic Canadian accents, little about the series deviates from typical serialized murder tropes. Canadian culture may indeed be distinct from US culture, but which components of the Canadian way of life must be protected from US "imperialism" are not very clear. "Taking a swipe at US cultural imperialism" (Henley, 2005), also shores up the market power of the big Canadian media firms (which seem to be opting for a cultural imperialism of their own) (Mirrlees, 2019a, p. 16). What exactly must we oppose in US cultural imperialism? Should Canadians opt for a nascent Canadian cultural imperialism?

Mirrlees (2019a) suggests that Canada has become "Hollywood North" because US studios can find locations that look American and cultural workers in Canada have lower wages. In addition, Canada has become more transnational (as defined earlier) with about 60 co-productions with studios in France, Germany, Ireland, Britain, and Australia (pp. 14–15). Perhaps Canada aspires to cultural dominance in Latin America? What other option does the Canadian media industry have for capitalist growth? Again, herein is the problem of identifying media ownership, production, influence, and culture as national, when the real, pressing communication and political issues are questions of social class, social relations, and social power contained and expressed through commercial media which structurally deny public access.

Here one might reasonably take the same approach to "cultural imperialism" inside the United States organized by the military-entertainment complex to influence American values and behaviors. As Linebaugh (2014) notes media monopoly and government power convergence appears in CIA (Central Intelligence Agency) cultural campaigns, including exhibitions, magazines, and orchestras for domestic consumption (p. 116). He argues that the CIA functioned as a Ministry of Culture with the support of Ford, Rockefeller, and Carnegie Foundation—modeling cultural imperialism in the hemisphere. One obvious point from Linebaugh's example is that cultural imperialism as a rubric may miss the more fundamental political economy question of which social class controls media structures and content "from points of production to the organization of reproduction… from commodity to division of labor" (p. 118), including education, advertisements, culture, and media—nationally and internationally.

It is perhaps unfair to ask media studies scholars to clarify our understanding of culture when decades of study by anthropologists and ethnographers have not reached a consensus (Agar, 2019). Raymond Williams (1989) offered a definition for media studies and sociology that "culture is a whole way of life" (p. 8). Jan Pieterse (2020) notes that culture is often summed up as customs and beliefs that are learned and shared as part of a social group (pp. 10-11). Cultural geographer Ben Anderson (2020) suggests that culture is primarily a "placeholder term" that informs contrasting orientations, some of which reify culture as an essential human difference, echoing colonialist assumptions (p. 608). Yet distinguishing individual cultures as specific ways of life has not always been categorical or even apparent. The Antiguan novelist Jamaica Kincaid (2000) wrote: "And what is culture anyway? In some places, it's the way you behave out in public; and in still other places, it's *just* the way you behave out in public; and in still other places, it's just the way a person cooks food. And so what is there to preserve about these things? For is it not so that people make them up as they go along, make them up as they need them?" (pp. 49–50). The outmoded concept of "traditional" cultural values and behaviors doesn't work anymore; there are no remaining "authentic" cultures; we are all a mix of cultures.

Granted, different cultures may have different meaning systems—the direct product of power struggles historical and contemporary—indicating the social relations of power within any society (Gramsci, 2000), so culture remains a site of political and social conflict. Historical anthropologist, Brian Ferguson has argued that "culture has cumulative development—and it needs language and symbols for this. You learn what one generation did, then you can do something on top of that. Everything we have in this world goes back to thousands and thousands of innovations, all of which have been based on the innovations that came before" (in Short, 2021). Often that means that a purported national culture represents the distillation of dominant social interests resisted by popular needs and practices. Even "nations and their borders are the outcomes of regional politics" (Pieterse, 2020, p. 14), while culture is the product of more historical contests over religion, ethnicity, and social class power. Benedict Anderson (2016) discards Asian values and other culturalist assumptions as reifications of national identities created by capitalist ideologues. Indeed, many assumptions about national cultures are actually colonial inventions that identified meanings, practices, and values filtered through a colonialist national identity that asserted indigenous ethnicity was the cause of inequality.

In general, culture regularly appears as a shortcut cultivating racial and ethnic difference as the cause of social and economic inequality, without identifying the concrete components that construct any cultural value, belief, or practice. Culture then becomes a concept which disguises social, political, and economic relations which are instrumental in constructing a "way of life." Recognizing culture as a way of life (with all of its ritual practices, artifacts, language, and social relations) underscores culture as an ongoing process of construction, learning, and practice. Culture cannot be separated from the social order; it cannot be frozen in time to find its authenticity. Actual relations, events, and practices can only be understood ideologically and culturally within existing social relations of power. Oftentimes the values and behaviors attached to nations and cultures as racist stereotypes appear in similar values and behaviors that are presumably defended in solidarity with resistance to cultural imposition. This raises a key question: which behaviors accurately express a national culture and which behaviors become reified as standing for a national culture? So in describing global media practices, if one wants to deploy "cultural imperialism" as an explanatory and predictive theory, both culture and imperialism need considerable unpacking to be meaningful and useful.

The Australian based Cultural Atlas (https://culturalatlas.sbs.com.au/) publishes "Core Concepts" of diverse national cultures to improve cross-cultural communication, but the stated concepts do not link values to any specific cultural behaviors. Solidarity, group orientation, interdependence, harmony, and diversity ostensibly define each of several cultures, including Brazil, Japan, China, India, and Mexico, but few would suggest these values indicate how citizens in those cultures lead their daily lives. Language, holidays, and rituals commemorating national histories, religion, and cuisine might provide better markers of cultural difference and identity. But even those provide little indication of which cultural practice describes fundamental differences when it comes to domination and subordination. Will eating burgers instead of shawarma undermine Indian culture? Does hip-hop radio destroy taverna music in Turkey? Does Tata Motors purchase of Jaguar replace British cultural values for mechanics and drivers? In each case, the demand to protect traditional cultures presumes citizens (not national media monopolies and government regulations) in diverse nations actually produce their daily culture. It also presumes that they prefer and defend other traditional practices, which might include child brides, clitorectomies, polygamy, the caste system, reliance on magic over medicine, machismo, ethnic and religious violence, and other cultural behaviors.

In his treatment of nations as "imagined communities," Anderson (2016) disrupts many national culture presuppositions, noting that imperialism predominated because the colonial capitalist class created, drafted, and promoted hegemonic cultural values—that expressed a national identity in language, education, administration, and culture (pp. 91, 114). National cultures have included poetry, literature, music, dance, and fashion that express proposed ethnic, race, and national identities—all conceived and advocated by the colonial and domestic capitalist class. What is "Nigerian" culture in a nation with 370 ethnic groups and languages? As noted earlier, traditional cultures are seldom national cultures; traditional icons are incorporated into national cultures by national elites for their own class interests. (Disney was accused of appropriating Mulan from *Chinese* culture, but Mulan was already appropriated by the Chinese empire during its 5th century conquest of *Mongolian-Turkic* communities in the north.) More importantly, today prevailing cultural practices of citizens in countries from China and India to Brazil and Mexico to Europe and the Middle East are largely defined by wage labor and consumerism, with some loosely articulated traditional domestic cultural highlights. None of this is to deny cultural differences or tradition, but does note that all cultural practices are the historical outcome of conflict and negotiation over meaning appropriated and constructed for social, political, and economic power.

Global consumer culture has been established. Working classes, peasants, and entrepreneurs everywhere rely on wages and salaries for survival. They must turn to the market for daily essentials. In short, the hegemonic social relations that organize our working lives, survival needs, and recreation are all constructed within capitalism, with many national and cultural variations. From a robust historical perspective, dominant behaviors and accepted norms result from and connect to social relations that represent and organize power: time clocks, flow charts of authority, decision-making protocols, wages or salary, and the personal consumption of advertised goods. In any language, under any religion, with any unique cultural markers, daily behaviors are organized by contemporary capitalism and predicated on wage labor and corporate ownership enforced by government laws and policing.

Nations and cultures are politically constructed: enforced by police, courts, jails, and other coercion; recruited with flags, parades, holidays, public pledges, and other practices and patriotic symbols; persuaded through news and entertainment media featuring heroes, worthy victims, and preferred national and ethnic identities; and reinforced by everyday practices of language, religion, recreation, and work. "We" are identified, recruited, persuaded, and socialized to be the "we" of a nation and a national culture. "They" are identified, evaluated, and positioned as the "they" which threaten us.

Popular culture is not folk culture. It is not authentic culture of the people. Popular culture of the late 20th century is lived in everyday practices activating beliefs and values interacting with our working lives, media, mass production, and consumption—all of which affect our languages, our stories, our music, our expectations. Those daily practices organized by existing social relations and cultural practices are not reducible to some geographically-specific US or Western values. The "local" culture of the entire world (with the exception of Cuba) is produced and constructed by local, domestic, and national corporate powers that influence their national governments and civil society organizations and control the means of production of wealth—increasingly in partnership with other transnational companies. The music and discourses of daily life are organized by transnational and national commercial media promoting ideologies and practices which incorporate working class challenges and cultural diversity into broader narratives for existing social relations. Thus, EMI Universal, the French-British music TNMC, produces Ghana's "high life" music and SonyBMG, the Japanese-German music group, produces and distributes American hip-hop. Likewise, to be economically successful even big budget "blockbuster movies need to play well on an international scale" (Richeri, 2016, p. 316), leading most studios to rely on spectacle and to feature more gender, race, ethnic, national, and cultural diversity to attract large audiences. Still, while media entertainment and popular culture may provide some respite and pleasure validating cultural diversity, the new global culture is thoroughly transnational, whether appearing in Chinese, French, German, or Yoruban.

Transnational Media

Globalization theories present oblique concepts of a stateless international empire, hybridity, and agency, all of which ignore the developing political economy of neoliberal capitalism. Neoliberal governments front for their own transnational capitalists, facilitating collaboration, unregulated markets, and unfettered profits. In contrast, cultural imperialism articulated more accurate explanatory and theoretical concepts. However, the conditions of cultural production have changed since the 1980s and 1990s. Capitalism of the late 20th century has changed. Global media relations have changed. Cultural imperialism has not been eclipsed by globalization, the collapse of national cultures, or the political decline of nation-state governments. Cultural imperialism has been superseded by culturally and politically collaborative transnational media.

In contrast to both globalization and cultural imperialism approaches, the appraisal presented in this book recognizes what exists: capitalism and its evolving social relations of power based on ownership, control, and leadership are hegemonic—having won wide consent of media owners, governments, labor, and audiences in most countries. This is not an adherence to some misconstrued Marxist determinism, but a recognition of the actual material conditions of media structures and practices and an historical understanding of the impulses and necessities which direct capitalism nationally, regionally, and globally. Genocide of Native Americans and the Israeli destruction of Palestine have created new historical conditions and relations of power. These conditions may be undesirable and ethically indefensible, but having been created, the imposed and material conditions formed a new reality that must be addressed as it exists, not as it used to be.

Imperialist colonial powers educated and socialized managers and administrators to a "system of tastes, opinions, morals, and intellect" with the beliefs, values, and behaviors of the hegemonic colonial power—long before cultural imperialism (Anderson, 2016, p. 91). As colonial nations became nominally independent, neo-colonial relations were administered by national compradors, elites who shared political and economic interests with their former colonial rulers. Cultural imperialism developed—not so much as imposed—and was welcomed by well-trained, assimilated colonials. Cultural imperialism predominated within developing nations wherever a domestic capitalist class leadership created, drafted, and promoted hegemonic cultural values and behaviors. Now, however, economic and media dominance (along with cultural imperialism) by the US and other monopoly capitalist nations, has been overtaken by transnational capitalism because millionaire and billionaire capitalists in the global South share common perspectives and common interest with transnational partners from the South and North.

Media as an industry has been pushed to transnationalism for survival. Domestic markets have topped out, even in the US. Profits taken domestically have reached their limit—and quite often do not even meet the costs of production. Cross-nation media distribution is required to secure larger audiences. Thus, media in the US and China, for instance, have been "making more Sino-American co-productions and increasing the investment from each country's companies in the other nation's film industry" (Richeri, 2019, p. 322), while Chinese studios have also partnered with Korean, Japanese, and even European filmmakers. New strategies emerged: film franchises with sequels and prequels; less dialog, more spectacle; more action and fantasy; more cultural diversity; and above all, joint ventures and partnerships among media across national borders.

The chapters which form this book illustrate how *transnationalism*, as a new stage of capitalism with national capitalist classes collaborating on global strategies, jointly influencing their national governments to privatize public resources, and cooperatively expanding foreign investment, joint ventures, and cross-border production and distribution partnerships. Importantly, and in tandem with other transnational industries, transnational media have organized new structures, relations, regulations, and a new international division of cultural labor. Thousands of creative workers across borders and cultures are employed and directed by the shared managements of transnational capitalist owners to produce, distribute, and profit from culturally diverse entertainment products. Creative workers are increasingly integrated into the industrial process, as individual work is computerized, standardized, and even replaced by AI (artificial intelligence) technology, creating "relations of domination and dependency" (Knoche, 2019, p. 295) that contribute to capitalist wealth but not the common good.

Media content production and distribution depends on the technology and the social relations of production and consumption that are structurally and ideologically organized. With digital technology, media content becomes consumption through limited access rights (streaming, copyright, individual rentals). Meanwhile, media production is determined by the relationship of owners of media production to the primary creators, writers, actors, producers, and technicians—a relationship corresponding to decision-making relations that assign the skills and available technology to the most profit-making formats and genres. The new transnational division of cultural labor means media corporations employ local contractors, assemblers, media editors, sound engineers, set designers, costumers, grips, and other workers to complete the production of media commodities—none of which is done exclusively within one nation or by one company. The actual social relations of media production and consumption are not national, but transnational; media content becomes available internationally through digital technology and platforms purchased by consumers. The means of production and distribution have changed dramatically with new platforms and formats, while the new transnational media enterprises remain capitalist owned and controlled. Notably, the relations between the owners and the producers and consumers of media (and all other industries) are always politically apparent in enacted government regulations and policies.

As explanations and examples in subsequent chapters confirm, regional media corporations produce content bolstering transnational capitalist relations and interests based on a new political economy of media, In this process, national cultures which were largely constructed by national capitalists (Mattelart, 1976) have become imbued with ingredients favorable to transnational capitalism. This global culture cannot be defined as American or Western. Seeking to legitimize wage labor, hyper-individualism, and social hierarchy, transnational media exhibit globalized capitalist market values and consumerist norms. Content in all genre, distributed across all media, present themes and values that have clear preferences for stories about an individual protagonist's self-interest, based in hierarchical systems (whether historical, contemporary, dystopian, or fantasy narratives), with an ideological and narrative defense of deference to authority. In fact, leaving aside language and setting, one would be hard pressed to identify the national culture of *Taken* (2014), *Hobbit* (2014), *Kita Kita* (2017), *Black Panther* (2018), or *Hotel Mumbai* (2019). In addition, because transnational movies are produced for profit, to keep production costs down most media genre rely heavily on spectacle rather than dialog or character development and feature clumsy appeals to diverse audiences by including token female, Black, Hispanic, Asian, and other characters presumably representative of those audiences. Moreover, science fiction and fantasy in particular present stories without explicit national or cultural characteristics or settings, attracting and amusing audiences without regard to their cultural proclivities other than entertainment and spectacle.

TNMCs also hope to maximize audience appeal by incorporating local cultures and radical content which offer an appearance of diversity and inclusivity while reinforcing a hegemonic capitalist ideology. Including critiques of the social system and its agents not only attracts diverse audiences, it allows multiple interpretations of the films' meaning. Viewers become immersed in the spectacles and attracted to the hegemonic values and behaviors essential to capitalism (Artz, 2013). The cultural norms and values of top transnational films transcend local and national cultures but do not serve to inculcate exclusively US, Western, or other identifiable national cultural imperialist interests. As Mirrlees (2013) concluded, "Even though TV shows and films circulate in a world system of nation-states, they are shaped by economic, political, and cultural forces and relations that are no longer contained within national boxes" (p. ix). Transnational media parallel and serve transnational capitalism.

One should also be concerned that opposing cultural imperialism in defense of national culture, national media, and national capitalists disarms and misdirects social movements capable of building their own democratic media systems and participatory practices. This is not a specious concern, but an important practical and political component of any critical media study of power. As Haynes (2018) recounts, the emerging youth audience in Nigeria is not interested in returning to traditional village culture, while commercial entrepreneurs offer only a variant of capitalist mass culture. Real communication alternatives can only arise from opposition to global *and* national commercial media ownership, both of which are based on labor exploitation, cultural cooptation, and capitalist profit. While disarming social movements is not the intent of any cultural imperialism proponents, the formulation itself obscures the actual social relations of production within and between nations which are constrained by social class conditions of ownership, control, organization, and political power. Do Brazilians have more access to media production if Disney and X-Men are excluded in favor of Marinho's Rede Globo telenovelas, sports, and news media? Across Latin America, Africa, and Asia, domestic landowners, industrialists, corporate managers, local entrepreneurs, and local and transnational media construct and promote an ideology of hierarchy, class inequality, and privilege based on individual wealth, closely linked with European ancestry and racism. In other words, cultural imperialism is less of an issue than which social classes actually have control over media production and distribution, including the structure, design, and content of broadcast, satellite, cable, internet, cell phone, and social media applications.

There is no "our" media, if there ever was a media representing the majority of citizens. There is no "their" media, if referring to any nation's media—which are consolidated by capitalist owners. "Their" media accurately refers to capitalist media. Commercial media never represented a nation's citizens, but has always served to advertise, privilege, and report on the corporate elite and their governments (Herman & Chomsky, 1988). TNMCs do not belong to or represent the interests of any national publics, including those of the industrialized nations of the global North. TNMCs are a crucial part of the transnational capitalist system, promoting market relations, deference to authority, and individual consumerism and self-reliance.

References

Adl-Tabatabai, S. (2017, August 27). Here are the 147 transnational companies that run the world. *Technocracy: News and Trends.* https://www.technocracy.news/147-transnational-companies-run-world/

Agar, M. H. (2019). *Culture: How to make it work in a world of hybrids.* London: Rowman & Littlefield.

Anderson, B. (2020). Cultural geography III: The concept of "culture." *Progress in Human Geography 44*(3), 608–617.

Anderson, B. (2016). *Imagined communities: Reflections on the origin and spread of nationalism.* New York: Verso.

Andrews, T. (2016, May 18). Real clownfish suffered after 'Finding Nemo,' so 'Finding Dory' raises concerns. *Chicago Tribune.* https://www.chicagotribune.com/nation-world/ct-finding-dory-blue-tang-population-20160518-story.html

Artz, L. (2013). Media hegemony. In M. Danesi (Ed.), *Encyclopedia of media and communication* (pp. 336–339). Toronto: University of Toronto Press.

Artz, L. (2015). *Global entertainment media: A critical introduction.* New York: Wiley-Blackwell.

Boyd-Barrett, O. (1977). Media imperialism: Towards an international framework for the analysis of media systems. In J. Curran, M. Gurevitch, & J. Woollacott (Eds.), *Mass communication and society* (pp. 116–135). London: Edward Arnold

Boyd-Barrett, O., & Mirrlees, T. (2020). *Media imperialism: Continuity and change.* Lanham, MD: Rowman & Littlefield.

Callinicos, A. (2009). *Imperialism and global political economy.* Malden, MA: Polity Press.

Countries and Their Cultures. (n.d.) *Nigeria.* https://www.everyculture.com/Ma-Ni/Nigeria.html

Danaher, K. (2001). *Ten reasons to abolish the IMF and World Bank.* New York: Seven Stories Press.

Davidson, N. (2016). *Nation-states: Consciousness and competition.* Chicago: Haymarket Books.

Fazio, M. (2020, November 23). "The Queen's Gambit" sends chess set sales soaring. *New York Times.* https://www.nytimes.com/2020/11/23/arts/television/chess-set-board-sales.html

Gerbner, G., Gross, L., Morgan, M., & Signorielli, N. (1994). Growing up with television: The cultivation perspective. In M. Morgan (Ed.), *Against the mainstream: The selected works of George Gerbner* (pp. 193–213). Hillsdale, NJ: Lawrence Erlbaum Associates.

Gramsci, A. (2000). *The Antonio Gramsci reader: Selected writings, 1916–1935.* D. Forgacs (Ed.). New York: New York University Press.

Harvey, D. (2005). *The new imperialism*. Oxford: Oxford University Press.

Haynes, J. (2018). Keeping up: The corporatization of Nollywood's economy and paradigms for studying African screen media. *Africa Today 64*(4), 3–29.

Henley, J. (2005, October 19). *Global plan to protect film culture. The Guardian.* https://www.theguardian.com/world/2005/oct/19/artsnews.filmnews

Herman, E. S., & Chomsky, N. (1988). *Manufacturing consent: The political economy of the mass media*. New York: Pantheon.

Iraq Business News. (2020). List of international oil companies in Iraq. *iraq-business news.* https://www.iraq-businessnews.com/list-of-international-oil-companies-in-iraq/

Kincaid, J. (2000). *A small place.* New York: Farrar, Strauss, and Giroux.

Knoche, M. (2019). The crisis-ridden capitalist mode of production as driving force for restructurations and transformations in and of the media industry: Explanatory theoretical elements of a critique of the political economy of the media. *TripleC: Communication, Capitalism & Critique 17*(2), 287–307.

Linebaugh, P. (2014). *Stop thief! The commons, enclosures, and resistance.* Oakland, CA: PM Press.

Lydia, O., & Damilola, A. (2020). Mass media and cultural imperialism: The Nigerian experience. *Global Journal of Education, Humanities and Management Sciences 2*(1), 91–102.

Mattelart, A. (1976). Cultural imperialism in the multinational's age. *Instant Research on Peace and Violence 6*(4), 160–174.

Meade, J. (2017, May 22). How "Hunger Games" changed archery forever! *Hunter's Friend.* https://www.huntersfriend.com/how_hunger_games_changed_archery_forever.html

Mirrlees, T. (2013). *Global entertainment media: Between cultural imperialism and cultural globalization.* New York: Routledge.

Mirrlees, T. (2019a). Canadian TV Goes global. In P. Sigismondi (Ed.), *World entertainment media: Global, regional and local perspectives* (pp. 11–19). New York: Routledge

Mirrlees, T. (2019b). The military-entertainment complex, US imperialism and. In Ness, I. & Cope, Z. (Eds.), *The Palgrave encyclopedia of imperialism and anti-imperialism.* https://doi.org/10.1007/978-3-319-91206-6_48-1

Moody, P. (2017). US embassy support for Hollywood's global dominance: Cultural imperialism redux. *International Journal of Communication 11*, 2912–2925.

Nkrumah, K. (1965). *Neo-colonialism: The last stage of imperialism.* London: Thomas Nelson & Sons.

Panitch, L., & Gindin, S. (2004). Global capitalism and American empire. In L. Pantich (Ed.), *The new imperial challenge* (pp. 13–33). London: Merlin Press

Patnaik, U., & Patnaik, P. (2017). *A theory of imperialism.* New York: Columbia University Press.

Pieterse, J. N. (2020). *Globalization and culture: Global Mélange.* 4th Ed. Lanham, MD: Rowman & Littlefield.

Phillips, P. (2018). *Giants: The global power elite.* New York: Seven Stories Press, 2018.

Prashad, V. (2020, November 28). Why imperialism is obsolete in Latin America. *Eurasia Review.* https://www.eurasiareview.com/28112020-why-imperialism-is-obsolete-in-latin-america-interview/

Richeri, G. (2016). Global film market, regional problems. *Global Media China 1*(4), 312–330.

Rugman, A. M. (2005). Globalization and regional international production. In J. Ravenhill (Ed.), *Global political economy* (pp. 263–290). Oxford: Oxford University Press

Schiller, H. I. (1976). *Communication and cultural domination.* White Plains, NY: International Arts and Sciences Press.

Short, A. M. (2021, January 22). War is not innate to humanity: A more peaceful future is possible. *Counterpunch*. https://www.counterpunch.org/2021/01/22/war-is-not-innate-to-humanity-a-more-peaceful-future-is-possible/

Sklair, L. (2001). *The transnational capitalist class*. New York: Wiley.

Smythe, D. (1981). *Dependency road: Communication, capitalism, consciousness, and Canada*. Norwood, NJ: Ablex.

Sparks, C. (2012). Media and cultural imperialism reconsidered. *Chinese Journal of Communication 5*(3), 281–299.

Tunstall, J. (1977). *The media are American*. New York: Columbia University Press.

UNESCO (United Nations Education, Scientific, and Cultural Organization). (2001). Universal declaration on cultural diversity. UNESCO.org. http://portal.unesco.org/en/ev.php-URL_ID=13179&URL_DO=DO_TOPIC&URL_SECTION=201.html

van der Pijl, K. (1998). *Transnational classes and international relations*. New York: Routledge.

Williams, R. (1989) Culture is ordinary. In *Resources of Hope* (pp. 3–18). New York: Verso.

Wood, E. M. (2003). *Empire of capital*. New York: Verso.

3

MEDIA IN INDIA

From Public to Private to Transnational

A handsome, chiseled young man leans in to kiss a fashionably-dressed beautiful young woman. The attraction is palpable. Romance surrounds the passion. Lips part… cut to dance scene! For decades affection on screens in India led to extravagant and colorful musical production numbers, reflecting the conservative mores of deeply religious and patriarchal society.

India is a caste stratified, multi-class, multi-religious, and multi-lingual society, with 31 languages and hundreds of dialects. Hindi is spoken by about 45% of the population, with some 100 million who speak English. The divisions are even more stark economically. There is a handful of millionaires and billionaires, with a growing middle class of hundreds of millions "aspiring to enjoy the comforts of a western lifestyle" (Rodrigues, 2010, p. 20). Yet, most estimates still find more than 300 million poor. According to Oxfam, an international research and advocacy group, India's top 1% of the population now holds 73% of the wealth, while the country's poorest half, saw their wealth rise by just 1% in 2018 (Business Today, 2019).

With more than 1.4 billion people, 50% whom under 25 years old, India is one of the world's largest markets (Tatna, 2019). Overall, India's growth rate was 4% in 2019, according to World Bank with 7.2% GDP growth in 2020 according to the Asian Development Bank. India's Commerce & Industry Ministry reported that 2020 Foreign Direct Investment (FDI) increased 40%, making India one of few major economies in world with rising FDI. Cross-border mergers and FDI grew especially in telecom, e-commerce, cloud computing, and IT, which includes television and film streaming services (Elegant, 2021). In the last three decades, hundreds of transnational corporations invested and expanded in India, hundreds more are wanting in. Media Partners Asia found that India attracts most of the television ventures by US media (Frater, 2018).

DOI: 10.4324/9781003162452-04

Increasingly Indian transnational media companies (TNMC) represent the success of neoliberal restructuring of global capital as it traverses national borders to make deals with partners-in-profit. To understand TNMC developments in their historical context, we begin with a brief background to privatization and foreign investment in India

The Neoliberal Turn

Following independence in 1947, India embraced the Non-Aligned Movement, an alliance of 120 Asian and African nations looking to avoid choosing sides during the Cold War. The Nehru-Ghandi governments adopted a pacifist perspective in international politics and cultivated a progressive, semi-socialist national policy. Government policy promoted national development through public ownership and regulation that curbed private capital and foreign investment, but did little to alleviate poverty, inequality, or the caste system (Mehta, 2011). Following the collapse of the Soviet Union and its favorable trade relations, India found itself economically disoriented. With its national protection no longer functioning and the global economy in disarray, India was cajoled toward neoliberal capitalism as a means to bolster its economy that was in danger of defaulting on global debt.

India officially joined the neoliberal project of global capitalism in 1991. Under pressure from the IMF and with the consensus of elite Indian capitalist groups (Sen, 2011, p. 145), the Narsimha Rao government weakened regulations protecting public institutions, sold national interests in transportation, public utilities, and state development projects, lowered import tariffs and offered financial incentives to foreign investors. Eighty percent of industries were removed from federal licensing and many industries were permitted 100% foreign investment.

The Indian government adopted, legitimated, and then instituted neoliberal social and economic policies, including the privatization of previously large scale national, public industries that had been part of India's development model for decades. The participation of Indian capital in the globalization of unregulated markets merged with the enthusiastic facilitation by the Indian government. Under the guise of using cultural resources to make India more competitive, the abrupt disruption of public media by satellite broadcast, cable television, and licensing of private media created an environment incentivized for transnational partners, massive FDI, and unlimited media consolidation (Punathambekar, 2013). The national was linked with the transnational as capital, labor, and media commodities were spatially and socially reconfigured.

Indian media joined with French, English, Chinese, Malaysian, and US media to produce television and film content for culturally diverse audiences. Neoliberal transnational capital became hegemonic—which meant its leadership won the consent of Indian capitalists, managers, and the rising middle class of professionals and entrepreneurs (Gramsci, 2000). The Indian nation, its media, and its culture allied with other transnational capital, labor, and cultural contributors (Yudice, 2005). India moved beyond geography per se because the mobility of capital reorganized the nature and practice of "national" media. National media still thrive in India, while film and television are more consolidated. News and entertainment content is created and assembled transnationally by managers and specialists in decentralized multiple locales collaborating on co-productions and distribution agreements or longer term joint ventures (JV). This transnational production and distribution provides a more flexible accumulation of wealth by capital from labor. Labor remains confined by national regulations and restrictions on movement, but capital and its commodities roam freely.

Indian capitalism and its government also reconfigured its relationship to the 50 million Indians in the diaspora, reinventing Bombay-Mumbai as a global cultural city inviting to transnational partners and the rapid development of private television, advertising, Internet, and telecommunication industries—in each case requiring increased levels of technology, skilled labor, and industrial convergence.

Recognizing that "television is a highly visible product that functions as the best marketing tool for the liberalization of the India economy" (Sinha, 1999, p. 27), the media market was opened to commercial privatization with few restrictions. As Daya Thussu (2016) noted, "in contemporary international relations, the capacity of nations to make themselves attractive in a globalizing marketplace for ideas, has become a crucial component of foreign policy" (p. 226). Media and entertainment were considered means for communicating a positive image for the nation, while serving the economic interests of its commercial media industry, offering economic benefits to a sizeable upper middle class, and validating the many cultures of the larger, multi-ethnic population.

Prior to neoliberal reforms, India had one national television station, Doordarshan. By 2009, 450 commercial broadcasts reaching 500 million viewers had elbowed the public station aside. Transnational media quickly expanded into India, building alliances with domestic broadcasters and producing programs in Hindi, Marathi, Tamil, and Telugu. Some like Zee TV featured a hybrid "Hinglish" language as all media sought content attractive to India's multi-lingual and multicultural audiences—audiences that are severely divided into privileged and impoverished social classes with different needs and expectations for media content and access (Rodrigues, 2010, pp. 18, 23). In the midst of these glaring social contradictions, a significant number of Indian films presented affluence as "the signifier for national value and pride," while corporate news channels represented and catered to the "ambitions and political niches of the upper middle-class post-global India" and major movie studios served as entertaining allies to neoliberalism (Mehta, 2011, p. 5).

By the time the Indian government opened media to unlimited foreign investment, transnational capital had already entered the rest of the economy through partnerships and JV. A transnational joint venture is attractive to both domestic and non-national corporations. These JV bring two or more partners from two or more nations together to achieve a common objective for commercial purposes. It may be a long-term agreement for a continuous process (such as forming a separate company) or on a limited basis for a short-term objective (such as a co-production of a single film). JV are highly flexible and often temporary, short-term. The form and duration of a JV depends on the decisions and resources of the parties involved. JV share expertise and liabilities, leverage resources, expand markets, and anticipate increased profit. In short, a transnational joint venture is a consensual alliance of two or more companies from two or more nations mutually sharing the complementary resources of the partners for commercial gain. JV may be "co-production projects as 'temporary systems' of production involving a range of firms, creative artists and technical services, with actors drawn from established pool of talent in project networks as more than temporary systems" (Hoyler & Watson, 2019, p. 45).

The emergence of these new transnational capital partnerships encouraged by the government and industrial leaders set the stage for further media deregulation and consolidation, because media and their entertainment content are constructed within and through circuits of capital, production cultures, and government policies. Likewise, media images and narratives of gender, power, and celebrity relate to civic values and national and regional politics. For example, in Indian media few Muslim actors, writers, or directors can be seen (Sen, 2015).

A brief overview of Indian capital's willing participation in the neoliberal project will help to clarify how transnational media corporate partnerships are not unique but parallel to other industry transformations.

Transnational Joint Ventures

Transnational JV, partnerships, and mergers have become standard in the contemporary Indian economy and occur in most every industry. Following the "Make In India" 2014 initiative (www.makeinindia.com) by Prime Minister Narendra Modi, foreign investments increased dramatically. In 2020, FDI to India reached $51 billion (Sabarwai, 2021). To attract investors to one of the largest consumer markets in the world, India invited more FDI in retail, pharmaceutical, consumer products, media, railways, as well as in defense manufacturing, aerospace, and other industries. Importantly, the government's regulatory policies were relaxed to facilitate investment.

Agriculture has long been the backbone of India's national development. About half of India's working population is involved in agriculture. However, with India's neoliberal turn in the 1990s, three of the largest transnational agro-industry corporations (Dupont India, Monsanto–Bayer, and United Phosphorous) invest heavily in India and manufacture seeds, insecticides, and pesticides. India produces tons of rice, milk, wheat, fruits, and vegetables for export, but there has been a rapid displacement of small- and medium-sized farms, as "seeds, mountains, water, forests, and biodiversity are being sold off" (Todhunter, 2016) to transnational investors and partners. The farmers are being squeezed further by Prime Minister Modi's 2020 privatization laws which oblige farmers to accept market prices set by the government, Cargill, Bayer, and their Indian partners.

Companies in other industries have struck partnerships, formed JV, and attracted sizable foreign investment—not under duress, but enthusiastically recognizing the political and economic leadership of transnational industries. For example, Tata Sons holds a 50:50 joint venture with Starbucks US, with "A Tata Alliance" operating a chain of coffee shops across India. The range of transnational partnerships in India is wide. Fratelli Wines is an Indo-Italian JV between the Secci brothers of Italy and the Sekhti and Mohite-Patel families in India. Fratelli combines Italian expertise and Indian grapes to produce wines worldwide. Aeronautics, consumer goods, construction, and many other industries in India illustrate the growth of multiple transnational production and distribution partnerships, with financing and profits shared among participating companies. The sections below highlight a few transnational operations by industry.

Aerospace and Airlines

- One Indian company with an abundance of transnational JV is Hindustan Aeronautics Ltd. (HAL), a government-owned industry, which has partners for making helicopters, wing fighter and civilian aircraft, defense systems and aerostructures, aircraft engines and other aeronautic and aerospace-related products. For example, HAL holds 50% of its joint venture with Edgewood Ventures of the US holding 26%. HAL and Edgewood also have partnered with Tata's Jaguar manufacturing aircraft engines for the Indian Air Force. With assets of almost $8 billion, HAL has production agreements with Sukhoi and Ilyushin in Russia to make fighter jets, US Boeing and transnational Airbus to make aircraft parts, Malaysian Su-30 for avionics, an Israeli company to make droned helicopters, and deals with other companies in Switzerland, Ecuador, Turkey and more.
- Tata Sons is a leader in transnational JV. Vistara is a JV between Tata and Singapore Airlines (SIA). Tata holds a 51% stake while SIA controls the rest. Vistara has carried some three million passengers since its launch. The two companies are pumping billions into Vistara to expand domestic operations, find international markets, and expand its fleet.

- Tata also owns 49% of AirAsia India, a JV with Malaysia-based AirAsia Berhad. The airline ranks as the fourth largest discount carrier in India.
- Tata Boeing Aerospace is a 2016 joint venture making Apache helicopter fuselages.
- Dassault Reliance Aerospace is a 2018 partnership between Anil Ambani's Reliance ADAG and Dassualt Aviation, a leading French aerospace company that manufactures military and business jets for 90 countries. The $80 million Dassualt Reliance partnership produces transport equipment, vehicles, and military hardware, serving as a hub for exporting to select Indian and French allies.
- BrahMos Aerospace, a JV between India's Defense Research and Development Organization (DRDO) and Russia's NOP Mashinostoryenia, manufactures missiles capable of carrying nuclear warheads.

Insurance

Insurance is a particularly fertile industry for JV, given its expected high return on investment. A few of the more notable transnational agreements include the following:

- Bharti AXA General Insurance is a JV between India's leading business group Bharti Enterprises and insurance major from France, AXA. The transnational Bharti AXA is the leading insurer in India.
- India's state owned Punjab National Bank (PNB) holds 30%, private India investors have 44%, and America's largest life insurer Metropolitan Life Insurance (MetLife) holds 26% of the joint venture, PNB MetLife India. PNB MetLife is one of the top life insurance companies in India.
- India's Max Life Insurance has a partnership with Japan's Mitsui Sumitomo Insurance.
- HDFC ERGO General Insurance is a JV between HDFC, India's top housing finance company, and ERGO International of Germany's Munich Re Group. HDFC ERGO offers auto, health, travel, home, and personal accident coverage.

Pharmaceuticals

India produces about 20% of the world's generic medicines and is the largest producer of vaccines, supplying over 50% globally. India makes 40% of generics sold in the US and 25% of all medicine in UK. India produces 60,000 generic brands and manufactures more than 500 different pharmaceutical ingredients. The country's pharmaceutical exports reached $19 billion in 2019. India allows *100% Foreign Direct Investment in pharmaceuticals* (*See* https://www.fdi.finance/sectors/pharmaceuticals). Here are several Indian pharma transnational JVs.

- Cipla, the leading Indian pharmaceutical producer has a joint venture with China's Jiangsu Acebright Pharmaceutical. Cipla holds 80% in the $30 million JV. The new company will manufacture respiratory products for the Chinese market (Liu, 2019)
- In 2018, a subsidiary of India's Aurobindo Pharma formed a JV with Shangdong Luoxin Pharmaceutical to manufacture inhalers and other products.
- Sun Pharmaceuticals bought into US Pharmalucence and Ranbaxy in 2014 to become one of the largest generic producers in the world. Sun joined InSite Vision US and acquired Britain's GSK's opiate business in Australia in 2015. Sun acquired a majority share of Biosintez as it expanded into the Russian market in 2016. Sun has production agreements with Japanese and other European companies, including JV with MSD Pharma in the UK. Sun Pharma also has two major licensing deals with China Medical System.
- Panacea Biotech has a JV with Chiron US developing and marketing vaccines.
- US Novavax and India's Cadila Pharmaceuticals have a JV manufacturing vaccines and other biopharmaceutical products in India.
- CPL Biologicals develops and manufactures vaccines, biological therapeutics and diagnostics in India using technology from Novavax and Cadila's JV.
- Novotech, an Australia based clinical research company has a JV with ETI Klinical for clinical research and data management services in India.
- ApoKos Rehab Pvt. Ltd is a JV between the Apollo Group, Asia's largest hospital and clinic caregiver, and KOS Group, Italy, which specializes in orthopedics and healthcare support.

This transnational process of consolidation is pushing out many smaller players that have no transnational partners, while larger firms like Sun, Cipla, and Aurobindo expand and consolidate through JV. In this new climate of transnational collaboration, Indian pharma companies find many suitors. PriceWaterhouseCoopers' (2010) report, "Global Pharma looks to India: Prospects for growth," noted that Indian companies are collaborating more with overseas players. Although there are many transnational deals between Indian and European or US firms, the most immediate expansion is regional transnational agreements. A recent report by Bank of America Merrill Lynch estimates that the number of JV between Indian and Chinese companies will continue to increase (Spencer, 2019). The Chinese government has further opened its pharmaceutical market and invited Indian firms to take part (Liu, 2019).

Auto

India became the fourth largest auto market in 2018 with sales increasing to 4 million cars. India is also the largest tractor manufacturer, second-largest bus manufacturer and third largest heavy trucks manufacturer in the world.

The industry saw a 25.5% jump in FDI from 2018 to 2019. With FDI government policy for auto allowing 100% FDI, investment in the industry amounted to $17.9 billion in FDI between 2000 and 2017—5% of total FDI (See https://www.fdi.finance/sectors/automobile). Below are a few notable JVs in automotives.

- India's largest auto manufacturer, Mahindra & Mahindra, formed a partnership in 2007 with Renault of France. The Indian firm owns 51% of this venture, which produces several Renault models in India. The vehicles are manufactured in India with French technology and components produced in India—exemplifying the new transnational model of production and distribution that combines management, labor costs, and profits from two national industries
- Tata Motors bought Jaguar Land Rover in 2008 and is the third largest automaker in India, with factories and partnerships in China and Slovakia. Fearing they were too small to compete with BMW, Audi, Mercedes and other automakers, Tata teamed with BMW in 2020 to produce the new all electric I-Pace Jaguar (Boston, 2019).
- India's Eicher Motors formed a joint venture (VE Commercial Vehicles— VECV) with Sweden's AB Volvo that includes five divisions, Eicher Trucks and Buses, Volvo Trucks India, Eicher Engineering Components and VE Powertrain. VECV produces a complete range of commercial vehicles, components and engineering design as well as the sales and distribution of Volvo trucks.

Telecom

India is currently the world's 2nd largest telecommunications market with a subscriber base of 1.2 billion following a rapid growth in the past decade. The industry had even more exponential growth over the last few years driven by affordable tariffs, wider availability, expanding 4G coverage, increasing consumerism, and a conducive regulatory environment.

The number of smartphone users in India crossed the 300 million mark in 2016, making it the largest phone market in the world. Subscribers are expected to reach 1.4 billion by 2020. The Indian mobile economy is growing rapidly and will contribute substantially to India's GDP, India had a 165% growth in app downloads from 2017 to 2019. As part of the government's deregulation policies, telecommunications is open to 100% FDI with 49% automatically allowed without government approval (See https://www.fdi. finance/sectors/telecommunications).

- Jio, is an Indian telecommunications company and subsidiary of Reliance Industries, owned by Mukesh Ambani, the richest man in India according to *Forbes* with a net worth $36.8 billion (Karmali, 2020) Jio operates a

TABLE 3.1 List of Top Investors in Reliance Jio (Singh, 2020)

Investor	Stake (%)	Invested (Mns.)
1. Facebook	9.90	5700
2. Silver lake	2.1	1338
3. VISTA	2.30	1500
4. General Atlantic	1.30	873
5. KKR	2.30	1500
6. Mubadala	1.85	1200
7. Abu Dhabi Investment	1.16	750
8. TPG	0.93	600
9. Catterton	0.39	250
10. Fund Saudi Arabia	2.3	1500
11. Qualcomm	0.15	97
12. Google	7.73	$4.5 billion

national LTE network with coverage across 22 regions in India. Jio uses only voice over LTE on its 4G network. It is the largest mobile network in India and the third largest in the world with over 400 million subscribers. In September 2019, Jio launched home broadband, television, and telephone services. Since April 2020, Reliance Industries has raised more than $21 billion by selling 32.97% equity stake in Jio Platforms. The 5G US giant Qualcomm was the latest partner, investing $97 million to acquire a 0.15% equity stake. One look at Jio's investors indicates its transnational relations, with investors from France, UAE, Saudi Arabia, and the US (See Table 3.1)

- A smaller TNMC, Byju, is an internet edtech application, valued at $1.8 billion. Byju investors include Mark Zuckerberg and Tencent of China. This transnational partnership made owner Byju Raveendran one of the newest billionaires in India (Karmali, 2020).
- Vodafone India contracted with Huawei on a $2 billion managed services deal
- Tata, like many major India companies, diversified as it consolidated. In 2008, Japan's NTT Docomo bought a 26% stake in Tata Teleservices for $2.7 billion. Tata was number 6 in Indian telecom at the time, with about 80 million subscribers. Tata Docomo added another 33 million by June 2010, but struggled to compete with larger telecoms. Tata Sons recently bought out NTT's share of the joint venture.

Media and Entertainment

The rapidly expanding media and entertainment industry exhibits similar transnational partnership and joint venture structures as other Indian industries. With the world's largest newspaper circulation and the world's largest film industry in terms of number of films made per year, India's culture industry continues its strong growth. Spurred by rising consumer demand, and improving advertising revenues, India's largest TNMCs are reaping huge profits. The emergence of multiple transnational media firms and their associated relations of production and distribution greatly affected the national media market. Finance, state policy, technology, media owners, creative and production labor, and industry conferences now are fully "bound up in a web of relations" (Curtin, 2003, p. 204) that exist at the local, regional, national, and transnational level. The social relations of production were reorganized to more efficiently accumulate wealth and maximize profit. Decisions on location, programming forms and techniques, contributions by writers, directors, and actors, and technical work on lighting, sound, sets, backgrounds, costumes, make-up, and post-production editing—all were reconfigured to centralize control, normalize acquiescent behavior, lower labor costs, attract consumers, and reap profits. Likewise, contracts with myriad others in production, distribution, and exhibition were streamlined to limit corporate responsibility. This hegemonic process of building consent for privatization and consolidation among disparate social forces in India was jointly constructed and enforced by Indian capital and its political representatives with support from transnational capital.

The media industry in India has grown faster than the nation's economy as a whole. With continued financing from transnational media and investors, media grew 13% in 2017. Where "slums sport satellite dishes, cell phones are no longer considered a luxury… and no protectionist policies towards importing movies" (Tatna, 2017) even more media growth is coming, justifying capital's enthusiasm for the neoliberal project in India. Unsurprisingly, there has been a gradual but unrelenting expansion and corporatization of media since the 1990s, when the government deregulated the culture industries. Government regulations allow FDI up to 74% in broadcasting, cable networks and mobile TV. Entertainment media like film and television can have up to 49% FDI without government approval, up to 100% with review (Mangaldas & Co., 2015).

Simultaneously with neoliberal reforms enacting privatization of public resources and increased foreign investment, media in India had the burden of articulating a nationalist rhetoric tethered to neoliberalism.

Corporate leaders and government politicians expected Hindu nationalism to work at two levels: "offering the cultural and ideological accompaniment to liberalization for the middle and upper classes" and "translating it into a religio-mythic narrative that would win popular consent" (Rajagopal in Sen, 2011, p. 146). In other words, neoliberalism was more than an imperative to privatize and globalize the Indian economy, it also had to culturally serve the free market by winning consent of the population for austerity, inequality, and social class hierarchy. Notably, media convergence within India indicates that entertainment content travels across and among television, film,

Internet, streaming, and mobile phone ownership structures and user access (Punathambekar, 2013). Thus, news, television, and especially Bollywood function to popularize a new national identity of individualism and consumerism within the parameters of traditionally conservative family values, caste distinctions, and a Hindi national identity (Dixit, 2021).

In India, the neoliberal push for global competition, privatization, and corporate profit resulted in national media conglomerates such as Reliance Entertainment's Network 18, Essel's Zee TV, Sun TV, and the Times Group—all of whom have partnered with multiple non-media firms in film and television production, satellite, cable, and gaming. Many Bollywood film companies also found foreign investors and partners: UTV with Disney; Yash Raj with Disney; Reliance and DreamWorks; Studio 18 and Paramount; Banjali Films with Sony; Ramish Sippy with Warner Bros.; Times Global and Reuters; NDTV and Vijay TV with News Corp's Star TV; and many others. This makes complete business sense for transnational media, which are "willing to forego pumping and promoting their own content to break into markets like India" (Rasul & Proffitt, 2012, p. 565). Each of these transnational partnerships adopted "rational systems of management and the formalization of business practices in production, financing, and distribution" which aligned with industry and government goals of "stream-lined, efficient, rational, and corporatized mode and culture of production" necessary for maximizing profits in a globalizing capitalist world (Punathambekar, 2013, p. 63).

Confirming that media's social function is *not* to serve the public interest, Vineet Jain, owner of *Times of India* (the largest English daily) and Times Internet, explained, "We are not in the newspaper business, we are in the advertising business," underscoring how media has become a transnational investment-driven industry as corporate managers and marketing managers became more powerful than bureau chiefs or content creators (Chishti, n.d.). In a few short years, private media expanded dramatically; it also became more concentrated. Five major newspaper chains hold one-third of overall circulation amassing $7 billion in yearly revenue. Newspapers branched into television with foreign investment reaching $6 Billion by 2018. In seven or eight states, more than 50% of readers and viewers receive news and entertainment from a single media monopoly. The largest firms have multiple media outlets: the *Times* owns radio, television, internet, magazines, and film production; Essel's Zee TV operates television, cable, film, newspapers, and internet sites; Star India (now part of Disney) has film production, television networks, internet sites, newspaper, cable, and streaming services. Each case illustrates the industrialization of media and culture as India commercialized. The next sections provide a brief overview of media newspaper, television, and film ownership and production in India.

Newspapers

India has the largest global newspaper readership; more than 120 million read 50,000 newspapers every day. India has 118,239 registered publications (newspapers and periodicals), and more than 570 million internet users—the second largest after China. Under current media deregulation 100% FDI in print publication is allowed. Several newspaper chains have TNMC JV. For example, Vice Media (a US-Canada TNMC with 26% Disney) and the Times of India Group have a 50:50 joint venture in television production, lifestyle programming, and the India pay-TV channel Viceland (TNN, 2016).

Two papers, Dainik Jagran and Dainik Bhaskar, each part of a publishing giant, are read by more than 35 million, because each daily subscription is estimated to have several readers (See Table 3.2).

Television

Until the 1991, public television Doordarhsan was the only broadcaster in India. Since the neoliberal reforms privatizing public resources and deregulating public control of broadcasting, more than 1500 television stations are available by cable, satellite, broadcast, and digitally. India has more than 200 million pay TV subscribers. India is now the second largest TV market in the world (See https://www.fdi.finance/sectors/media).

Indian television was quickly overtaken by dozens of transnational private broadcasters who found willing national partners eager to restructure the entire Indian media environment. As domestic media branded, syndicated, and franchised their corporations to participate in new transnational regimes of risk, speculation, and profit, they also continued to involve the existing social and financial relations within India. Transnational media did not replace national or local producers, but attracted, partnered, and educated them in corporate

TABLE 3.2 Leading Newspapers India (2019)

	Newspaper	Language	Headquarters	Circulation
1	Dainik Jagran	Hindi	Kanpur	6,866,070
2	Dainik Bhaskar	Hindi	Bhopal	5,242,900
3	The Times of India	English	Mumbai	2,880,144
4	Malayala Manorama	Malayalam	Kottayam	2,308,612
5	Amar Ujala	Hindi	Noida	2,261,990
6	Hindustan Dainik	Hindi	New Delhi	2,221,566
7	Rajasthan Patrika	Hindi	Rajasthan	1,788,420
8	Eenadu	Telugu	Hyderabad	1,614,105
9	Dina Thanthi	Tamil	Chennai	1,472,948
10	The Hindu	English	Chennai	1,415,792

collaboration and decision-making structures and practices. Television and movies needed to continue their appeal within India as their economic base, while their transnational goals looked to create and market content with global appeal—to the diaspora as well as other audiences in other nations.

Although to date there is no comprehensive national media policy regulating cross ownership, mergers, acquisitions, and media consolidation (Chishti, n.d.), India's existing FDI policy permits majority ownership by TNMCs in cable and direct broadcasting and television production. Disney's Star TV network has Hindi, Telegu, and Tamil broadcasts as well as Star UTsav Plus with more than 3 billion pay-TV viewings per week (Statista, 2021). Sun TV (853 million viewings each week) is the second most watched station, the largest pay-TV station and has its own movie production studio, as well as cable, 70 radio stations, 2 newspapers and the streaming platform SUN NXT. Essel's Zee TV Network broadcasts three stations in Hindi, Telegu, and Tamil that collectively have 1.8 billion viewings each week. Reliance Industries Network 18 has its own television station, Colors, which attracts about 600 million viewings each week. Sony Pal has similar numbers. Doordarshan, the public service television network, reaches millions of viewers with its classic reruns and sports broadcasts, but its audience has declined. In less than 20 years, India shifted from a public broadcasting system and mostly family-run film studios to an advertising-driven, commercial, consumerist system of national media monopolies with multiple transnational partnerships. Since the 1990's neoliberal reforms opened India to private television, five media networks dominate Indian television, one is US-owned that airs many Indian co-productions, one remains a locally-owned Tamil language company with occasional JV, and three are transnational media.

Star TV

Star TV (Satellite Television Asian Region) began as a joint venture between two Hong Kong investment companies in 1990. Three years later Rupert Murdoch's News Corporation had acquired full ownership. Star TV soon offered Hindi, Marathi, Malayalam, and Telugu channels and programs, as well as Star CJ, a joint venture in Korea.

With the 2019 purchase of 21st Century Fox, which included Star India, Disney became the largest TV producer and broadcaster in India. The Disney Star India network broadcasts over 60 channels in seven languages and claims a reach of four billion viewers every week across India and a hundred countries (Bhushan, 2015). In 2018, Star TV took in $1.2 billion in revenue. Disney's Star also has 30% stake in Tata Sky satellite (a joint venture with Temasek Singapore) with 600 channels (BQ Desk, 2017). Since 2011, Star TV has been in a joint venture with Zee TV—the two networks offer 78 channels on MediaPro. Star TV broadcast drama, crime, and comedy series in Hindi, Telegu, Tamil, and Marathi, among other languages. Star TV also airs leading US television fare, such as *Modern Family*, *Blacklist*, and *The Office*. Star TV broadcasts the India Premier League cricket games. Disney has multiple pay-TV stations broadcasting its content across India and South Asia. For example, Disney Channel, Hungama TV, Marvel HQ, and Disney Junior are all pay channels. Disney-Star TV has become the dominant television content distributor in India, with co-productions in Hindi, Tamil, and other Indian languages receiving the largest audiences. Disney and Star TV have formed several JV with Indian animation studios, including Green Gold on *Chorr Police*; Toonz Animation on *Gaju Bhai*; and with Graphic India on the 2021 *Legend of Hanuman*, among others.

TV 18/Viacom 18

Mukesh Ambani, Anil's brother, also ventured into media, entertainment, and telecommunications. The television and film studio Network TV 18 is owned by Mukesh Ambani's conglomerate Reliance Industries. 2018 revenues were $760 million. A joint venture Network18-CNN was established in 2005 with the US Cable News Network (CNN) which was a Time-Warner company that distributed satellite TV channels like CNBC-News18, CNBC Awaaz, CNN-News18 and IBN7. Network 18 owns two cable networks in India, DEN and Hathway. Recently, Ambani expanded it e-commerce reach by purchasing retail and on-line giant Future Group for $3.8 billion, elbowing out US Amazon which wants in on the lucrative and growing Indian commerce (Sethi, 2021).

In 2007, Network18 and ViacomCBS formed Viacom 18 to distribute popular satellite TV channels such as Rishtey, MTV, Colors, and Colors HD, among others. Viacom 18 owns a streaming service Voot which has over 100 million subscribers. Viacom 18 broadcasts television in Hindi, Tamil, Telugu, Marathi, Bengali, Punjabi, and four other regional languages with almost 600 million viewers each week. In 2019, Viacom 18 reported $71 million in revenue (See https://www.tofler.in/companylist/maharashtra).

In 2012, TV18 and Viacom18 formed another 50:50 joint venture, IndiaCast, to distribute 57 channels. IndiaCast leveraged Viacom's global reach by consolidating domestic and international channel distribution, content syndication, and adding new media platforms like IPTV and mobile— providing content for Ambani's Jio cellphone network (Reporter, 2012). The transnational IndiaCast distributes all the channels of both media—CNBC, CNN-IBN, CNBC Awaaz, IBN7, Colors, MTV, Nickelodeon, Sonic, VH1, Comedy Central, Colors HD—and all the channels of Eenadu, which had already partnered with TV 18. In addition, IndiaCast distributed Sun Network channels (and Disney channels in Hindi-speaking markets, until Disney purchased Star TV in 2019).

In 2018, Network TV 18 paid $20 million to buy a 1% stake in Viacom18 establishing majority ownership with 51%. Viacom 18 has 44 television channels across 80 countries in 6 languages, with operations in broadcast, digital, film, merchandise and live events—earning $477 million in 2016 (Frater, 2018). Viacom 18 distributes its Colors TV to the US and Malaysia, as well.

Sony Pictures Network (SPN) offered to purchase 74% of the Network 18/ Viacom 18 JV in 2020 (Jha, 2020). The merger would have given Sony access to the 350 million subscribers on Reliance Industry's Jio platform, but Ambani rejected the offer finding the existing TNMC Viacom 18's content sufficient for Jio and a planned expansion in digital media streaming by Reliance.

Media commentators in India warned that while consolidations enable broadcasters to capitalize on their partner's synergies, "a lot of non-performing channels will fold up" (Shashidhar, 2020). Essel's Zee Entertainment which still owns 66 channels across 171 countries struggles with its regional television focus, while Comcast, Amazon, Tencent, and Alibaba have expressed interest in partnering with Zee (Ramachandran, 2019). The portent is clear: national commercial media with transnational partners survive and expand.

Zee TV

Zee TV and Zee Entertainment (which includes Zee Studios) has interests in television, print, internet, film, and mobile content. Zee is owned by the Essel Group, an India media conglomerate owned by the Chandra/Goenka family (Media, 2020). Chandra was elected to the Indian parliament supported by the Bharatiya Janata Party (BJP) which has been pushing neoliberal policies under the Narenda Modi government since 2014.

Zee TV broadcasts 44 channels in eight different languages across the country, including Zee Telugu, Zee Kannada, Zee Cinema, and Zee Bollywood, among others, with affiliated channels in Nepal and Bhutan, reaching almost 2 billion viewers each week. In 2016, Zee partnered for broadcast in Germany in 2016 and launched the Zee Mundo channel in Latin America, followed with expansion to Poland in 2017. The owner's family also operates satellite network Dish TV India. Zee Media has film and video production studios, which until 2018 had a distribution joint venture with the US Turner Broadcasting System for India. Zee also runs a film school called ZIMA, Zee Institute of Media Arts. The Essel Group owns 69% of Zee Media Corporation Limited with the remaining 31% of shares publicly traded. Zee purchased Reliance ADAG television stations Big Magic and Big Ganga, along with 59 radio stations in 2018. In 2019, Invesco US bought 11% of Zee Entertainment (Thomas, 2019). By global standards, Zee is an active mid-major TNMC.

Sun TV

Sun TV was launched in 1993 in Chennai as the first commercial station in Tamil and remains the dominant network in the region with over 800 million viewers across India each week. The Sun Network has 32 TV channels in Tamil, Telugu, Kannada, and Malayalam in South India and in Bengali in the North with satellite stations in Australia, South Africa, Asia, Europe, and US. The Sun Network which owns two cricket teams, has 70 radio stations, two newspaper and five magazines, as well as a small film studio—all in Tamil. Almost all of Sun's television programs are either produced in house or co-productions with other Indian studios. Sun Network's total revenue in 2020 was about $140 million.

In 2016, Sun partnered with US-based YuppTV to stream 10 channels in 4 languages to West Asia and North Africa (Leena, 2016)—marking Sun's first foray into a transnational joint venture.

Sony Pictures Networks India (SPN)

SPN is the Indian division of the Japanese-based global electronics manufacturer and media giant, Sony. Arriving in 1995, Sony was one of the earliest TNMCs to find media partners in India (and also co-produced the first Indian TNMC film, *Saawariya* in 2007). Today, Sony's SPN broadcasts 24 television channels to India, including pay-TV channels Sony SAB, sports channels Sony Six and Sony Ten, and Sony Yay (for children). SPN also offers the Internet streaming Sony Liv in Hindi, Tamil, and English (with 20 million subscribers) and operates Sony Entertainment Television (SET India), a YouTube channel with 100 million subscribers. SPN broadcasts several BBC shows, ESPN, a few Disney Fox AXN programs, and Bengali, Tamil, and Marathi programs. In 2020, Sony partnered with India's only copyright organization to broadcast millions of Indian music productions and lyrics on its networks.

SAB airs mostly co-productions of situation comedies such as *Maddam Sir, Tera Yaar Hoon Main, Kaateli, Wagle Ki Duniya,* and *Jijaji Chhat Parr Koli Hai*; fantasy series *Baalveer* and *Hero*; and news stations, among others. SET broadcasts UK-German RTL Freemantle-Indian co-production *Indian Idol* and Sony-Frames Production *Super Dancer*, a kids reality contest show.

Sony Southeast Asia broadcasts to Pakistan, Singapore, Hong Kong, Korea, the Middle East, New Zealand, and Australia. Overall, SPN channels are available in 167 countries and reach 700 million in India—making Sony a major TNMC in India and the world (Business Wire, 2020).

Television for Kids

While many cartoons and children's show on Indian TV are either nationally produced in regional languages or imported and language-dubbed US series, DQ Entertainment has become an important TNMC in television animation production that has moved into making feature film. DQE is known for *Casper's Scare School, Benjamin Bear, Leonardo,* and *Pet Pals,* television animation series co-produced with *Lyoko* animation creator Moonscoop France (now Ellipsanime), Grupo Alcuni Italy, Classic Media US, Amberwood Entertainment Canada, and several European studios. DQE has produced and distributed many iconic TV series such as *Iron Man, Mikido, Pinky & Perky,* and *Mickey Mouse Clubhouse, Chum-Chum, New Adventures of Lassie, The Little Prince,* and many others for leading broadcasters in Europe, the US, Asia, and the Middle East. DQE's own licensed and globally successful animated television series *Jungle Book* entered its 3rd season in 2019. A full-length feature film (released in English, Hindi, Tamil, and Telugu) based on the series attracted large audiences in 2017, grossing $39 million. The television series is co-produced and distributed by global kids broadcasters. ZDF Germany, DeA Kids-Italy, TF1-France, Canal+ France, Telequbec and TVO-Canada, JCCTV-Middle East, and Nickelodeon India are a few of the partners in this transnationally-produced animated series that broadcasts in over 160 countries worldwide.

In 2019, European and Global Licensing (EGL) Netherlands was named the global toy licensee for DQE's *Jungle Book* and *Peter Pan* franchises. Under the terms of the agreement in collaboration with DQE, EGL will design, produce and market a wide variety of plush and figurine toys inspired by both brands. EGL will hold the worldwide rights, excluding the territories managed by DQE's co-production partners (AnimationXpress, 2018).

DQE has had partnerships with many media companies, including Nickelodeon, Disney, BBC, Discovery, Electronic Arts, TF1 France, ZDF Germany, RAI Italy, Sony, NBC Universal, Mattel, ABC Australia. DQE has a subsidiary in Ireland, a full partnership with Method Animation France, and a joint venture with Sun TV India for producing and distributing its animation series in Tamil, Telugu, Malyalam, and Kannada languages for regional Indian television. DQE and France's Moonscoop (now Ellipsanime) co-produced an animated *Robin Hood* series in 2014 with TF1 in France and Minika TV in Turkey. DQE also co-produced the long-running French comic series *Lanfeust* with Gaumont Alphanim. The following year DQE partnered with SeaWorld Parks and Rollman Entertainment US to co-produce 7 *Dwarfs and Me* and *5 Children and It* with Method Animation France. For more than 10 years, DQE has produced *Keymon Ache* for Nickelodeon India. In all, DQE has more than 90 partners in production, distribution, and licensing (DQE Entertainment, 2010). In 2018, DQE announced plans for indoor theme parks in India. These TNMC partnerships have placed DQ Entertainment in the mix of thoroughly global television producers that have a pronounced non-specific cultural aura (Iwabuchi, 2002).

Several other TNMCs have partnerships in television production. In 2020 Reliance Animation signed with Warner's Pogo TV on *Smashing*

Simba. Reliance Entertainment and Shetty Pictures produces *Golmaal, Jr.* for Nickelodeon India and *Little Singham* for Discovery Kids India. Cosmos Maya Singapore has a long-term partnership with Nickelodeon India for *Motu Patlu* and *Shiva*, with Amazon and Disney's Hotstar + for *Selfie With Bajrangi*, and in 2020 with Disney's Hungama TV for *Chacha Bhatija*. Sony's Yay TV partnered with India's Ssoftoons on the animation *Paap-O-Meter*. Cartoon Network India maintains its 10 year partnership with Malaysia's Animasia Studio on *Roll No. 21*. Many more short term JV and agreements have been formed over the last 20 years, as TNMCs jockey and search for new television cartoon series that will attract large audiences and advertisers.

Language and Co-Productions

Although Disney, Nickelodeon, and Sony air US television programs, the highest rated shows are consistently co-productions between TNMCs and national television studios. In December 2020, the top TRPs (Television Rating Points) reported by India's Broadcast Research Council were all Indian language programs (See Table 3.3).

Each of these top ten shows are co-productions between TNMC networks and Indian television studios (Nagarathna, 2020). Rather than imposing US or Western programs on Indian viewers, TNMCs have recruited Indian partners to create and produce television programs that link individualism and consumerism with familiar Indian family situations, recognizable daily activities, and geographically national scenes. These are hegemonic narratives that seek consent and collusion from viewers for patriarchy and authority. With creative adjustment, television studios have moved the family patriarch from a feudal authority to a more modern, corporate and entrepreneurial gloss of warmth, love, and wisdom. Indian television melodrama "displaces all socio-cultural struggles into the domain of the family" with their emphasis on "consumer choices and the overvaluation of the consumer

TABLE 3.3 Most Viewed Television Shows in India December 2020

Network	Title	Genre
1 Star Plus	Anupamaa	Drama with female lead
2 Zee TV	Kundali Bhagya	Family drama
3 Star Plus	Imlie	Drama
4 Star Plus	Ghum Hai Kisikey…	Family drama
5 Zee TV	Kumkum Bhagya	Family drama
6 Sony SET	Indian Idol	Reality contest
7 Sony SAB	Taarak Mehta Ka…	Family comedy
8 Star Plus	Yeh Hai Chahatein	Romantic drama
9 Colors Viacom	Shakti	Family drama
10 Star Plus	Saath Nibhana…2	Drama

TABLE 3.4 Number of Films Produced (2018)

India 1813
Nigeria 1844 (2013) (Bright, 2015)
China 1082
US 613
Japan 576
(All data from Statista.com)

as citizen" (Sen, 2011, pp. 148–149). Television themes and values are replicated in weekly series, but film provides more spectacle and diversity on a much larger screen.

Film

India produces more than 1500 films each year—the most of any country in the world, followed by Nigeria, the US, and China (See Table 3.4). According to *Forbes*, India also became the largest film industry in terms of annual viewers several years ago (McCarthy, 2014). Produced in more than 20 languages, Indian film audiences surpass 2 billion yearly with more than $2 billion in box office revenues (See Tables 3.5 and 3.6). In the last several years, Indian films have grossed millions globally and attracted millions of viewers. Box office revenues are much lower than in China, the US, or Europe due to low

TABLE 3.5 Number of Tickets Sold/Size of Audience (2019)

China	1.72 B
India	1.51 B
US	1.17 B
Mexico	352 M
Korea	240 M
(All data from Statista.com)	

TABLE 3.6 Leading Box Office Revenue Worldwide (2019)

Country	Box Office Gross
US	11.4 B (2020, 9.4 B)
China	9.3 (2020, 9.9 B)
Japan	2.4
UK	1.6
Korea	1.6
France	1.6
India	1.6
(All data from Statista.com)	

TABLE 3.7 Average Ticket Prices
2013 in US Dollars (UNESCO
in Dastidar & Elliot, 2020)

India	0.81
China	5.74
UK	8.13
US	10.90

ticket prices ($1 to $4) (See Table 3.7). India's film industry has been called Bollywood, a term now "synonymous with vividly colored films featuring complex dance routines, singing and spectacular large cast scenes" (Dastidar & Elliot, 2020, p. 97). Rini Mehta (2011) observed that song and dance substituted for any display of affection, including kissing, which were banned by India's official censor board (p. 9). While musicals continue to attract large audiences, in the last decade, Bollywood's TNMC co-productions have featured some other global trends. Action movies with less dialog and animated movies are drawing large crowds in India (Tatna, 2017)—reflecting the changing tastes of audiences responding to consumer appeals in advertising and film images and narratives.

Like China, Korea, and other nations that adopt neoliberal economic policies, in India the film industry attracts many investors, which leads to greater competition for domestic films from large budget transnationally co-produced films that audiences seem keen to watch. Bollywood film practices developed from TNMC partnerships express new cultural renderings appropriate for a growing consumerism. The resulting changes are noticeable: a reliance on high profile star actors; increased production of sequels and franchised film series—most of which are action movies (See Table 3.8); and more marketing for film releases, especially during major holidays (Dastidar & Elliot, 2020, p. 100). Additionally, recurring themes and messages in TNMC films emphasize individualism and self-interest while reinforcing social hierarchy, which will be discussed in the Dominant Themes section.

TABLE 3.8 Top Active Film Franchises in India

Title	Last film	Box office	Genre
Baahubali	2017	$410 M	Action
Cop Universe	2018	$176 M	Action
Dabanng	2019	$160 M	Action
Tiger	2017	$150 M	Action
Housefull	2019	$130 M	Comedy
Golmaal	2017	$108 M	Action
Race	2018	$95 M	Action
Baaghi 3	2020	$86 M	Action

Beyond action movies and animation, top US studios without local partners were not successful in India due in large part to the cultural dissonance
of the language and unfamiliar content—the same problems facing Indian
film studios that do not produce multi-lingual films for a national audience
that effectively lacks a common language. The transnational pull encourages
Indian media to produce higher quality films with variations on a standardized global template that will appeal to mass audiences. Such an adjustment
needs significant resources for production and funds for increased marketing
to domestic and global audiences. Government incentives for foreign investment and partnerships will spur further TNMC developments (Dastidar &
Elliot, 2020, pp. 109–110). Ongoing invitations for transnational investment
indicates the exuberance of India's corporate leaders for more TNMC productions and exports.

As a consequence of neoliberalism and the development of transnational
media relations, the Indian film industry has been transformed from one
of horizontal, independent, family-owned production (Lorenzen & Täube,
2007) into "Bollywood" as the Indian government promoted "culture as a
resource" to meet the "demands of the new circuits of capital" which include
media partnerships with foreign media and investors. The former network of
local financiers, independent producers and distributors, family-owned companies, and small cinema exhibitors was overtaken by privatized studios working with a growing advertising industry (Punathambekar, 2013, p. 48) and
teaming with global and regional partners.

Bollywood is an instance of transnational alliances resulting from many
forces: political, economic, and cultural as well as the technical. Bollywood
intersects with production and circulation of media in China, South Asia,
Nigeria, and across the Middle East and Europe. Indian media and its government normalized corporatization, opened the film and television industry
to advertising and marketing, and invited media partners from everywhere.

"India's media space is defined by rapidly evolving, complex and surprising
connections within and among industry practices, state policy, new media
technologies and platforms, and a space of consumption and participation that
criss-cross regional, national, and transnational boundaries and affiliations"
sharing connections with radio, television, and digital media (Punathambekar,
2013, p. 5). Bollywood is a transnational zone of cultural production shaped by
multiple sites of mediation, including the physical operations and social worlds
of labor, industry professionals, state policies, and technology that organize
capitalist relations of production.

This is not leveling the field as Friedman (2006) asserts nor does it extend
Western imperialism as others argue. This is transnationalism with the active
participation of media in Mumbai, as well as Telugu and Tamil language media
in Hyderabad and Chennai, all of whom have established co-productions,
received foreign investment, and distributed their content regionally to China,

Indonesia, Malaysia, and Singapore and then further to the Middle East, Europe, and Africa.

To bolster its transnational commitment, India has signed film co-production treaties with many countries (Italy, UK, Germany, France, Brazil, New Zealand, Poland, Spain, Australia, and others) which provide tax credits and rebates for firms jointly producing films using Indian labor, actors, and locations. In 2014, India signed an agreement with China to bring the two countries film industries together to "pool their creative, artistic, technical, financial, and marketing resources to co-produce films" to help Indian movies gain greater market access (Bhushan, 2014b). In July 2014, India's most successful film *Dhoom 3* was released in China via local distribution company HGC Entertainment. In 2011, Reliance Entertainment's comedy hit *3 Idiots* had a favorable run at the Chinese box office, collecting nearly $3 million. Transnational collaboration among regional media has become more pronounced as small media seek partners for competition with globalizing TNMCs.

China is perhaps Indian media's most active neighbor in transnational partnerships. Previously, Disney/UTV/Aamir Khan's TNMC movie *Dangal* (2016) about Indian wrestling was hugely successful in China ($190 M). Following Aamir and Salman Khan's previous action thriller *Dhoom 3* (2014) by Yash Raj Films and Disney/UTV distributed *PK* (2014) which were also hits in China, *Dangal* sparked a wave of Indian-movie fever that prompted Chinese distributors to bring a series of Indian films to China (Yau, 2018).

Like Hollywood movies, Indian movies are subject to China's quota system which restricts foreign movie releases in China in support of local production. Foreign releases are handled by state-owned distributors China Film Group and Huaxia Film Distribution. In recent years, due to the lessening of the quota system and rising number of TNMC imports, the two companies have subcontracted promotion and distribution work to private companies like Beijing Chuangshixing. Chuangshixing's He told *The Beijing News* last year that his company does not choose films that are too "Indianised" and Bollywood for China release as local audiences won't understand them. Still, "we help popularize them among Chinese audiences who no longer think that Indian movies are just big song-and-dance productions" (in Yau, 2018), perhaps explaining why more Indian media are producing more drama, comedy, and action movies and why Indian TNMC films in China have found willing partners and receptive audiences (Patranobis, 2019).

India and Canada have a co-production treaty opening both industries to government financial assistance, tax concessions and inclusion in domestic television broadcast quotas, and co-productions being treated as national films. The agreement aimed to offer India as a shooting location for Canadian films, while boosting exports of Indian films to Canada (Bhushan, 2014a). The Indian government advocates co-production agreements hoping to draw transnational investment to develop India's media industry and bolster its cultural image.

Cinema, as the primary means of entertainment in India, already seems to have an outsized influence on its culture. "Attend any Indian wedding and you will find the ladies attired in the finest garments modelled after Bollywood fashion and revelers dancing to throbbing hit songs during the 'baraat'... Any outfit adorned by an actor or actress in a hit movie immediately becomes a prime sartorial trend for tailors to reproduce. The fashion industry capitalizes on this trend by launching their clothes and jewelry in movies. Top stars are made brand ambassadors to endorse fashion products" (Mandaiker, 2014). In the glitz and glamour, conservative cultural values of arranged marriages, the caste system, and unquestioned authority remain, but individualism and consumerism is irreversibly replacing traditional values (Rashtra, 2020). The hegemonic function of media entertainment is quite pronounced in Indian media as it integrates popular music, Indian fashion, and political challenges to the status quo within comedy, action, and drama that lauds individual heroes, personal romance, and historical myths promoting narcissism, hierarchy, and deference to established authority. At the end of this chapter, some of the most popular movies since 2016 will illustrate these claims.

Thirty-four of top 50 grossing movies in India have been produced since 2016 (See Table 3.9). Only four US movies attracted large audiences in India during the same period: Disney's *Avengers*, *Jungle Book*, and *Lion King*.

Yash Raj, one of India's largest film groups, produced 3 of the top 10 films. Yash Raj has had several co-production partners—Disney, Sony, a theme park with Dubai—but continues to produce successful films on its own.

The Indian film industry is dominated by Bollywood, the Hindi-infused Mumbai film center, which raises 43% of the industry's revenue. Regional

TABLE 3.9 Top India Films Global Box Office Since 2016

Rank	Film	Gross	Language	Year
1	Dangal★	$340 M	Hindi	2016
2	Baahubali 2 a	$260 M	Telugu	2017
3	Secret Superstar★	$154 M	Hindi	2017
4	2.0 a	$115 M	Tamil	2018
5	Sultan y	$89 M	Hindi	2016
6	Tiger Zinda Hai y a	$87 M	Hindi	2017
7	Sanju★	$83 M	Hindi	2018
8	Padmaavat★	$83 M	Hindi	2018
9	War y a	$67 M	Hindi	2019
10	Andhadhun★ a	$64	Hindi	2018

★ Five of the top 10 films were transnational partnerships

a Action movie – five of top 10 films were action movies

y Yash Raj Films production

Tamil and Telugu films together add 50% and international films receive 7% of annual film gross revenue (Jain, Soneja, & Ahluwalia, 2016, p. 9). Deloitte's 2016 report predicted more growth due to investments by foreign studios, the expansion of multiplex theaters, and the emergence of digital streaming.

When we consider the wide range of companies and professionals in India, "it becomes clear that every domain of Bollywood, including production, distribution, marketing and promotions, and exhibition involves negotiations among actors and institutions enmeshed in multiple asymmetric, and seemingly incongruent cultures of capitalism" (Punathambekar, 2013, p. 180). Across India the "technological and industrial convergence" of film, television, radio, telecommunications, and Internet have all journeyed toward transnational partnerships.

Major film studios are Yash Raj Films, Dharma Productions, Red Chillies Entertainment, Aamir Khan Films, Balaji Motion Pictures, ErosSTX, Sony, Viacom/Network 18 Motion Pictures, Disney Star India, Sun Pictures, and Reliance Entertainment—all of whom have significant co-productions with studios from other countries. Dozens of other India film studios that have emulated the forms and norms of TNMCs have produced box office successes, especially with their action movies.

Leading movie producers in India, even if not consistently making transnational deals, accommodate and assimilate to transnational media structures and practices. Reliance Media Works and its various affiliates, Reliance Entertainment and its diverse media holdings, Viacom-Network 18, Essel's Zee Entertainment, and even remaining family-owned media like Yash Raj and Dharma illustrate clearly the new media order that is not constrained within national boundaries. Transnational deals offer too many economic and cultural benefits to its corporate participants for even skeptical self-defined "Indian" capitalists to resist.

Yash Raj Films

Established in 1970 as a Yash Chopra family enterprise, Yash Raj Films (YRF) is one of the largest and most successful family-owned film studios in India. YRF has produced the highest grossing movie in 3 of last 8 years. The company not only produces its own films, it is a major overseas distributor of films by other studios, including film franchises: Green Gold Animation's *Chhota Bheem* (2013, 2019) films based on the popular TV series that is still aired on Warner's Pogo TV; the $100 million action films *Dabangg* (2010, 2012, 2019); and the Warner Bros./Wingnut New Zealand co-produced films *The Hobbit* (2012, 2013, 2014).

YRF has grown to a media conglomerate with offices in New York, London, and Dubai. It has its own music and home entertainment labels, cel design and post-production facilities, internet, digital, merchandising and marketing divisions, as well as in-house units creating television software, ad films, and music videos. YRF has built its own state-of-the-art fully integrated studio, producing an average of 6 films a year. Yash Raj is also building a theme park in UAE as part of a joint venture with Abu Dubai.

Among its many co-productions, Yash Raj partnered with Disney on the animated feature *Roadside Romeo* (2008) and two other films. The studio has an agreement with the transnational Tata to use its Elxsi visual computing labs to provide animation and visual services for film production. YRF also joined with Pakistan's Lightingale Productions on the action-romance *Teefa in Trouble* in 2018, following two previous Pakistan-India co-production and distribution deals, the romantic comedy *Mere Brother Ki Dulhan* (2010) and action-comedy *Kill Dil* (2014). In 2013, Yash Raj signed a joint venture distribution agreement with Nikkatsu Corporation, the oldest film studio in Japan, which also has JV with Canada's IMAX, Disney's Star India, and Dell. With Yash Raj Entertainment, Nikkatsu began producing films for global distribution with known celebrities: Olivia Wilde in *The Longest Week* (2014), distributed by Germany's Pro-Sieben Gravitas Ventures and *Grace of Monaco* (2014) starring Nicole Kidman, a co-production of YRF, Canal+, Weinstein, and Gaumont with co-disribution partners in Italy, France, Switzerland, and the US. Meanwhile, the studio has embarked on transregional partnerships to produce films in Telugu and Tamil.

YRF has benefitted from India's co-production agreements using local crews while filming *Dhoom 2* (2006) in Africa, Brazil, and Fiji, *Dhoom 3* (2013) in Germany, the US, and Switzerland, and *Tiger Zinda Hai* (2017) in Iraq and Syria. The studio also found transnational investors like Pepe Jeans, Coca-Cola, and Mountain Dew for its *Dhoom* movies; and product placement deals with BMW and Audi for *War* (2019). In what is essentially a full-length advertisement released as a comedy, Suzuki invested heavily in *Mere Dad Di Maruti* (2013). The 2016 hit *Sultan* also featured several product placements loosely connected with the story about an Indian wrestler.

Although Yash Raj Films produces many romantic comedies, in the last few years the studio has been releasing action-adventures that follow what has become the global "crisis-hero-hierarchy saved" template, such as: *Tiger Zinda Hai* (2017); *Thugs of Hindustan* (2018) and *War* (2019)—both co-produced with Canadian theater company IMAX; *Mardaani* (2019); and *Prithviraj* (2021). A few of these will be included in the Dominant Themes discussion toward the end of this chapter.

Dharma Productions

Dharma Productions is another family-owned (the Yash Johar family) film production company which has been growing since its 2001 hit *Kabhi Khushi Kabhie Gham*. Dharma has produced mainly romantic comedies in the iconic Bollywood musical tradition featuring leading actors. In 2015, Dharma distributed *Baahubali* which became one of the highest-grossing Indian films ever, and now is a four language (including English) five-season animated series on Amazon Prime. In 2015, Dharma signed a 9 picture co-production deal with Fox Star Studios (Bhushan, 2015). Following the global TNMC trend for profitable action adventures, Dharma began producing action films, including co-productions with Fox Star Studios *My Name is Khan* (2006) and *Kalank* (2019); the Cop Universe action franchise series *Simmba* (2011, 2014, 2018) with TNMC Reliance Entertainment; *Ittefaq* (2017) with Red Chillies Entertainment; *Dhadak* (2018) with Zee Studios; and a female-lead spy thriller *Raazi* (2018).

In 2019, Dharma partnered with Netflix in a multi-year deal to produce fiction and non-fiction series and films (Joshi, 2019). Dharma scheduled several action films for 2021 with releases of superhero action (*Brahmastra*) with Disney Star, cop action (*Sooyarvanshi*) with Reliance Entertainment, war action (*Shershaah*), and even a romantic sword and sorcery action movie (*Yoddha*). The themes and messages of Dharma's action films are discussed in the Dominant Themes section at the end of this chapter.

Disney/Fox Star/UTV

As Fox Star, the studio had multiple co-productions with several Indian television and film studios: Dharma, Phantom Films, Reliance Entertainment, Vishesh Films, Excel Entertainment, and Endemol India, a Dutch/French joint venture. For 20 years, Fox Star exemplified transnational media in its robust joint production and distribution partnerships with Indian media large and small (See Table 3.10).

In 2012, Disney and UTV co-produced Green Gold Animation's *Arjun Warrior Prince* and its television series *Arjun-Prince of Bali* (2014–2017). UTV (a Disney partnership and later subsidiary) co-produced the hit *Chennai Express* (2013) with Red Chillies Entertainment, the international German, French, US, and Indian movie *The Lunchbox* (2013), and a dozen more co-productions until 2017, when Disney restructured its India operations. Disney India coproduced the 2017 hit *Dangal* with Aamir Khan Studio.

In 2019, Disney bought 21st Century Fox, which included Star TV India that became a Disney subsidiary. Disney also owns the streaming Hotstar+, Fox Star, and UTV Film studios. Fox Star mostly co-produces with other studios and UTV distributes Indian films.

Red Chillies Entertainment

Red Chillies Entertainment (RCE) began as a visual effects studio (that also owns the Indian and Caribbean Knight Rider cricket teams) founded by superstar Indian actor Shah Rukh Khan and his wife Gauri Khan in 2003.

TABLE 3.10 List of Fox Star Co-Productions and Distributions (2016–2021)

2016 Fox Star had multiple distribution partnerships, including:	
Kapoor & Sons	with Dharma Studio
Traffic	action film with Endemol India
Baar Baar Dekho	action film with Excel Studio
2017 Fox Star had 2 co-productions:	
Juduaa	action film with Nadiadwala Grandson Entertainment
A Gentleman	action film with Fox Star Studio
2018 Fox Star had 1 coproduction:	
Baaghi 2	action film with Nadiadwala Grandson Entertainment
2019 Fox Star had 10 co-productions, including:	
Kalank	with Dharma Studio
Student of Year 2	with Dharma Studio
India's Most Wanted	action film with Raapchik Films
2020 Fox Star had 5 co-productions, including	
Baaghi 3	action film with Nadiadwala Grandson Entertainment
Shikara	with Vinod Chopra
2021 Fox Star had 2 co-productions, including	
Brahmastra	action film with Dharma Studio
Tadap	action film with Nadiadwala Grandson Entertainment

Red Chillies almost immediately began co-producing films with more major Indian studios as well as transnationals like Disney's UTV. The studio has had major successes: *Don 2* (2011) co-produced with Excel; the award-winning *Chennai Express* (2013) with Disney's UTV; and *Dear Zindagi* (2016) with Dharma. In 2015, RCE joined with Sony for co-production of television, digital, and film content to broadcast on Sony's SET, SAB, MIX, and other Indian television stations. Red Chillies expanded its global reach with a transnational partnership with the world's largest streaming site, Netflix. *Bard of Blood* (2017) and *Class of '83* (2020) are the first two movies produced under their long-term agreement.

ErosSTX

ErosSTX is an Indian-US transnational JV in film, television, and digital production. Eros was established in 1977 and only entered the streaming market in 2012, but by 2020 had 36 million subscribers. ErosSTX made several successful co-productions with Chinese, Pakistani, and Korean studios, including *Xuanzang* (2016), *Wrong No. 2* (2019) and in 2020 *Heo Hwang Ok Embrace of Gaya*, (bi-lingual with Korea's Say On Media/B & C Group) (Bollyspice Editors,

2019) and *Zookeeper* (co-produced with China's Peacock Mountain). Peacock Mountain was distribution partner for several Indian films released in China, including blockbuster hits, *Dhoom 3* (2013) and *Baahubali* (2015). These regional transnational ventures have a potential audience of 2.5 billion. Eros also teamed with Viacom in 2014 to distribute several films outside India (Shackleton, 2014). In 2018 another leading TNMC, Reliance Industries (which is partnered with Viacom) purchased 5% of Eros and formed Reliance Eros Productions. Eros also has a long-term partnership with the TNMC Universal Music Group (a joint venture by France's Vivendi and China's Ten Cent) to promote pop music in India. STX was founded as a film, TV, and digital producer in the US in 2014, releasing over 30 films earning $1.5 billion by 2020.

The shared management joint venture ErosSTX formed in 2020 was valued at $660 million. As the *Hollywood Reporter* noted the merger was "an ambitious Hollywood indie studio with worldwide theatrical distribution arrangements, combined with an old-school Bollywood film studio that also happens to own a wide-reaching local streaming service"—making a competitive mid-major transnational media operation (Bhushan & Brzeski, 2020) producing and distributing films across Asia and to the US.

Dreamworks/Reliance

Reliance Entertainment is the media and entertainment arm of Anil Ambani's Reliance ADAG group which also operates shopping malls, aerospace and weapons industries, dairy, and theater exhibition. (Reliance ADAG is separate from Anil's brother Mukesh Ambani's Reliance Industries which owns Network 18). Reliance Entertainment is one of the largest and most active TNMCs emerging from India. Reliance Entertainment produces and distributes film, television, digital, and gaming platforms.

In 2008, Reliance Entertainment invested in DreamWorks Pictures (with DreamWorks Animation remaining a Comcast Universal company). DreamWorks Pictures signed a long-term, 30-picture distribution deal with Disney's Touchstone Pictures, giving Disney a 10% distribution fee. The deal also included co-funding via a $175 million loan from Disney to DreamWorks for production and access to Disney's pay television agreement, then with Starz, part of the American-Canadian transnational media venture Lionsgate. In 2009, DreamWorks received another $325 million from Reliance Entertainment with an additional $325 million loan as part of a three-year $825 million partnership to produce up to six films a year. By 2011, DreamWorks output was substantial: *Cowboys & Aliens, The Help, Real Steel,* and *War Horse,* all of which found box office success. Reliance invested $200 million more in DreamWorks in 2012 as the studio released other co-productions including Oscar-nominated *Lincoln* (2012) with 20th Century Fox and the Coen Brothers' *Bridge of Spies* (2015). DreamWorks formed a deal with the German-British transnational

Mister Smith Entertainment to distribute its films in Europe, the Middle East, and Africa, while Disney continued to distribute in North America, Latin America, Australia, Russia, and parts of Asia.

In 2015, DreamWorks Pictures ended its distribution pact with Disney and entered a larger transnational partnership with Spielberg, India's Reliance Group, Canada's media transnational Entertainment One (eOne) (which merged with US toymaker Hasbro in 2019), and the US-based social message filmmaker Participant Media to form Amblin Partners. Each of the partners has multiple transnational co-productions and JV, including in Spain, Colombia, Abu Dhabi, Australia, Netherlands, Japan, and more. Amblin immediately signed a five-year distribution deal with Comcast Universal. The first project was Reliance DreamWorks *Girl on the Train* (2016) which made over $175 million. China's internet giant Alibaba bought a minority stake in Amblin in 2016 with co-financing for Amblin and DreamWorks films and to market and distribute their films in China. A year later, Comcast Universal also acquired a minority share in Amblin, reuniting DreamWorks Animation with DreamWorks pictures in a new Canada-China-India-US TNMC partnership. Amblin continues to partner on other films like *Jurassic World* (2015) with China's Legendary Pictures, *The BFG* (2016) with Disney, *Ready Player One* (2017) with Warner Bros. Pictures, and *Men in Black: International* (2019) with Abu Dubai's Image Nation, among many others. Through Amblin, Reliance DreamWorks has also co-produced many television series for CBS, ABC, NBC, and CW, and delivered streaming content for Netflix and Amazon.

In addition to DreamWorks and Amblin films, Reliance Entertainment has produced several other successful films through additional transnational JV. The *Hundred Foot Journey* (2014) made by Imagine Nation, Harpo Films, and DreamWorks earned $100 million. *A Dog's Purpose* (2014), a Reliance-Amblin-Mister Smith JV earned $200 million. The Post (2017) produced with 20th Century Fox and Amblin (distributed by Mister Smith) drew almost $200 at the box office. The 2019 Golden Globes and Oscar winning *Green Book* (2018) earned $325 million as a transnational co-production by Reliance, DreamWorks, and Alibaba, among others. The 2020 Academy Award nominee and Golden Globes winner *1917* (2019) was also a transnational film project of UK's Neal Street Productions, Amblin, DreamWorks and others, earning $385 million.

To further its transnational activities, Reliance Entertainment is primary equity holder in Lava Bear Films, which produces several films each year with creative partners from China, Australia, Mexico, Canada, and the US. As a Reliance subsidiary, Lava Bear also has a network of production and distribution partners: Italia Films (serving the Middle East, Greece, and Turkey); Nordisk Film; Revolutionary Releasing (for Eastern Europe); Sun Distribution (Latin America); and Entertainment One (in Canada, UK, Belgium and the Netherlands). Lava Bear co-produced the Mexican-French thriller *Disierto* (2015) with CG Cinema France, the French telecom giant

Orange Studio, and the Mexican-American film studio Esperanto Kino. *Disierto* won the International Film Critics Prize at the 2015 Toronto Film Festival. In 2016, Lava Bear released *Shut In* (starring Naomi Watts) transnationally co-produced with France's Canal+ and distributed by EuropaCorp. That same year, Lava Bear co-produced two other films: the Mandarin language action drama *The Body Guard* with China's EDKO, Hong Kong's Focus Films, and a subsidiary of the Asian social media giant Tencent; and the $200 million hit *Arrival* (starring Amy Adams and Forest Whittaker) co-produced with US Film Nation and distributed by transnational Sony Pictures. Lava Bear's latest film, *American Animal* (2018), is a docudrama co-produced with Britain's Film4 Productions and Al Film UK.

Reliance Entertainment bought 50% of Phantom Films in 2015 and co-produced several movies with Balaji, Viacom, and Sony. After a major controversy during India's MeToo movement, Phantom Films was dissolved as two investors were bought out. In 2021, Reliance invested 50% in a new post-Phantom firm called Mad Man Ventures, planning for the new studio to begin co-productions of quality films soon (HT Entertainment Desk, 2021).

Reliance ADAG also owns Reliance Media Works (RMW), a visual effects and digital production company. In partnership with China's Galloping Horse Films, RMW purchased the US Digital Domain in 2012. In 2014, RMW merged with Prime Focus India to become the world's largest media services company with operations in US, UK, Canada, China, Singapore, and India. RMW contributed to *Spiderman, Transformer,* and *Smurf* movies and post-production partnerships with Ethyrea Films and Turner International. RMW runs the television studio Big Synergy which produces programs and game shows in nine languages, including JVs with Discovery, Disney, and large India media like the Times Group and Balaji Telefilms. In 2020, Anil Ambani declared personal bankruptcy, but most of his entertainment operations have not been directly affected.

Viacom 18 Motion Pictures

Viacom 18 Studios is a subsidiary of the 2007 joint venture between Mukesh Ambani's Reliance Industry's TV 18 and Viacom CBS. Viacom 18 distributes Paramount films in India and Bangladesh. Since 2016, the studio has produced 38 films, including several in Telugu, Marathi, Malayalam, Tamil, and other regional languages (See Table 3.11). A few of the 10 action films produced in the last 5 years are included in the Dominant Themes section below. With Bhansali Productions, Viacom 18 Studio co-produced and distributed the 2018 hit *Padmaavat*, which had a $70 million box office. Viacom 18 owns Voot, the subscription video-on-demand platform, that is available on Ambani's Jio phone network. Voot airs Colors TV, MTV, and Nickelodeon shows, with content available in multiple languages like Kannada, Marathi, Bengali, Gujarati, Telugu and Tamil. The studio has multiple co-productions with other regional media.

TABLE 3.11 Partial List of Viacom 18 Studios Films (Produced and/or Distributed) 2016–2021

2016
Motu Patlu: King of Kings (coproduction w. Cosmos Maya Singapore)
Santa Banta Pvt. Ltd. (action comedy)
Force 2 (action, co-production Sunshine Pictures, JA Entertainment w. Viacom distributor)

2017
Rangoon (action, co-production w. Nadiadwala Grandson Entertainment)
Toilet (co-production w. KriArj, Friday Films, and Reliance's Plan C Studios) $45 M box
Aval (House Next Door) (co-production w. Etaki Entertainment)) in 3 languages

2018
Padmaavat (action, co-production w. Bhansali Productions) $82 M box
Andhadhun (action, co-production w. Australia Matchbox Pictures) $64 M box
Baazaar (action, co-production w. Emmay Entertainment and Mittal Steel's B4U)

2019
Romeo Akbar Walter (action, w. partners Kyta, Red Ice, VA Films and Eros International)
The Body (action, co-production w. Azure Entertainment)
Thambi (in Tamil) (action, co-production w. Parallel Minds)
Kodathi (in Malayalam) (action, co-production w. RD Illuminations)

2020
Viacom 18 produced 3 films in Hindi, Tamil and Telugu

2021
Viacom 18 produced several comedies in Malayalam, Tamil, Kannada, Telugu, and Hindi
Cobra (in Telugu) (action, co-production w. Seven Screen Studios)

Other Notable TNMCs and JVs

There are many more JV and regional transnational television and film co-productions. Space does not permit a full account of all the partnerships and the movies produced, which are constantly changing and expanding. The following selections are only intended to demonstrate the complex and uneven growth of TNMC activity from and in India.

- Sony's 2016 *Chalk N Duster* was co-produced with Surani Pictures and the cricket bio-pic *Azhar* was made with Balaji Pictures.
- Sony partnered with KriArj Entertainment in the production and distribution of the hit *Padman* (2018).
- *Monkey Master* (2020) was an India-China project of Graphic India and China's Shinework Pictures.
- For several years from 2019, Cosmos Maya, the Singapore-India animation studio jointly produced *Eena Meena Deeka* with the British studio, WildBrain. As an animation non-language production, *Eena Meena Deeka* appeared on video-on-demand (VOD) platforms and Netflix to large audiences in India, Europe, and Latin America (Middleton, 2021).

- Bertlesmann's RTL Freemantle/UK has been co-producing television programs in India since 2009, including top reality contest shows *Indian Idol* and *India's Got Talent,* as well as scripted dramas like *Code Red* and *Private Investigator,* among others.
- RTL Freemantle India has several JV with Amazon, Disney's Star India, Viacom 18, Sony's SET, and other regional Indian broadcasters.
- *Namaste Walhala* (2020), although not the first Nollywood-Bollywood collaboration, was widely marketed and critically-applauded. In English and Hindi, with a few smatterings of Igbo, Hamisha Ahuja's Nigerian Forever 7 Entertainment filmed the standard rom-com mostly in Nigeria using multiple Indian actors and technical staff. Thussu (2016) suggests that the Bollywood's family and community-oriented values, dress, gender separation, and limited sexual content will be culturally accessible to many Africans (p. 230), but the production of thrillers, action, and horror movies indicates that Indian transnational media are eyeing a more consumerist market.
- Transnational Indo-African media relations are growing: Tata Communications is a major shareholder in Neotel, a large South African network; Indian television channels appear on pay-TV in Africa; and many Bollywood movies are filmed in South Africa, while Indian exports to Africa are growing (Priyadarshi, 2015).
- Krayon Pictures producer of the animated hit *Delhi Safari* (2012) teamed with China's Heshan Media to make a sequel *Beijing Safari* in 2015.
- Salman Khan's Rockline Entertainment co-produced *Top Cat Begins,* a 2015 prequel to *Top Cat: The Movie* (2011) with Mexico's Ánima Studios
- The Indian animation studio Assemblage Entertainment co-produced *Blinky Bill* (2015) with Australia's Flying Bark Productions and Telegael Ireland. The studio also joined with Telegael and the US/French studio Splash to make *Norm of the North* in 2016 that grossed $30 million. Those same TNMC partners produced three DVD sequels in 2019 and 2020.
- Green Gold Animation, the studio that created the popular *Chhota Bheem* television series has partnered with Amazon Prime Video to air 4 feature films and episodes from its 12 years of broadcast.
- Animation film *Bunyan and Babe* (2017) was co-produced by Exodus US and India's Toonz Entertainment.
- *The Swan Princess* (1994–2020) was a joint venture of Sony, Nest US, and Crest Animation India (now TNMC Splash Entertainment).
- After Salman Khan filmed *Kick* (2014) in Warsaw, India signed a co-production agreement with Poland, leading G7FilmsPoland to co-produce *No Means No* (2021) with Vikash Verma directing.

One important note about Indian TNMCs: they have many partnerships other than with US media, largely in the region including China, Malaysia, Singapore, Australia, as well as with media in Europe and even Latin America.

India is becoming a major participant in transnational media entertainment. Ernst & Young India's "A Billion Screens of Opportunity" reported that India is the growth leader among major emerging markets and developing economies, surpassing China in terms of real GDP growth in 2014 and maintaining that level ever since (Harrison, 2021). So the transnational focus on India is hardly surprising. Unlike China, there isn't a limit on the number of movies imported, and the untapped market remains huge, as do the opportunities for growth in a country where the literacy levels are rising and the population is younger than most.

As internet streaming services expand globally, India's 600 million and growing internet users will be very attractive. "Netflix and Amazon Prime add subscribers every day (probably not all paying customers), and the local Disney+ Hotstar, which is cheaper, is also popular. Both Netflix and Amazon successfully produce Indian content as well. Presales of digital rights to Indian films are routinely snapped up by them" (Tatna, 2019). Amazon with 5 million and Netflix with 2 million subscribers have some catching up to do in India. TNMC Viacom 18 has over 20 million subscribers to its Voot service, Sony Liv has 15–20 million, and Disney Hotstar has 8 million with 400 million monthly viewings (Binged, 2020). Meanwhile, satellite rights in India are routinely sold to Hollywood studios. As part of their transnational practices, India studios are also buying rights to Hollywood stories for a percentage. In 2020, during the coronavirus pandemic, the total box office in India was still $1.9 billion. The value of the film industry reached $26 billion in 2020, based in part on the advertising industry's heavy investment in cinema (Keelery, 2020b). Transnational media collaboration will only expand from here.

Transnational Media and India

This overview of how India media has developed since the introduction of neoliberal reforms in the 1990s illustrates the breadth and depth of transnational investment and collaboration. From television, to film, and internet streaming, the emergence of TNMC leadership in India's media environment and the global outreach of the India-affiliated TNMCs strongly suggests that Indian capitalist consent to media globalization is much different than the contours of cultural imperialism. While Schiller (1976), Mattelart (1976), and more recently Boyd-Barrett and Mirrlees (2020) have noted that US media aim to win consent from other national media and capital for US values and structures, the current impetus arises more from domestic Indian capital than from any external pressure or seduction by the US or the West. India is a capitalist country, with its own 1% elite, and its own media monopolies. These conditions predate neoliberalism and represent the enthusiastic embrace of commercialization, consolidation, and transnational collaboration as means for accumulating wealth from labor anywhere. The content of Indian cinema and Indian television programming cannot be reduced to US imposition or

US cultural imperialism. While large audiences view Disney, Nickelodeon, and Warner television programming, Indian media produce content that attracts millions more viewers (See Tables 3.3 and 3.8). Indian, US, Dutch, British, German, French, and other media capital compete for market share and profits, but they also collaborate to maximize their take. In the process, a non-Western-specific popular culture is being assembled, with some thematic resemblance to US and European contemporary values and representations. Ironically, those representations, images, and values comport with dominant contemporary Indian cultures, including its many regional varieties. Action movies, animation television and feature films, reality TV, drama, and popular music in India reside within the flexible transnational frame rather than any US or European culturally-specific box. Identifying some of the predominant themes in select Indian media productions reveals the contours of the new, global transnationalized popular culture.

Dominant Themes in Indian Film

Action films attract some of the largest audiences in India. Seven of the top eight film franchises in India are action movies (see Table 3.8) and most of the top grossing films since 2017 have been action movies, including the eleven selected here: the epic action hit *Baahubali 2: The Conclusion* and *Tiger Zinda Hai* in 2017; the sci-fi action film *2.0* and *Andhadhun* in 2018; *War, Saaho, Uri: The Surgical Strike, Simmba*, and *Dabanng* in 2019; and *Tanhaji* and *Baaghi 3* in 2020 (See Table 3.12).

TABLE 3.12 Top Action Films 2017–2020

Year/film	Production companies
2017	
Baahubali 2: The Conclusion	Arka Media Works
Tiger Zinda Hai	Yash Raj Films
2018	
2.0	Lyca Productions
Andhadhun	Viacom 18, Matchbox Pictures
2019	
War	Yash Raj Films
Saaho	UV Creations
Simmba	Reliance, Dharma Studio
Uri: The Surgical Strike	RSVP
Dabanng	Salman Khan Films
2020	
Tanhaji	T-Series, Devgn Films
Baaghi 3	Disney Fox Star, Nadiadwala Grandson Entertainment

Four of these action movies are the latest sequels in successful franchises. All have also attracted audiences outside India, in part because spectacle, action, chase scenes, and fights need little translation, while more overt political perspectives can be subsumed within the excitement of the action as the hero dispenses with the villains.

The goal here is to identify the primary themes apparent in the narratives of these ten films as representative of Indian media productions and its correlation to transnational media film productions. In film studies, "action cinema practically does not exist unless it is employed under the auspices of the pejorative 'mindless' qualifier," positing that scholars should not waste their time seriously engaging such "lowly" cinema (Barrowman, 2013). Yet, analyzing the content of the most popular cinema provides important observations about the cultural norms and values used by media producers and—given the large audiences—some insight into the cultural values of those millions of viewers who willing consume the film content and its ideology. Codifying the dominant themes in a representative collection of Indian movies also provides vital information for assessing to what extent the content selected and distributed by Indian media varies from or parallels content produced and distributed by more global TNMCs. The comparison of productions is one indication of whether or to what extent Western cultural imperialism is imposing, bribing, or otherwise disrupting any identifiable national culture.

Without arguing whether action movies are "mindless" or escapist or credible cinema, the primary point here is transnational media and most national media have discovered that action movies attract and please large audiences. Given the high cost of producing movies that can appeal across borders, transnational media are committed to whatever genre and formula that appeal to diverse audiences. Codes and conventions of action movies provide an easy and effective template: spectacle, explosions, chase scenes, fight scenes, special effects, heroes, villains, authorities, and violence—which travels well without translation or cultural confusion. This action template appears in many genre: science fiction, war, comedy, historic epic, spy, fantasy, martial arts, revenge and vigilante, and more. Action frames can creatively be included or superimposed on romance, drama, sports, even animation. Essentially action movies present lots of physical conflict (Lichtenfeld, 2007). Fist fights, sword fights, gun fights, explosions, crashes, fights with weapons and machines, and any other spectacle imaginable that moves the story and audience.

Action movies not only express the physical, they also reveal the political, cultural, and ideological preferences of the producing media. Not surprisingly, these political and ideological messages are consistent across commercial film studios both national and transnational. The top movies from Indian media and Indian transnational media contain the same dominant themes suggesting the hegemonic pull of transnational capitalism. National media desiring the success and profit-making of leading transnational players not only consented to neoliberal reforms allowing foreign investment, they requested JV, partnerships, and shared management in production and distribution. Ronnie Screwvala founded the UTV film studio in 1996, shortly after the government opened India to increased foreign investment. UTV quickly co-produced successful films with Fox, Sony, and Disney for India, Asia, and the United States. Reliance ADAG and Reliance Industries also directly engaged transnationals, partnering with DreamWorks and Viacom CBS. At the same time, successful national Indian media such as Yash Raj Films, Salman Khan, and T-Series dabbled in JV and then followed transnational media's lead, producing more action movies with similar tropes and themes that were commercially successful. Films by Yash Raj, Arka Media Works, and Lyca feature non-national and non-specific cultural values and themes. After Screwvala sold control of UTV to Disney, he continued to apply TNMC formulas and subsequently has produced commercially-successful action movies such as *Uri: The Surgical Strike* (2019) and others with his newly formed RSVP studio.

Several questions arise from current transnational media arrangements and productions. First, do TNMC formations and practices have any recognizable effect on national media film content? Do themes in Indian media and Indian transnational media feature explicit or implicit indications of US media influence or content expressing identifiable US cultural values? Finally, and perhaps most importantly, what themes, cultural values, and political prescriptions in film content support or advocate neoliberal transnational capitalism? These three questions address the relations between the political economy of transnational media and their political and ideological appeals that are intended to win consent from mass audiences.

Action movies also feature hegemonic appeals to their audiences by integrating critiques of inequality and corruption, diverse cultural representations (Tamil, Telugu, Malayalman, among others), and idealistic possibilities within larger thematic narratives and plots that conclude by reinforcing authority. The global attraction of action movies and their prevalence among transnational and Indian media indicates the success of TNMC cultural hegemony—which is much more and much different than US or Western cultural imperialism. In India, the dominant social relations of capitalism are often clothed in both nationalism *and* universalism. Consequently, successful action movies, whether set in historic epics, science fiction, or contemporary crime action (like top grossing films of 2017–2020 in India), include contradictory social and cultural expressions.

"Action movies consistently provide direct actions and fantasies that in part challenge the status quo in the abstract and villainy in general, providing entertaining stories that include opposition and resistance to unacceptable social conditions" (Artz, 2015, p. 197), whether with good-hearted anti-heroes (Simmba, 2018), complicated plot twists with double-agents (War, 2019) or royal privilege that circumvents and justifies behavior (*Baahubali*, 2017).

Of course, action movies do not usually prompt reflection on complex social problems, instead, military equipment, missiles, planes and other objects, such as "cameras, listening devices, computers, cell phones, automobiles, trains, etc.—are given vitality in the film, but life is largely drained from the people" (Walsh, 2007). The essence of human life in action movies is often reduced to the exceptional skills and violence performed by the protagonists. Violent direct action achieves its goals, clarifying and confirming the ethical rightness of the action heroes destruction of evil. Ultimately, existing authorities and hierarchies are defended, even when civil rights and legal niceties are ignored. The hero and the viewer knows who is evil, justifying any measures necessary to dispense vigilante justice. Action films like *Tiger Zinda Hai* (2017), *Uri* (2019), and *Baaghi 3* (2020) provide entertaining plots and actions that parallel the Indian government's justification for military action in Kashmir, Pakistan, Syria, and arguably even against protesting Sikh farmers in Delhi in 2021. This hegemonic construction invites audiences that consent to brutal action on the screen to transfer their consent to military combat and police action in the street. As a prominent part of TNMCs content, action movie ideology corresponds to the rationale for military interventions by national and international forces against challenges to the neoliberal capitalist order.

Even in science fiction, fantasy, or historically-inspired action films, TNMC writers and producers address contemporary issues of inequality, group identity, normative behavior, and representations—as determined and financed from the world view of TNMC owners. In movies, action heroes appear at times of crisis: invasions, wars, terrorist attacks, disruptions to hierarchies, corruption, and threats to public safety. In Yash Raj Film's *Tiger* franchise (2012, 2017), special forces agents from India and Pakistan romantically temper their nationalism, save travelers in Ireland and nurses in Syria. In Salman Khan's *Dabanng* franchise (2010, 2012, 2019), semi-corrupt cop Chulbul metes out justice against even more corrupt cops and gang members. The TNMC coproduction franchise of Fox Star and N. Grandson Entertainment, *Baaghi* (*The Rebel*) (2016, 2018, 2020), has special forces veteran Ronnie repeatedly rescuing kidnapped relatives. Recent action films by TNMCs Viacom 18/Reliance Industries and Reliance Entertainment/Dharma and Indian media Yash Raj, T-Series, and Arka Films, among others, feature the same template: threat and crisis; hero with skills takes vigilant action; hierarchy and authority protected.

In each case, all challenges to various authorities, whether royalty or government, are deemed threatening, irrational, duplicitous, and dangerous to all. A more democratic approach might find that inequality, poverty, homelessness, and other societal dysfunctions deserve collective resistance. Instead, both Indian media and Indian TNMC critiques are voiced solely by villains or secondary characters: only ISIS opposes the US occupation of Iraq in *Tiger Zinda Hai* and *Baaghi*; Kashmiris fighting for independence are cast as irrational terrorists in *Uri*; and challenges to rightful kings appear as treacherous and ruthless in *Baahabuli* and *Tanhaji*. In *2.0*, criticisms about the environmental consequences of cell phone producers and providers are reduced to the ravings of the madman Pakshi who traps 80,000 people in a football stadium.

Recurrent dominant images, representations, and story lines comprise an important part of the repertoire of TNMCs and their national media emulators. Recurring images of special forces, vigilante heroes, and royal heirs in action movies suggests to viewers that unaccountable, semi-secret government military activities are legitimate. Or at least entertaining. Irony, satire, and clever banter contribute to action movie claims that "only one, morally righteous side exists"—that of the government operative or chosen hero using extralegal measures (Keeton & Scheckner, 2013, p. 56). Even with all their genre and plot variations, action movies promote the interests of neoliberal transnationalism that must enforce its social inequality on the world. Action movies contribute to political apathy by "revealing social injustice, cultural bias, government incompetence and corruption in de-politicized narratives that champion the movie star character and debase democracy, the public, and humanity itself as ineffectual and unimportant" (Artz, 2015, p. 198). By identifying with the action hero, audiences begin to deny their own power, their own ability to right wrongs and make social change. Ronnie, Chulbul, and Tiger will be back to save their friends or the nation, but their heroic returns depend on continued social inequality and corruption. In action films, in the end nothing changes—except the momentary pleasure of the audience.

Transnational media and their hegemonic leadership in commercial film and television production assure that the themes, values, and ideologies useful for capitalist social relations prevail in entertainment and public consciousness. This is not to suggest that media content directly effects audience understandings or political leanings—those are more directly subject to lived experience—as protesting farmers in Delhi reveal (Schmall, 2020). Still, the engaging spectacles, visual effects, and simplistic narrative fantasies of TNMC-led action movies, ironically launch audiences toward political passivity and extreme self-interest. "The inequality of life, the tacit acceptance of authority, and our presumed powerlessness in the face of overwhelming structural practices are reinforced as common sense through the entertaining spectacle of direct action against evildoers" (Artz, 2015, p. 199). Dominant themes of the top Indian action movies may not appear fully in each film, but in the aggregate five themes consistently appear in the ten representative action films from Indian media and TNMCs: (1) danger and threats are everywhere; (2) average citizens are incapable of defending themselves; (3) heroes with special skills are needed; (4) hero violence is justified; and (5) hierarchy and authority must be defended.

Unpacking these five themes reveal the correspondence between the political economies of TNMCs and Indian media while illustrating the parallel content both produce for audience consumption.

1. *Danger and Threats Are Everywhere*

Most international airports announce a warning to passengers: "If you see something, say something." Danger is everywhere, possibly in a forgotten suitcase. Action movies echo and amplify those alerts. Be afraid, very afraid. Society is on the verge of collapse. Evil lurks. In action movies, daily life is unexpectedly but repeatedly and violently disrupted. Corruption, crime, invasion, terror, and crazed villains set the opening scenes. The second highest grossing Indian movie of all time, *Baahubali 2: The Conclusion* (2017), continues the fictional ancient Indian epic story of a warrior prince. From the beginning, palace intrigue and treachery threaten the rightful and beloved king, as invasions from neighboring bandit kingdoms recur. In Iraq, ISIS holds Indian and Pakistani nurses hostage setting the scene for *Tiger Zinda Hai* (2017). In action movies, even cell phones can be dangerous. In the sci-fi hit *2.0*—the top grossing film in 2018 with $115 million box office—vengeful villain Pakshi collects the electromagnetic radiation of individual phones to attack politicians and the public.

Danger is everywhere. Police cannot be trusted. Beautiful, refined women are treacherous. A piano player's life is upended in Viacom's Indian co-production *Andhadhum* (2018) when he witnesses a woman kill her husband with the help of a corrupt cop. She drugs the piano player, who is taken to an organ harvesting clinic. Yash Raj Films produced two of the top movies in 2019, *War* and *Saaho*, both of which present imminent danger. *War* opens with a rogue sniper killing his own secret agent employer (translation: even well-trained spies cannot be trusted). Official crimefighters offer little security, either. Following a crime boss murder in a fictional futuristic gangster city, a presumed team member turns out to be a thief. Reliance Entertainment, partner in DreamWorks and Amblin Productions, produced the anti-hero action film *Simmba* (2019). Simmba is corrupt, but crimes of murder and rape go too far for him. Unexpectedly, blood-thirsty terrorists kill 19 "innocent" Indian soldiers occupying Kashmir in Screwvala's RSVP hit, *Uri: The Surgical Strike* (2019). The dangers and threats confronting Indian audiences recount similar threats and crises facing all other nationalities depending on the TNMC target audience. In action films, existential dangers, whether to a family or a nation, transcend time periods. *Tanhaji* (2020), the T-Series and Devgn co-production recounts the invasions in 1665 by a Mughal emperor against the Marathas, an early confederacy on the Indian subcontinent before 19th century British colonialism. The invasion endangered not just the Maharaj's power, but the peace and security of the population. The last of the top films from 2017 to 2020 is the third film in the *Baaghi* series produced by the TNMC formed by Fox Star and N. Grandson Entertainment. Each *Baaghi* movie begins with a kidnapping—first the hero Ronnie's girlfriend, then his girlfriend's daughter, and finally Ronnie's brother is kidnapped by terrorists in Syria. No one is really safe. Villains kidnap women, children, and family members. Action movies are not the only productions for global audiences by TNMCs and Indian media, but they have been audience favorites. Given the continuing success of several franchises and the transparent operating principles in action movie narratives, millions receive an overarching message of direct action against threatening villains that sounds very much like the national government's entreaties to citizens: trust no one, villains are plotting attacks, danger is everywhere, be afraid.

2. *The Public is Incapable, Passive*

The 21st century has been characterized by mass democratic social movements from the Pink Tide in Latin America, the Arab Spring, uprisings against military dictatorships in Myanmar and Thailand, and even in the heart of India as farmers demonstrated for more than three months against Prime Minister Modi's attempt to further privatize agriculture (Suhrawardy, 2021). However, no commercial media production has been inspired by these truly heroic struggles for democracy and humanity. Instead, TNMCs and Indian media action movies narratively avoid any possibility for citizen participation or democratic action.

The unconcealed message within TNMC action movies, including all ten of these top grossing Indian films, communicates that citizens are incapable of defending themselves, and such attempts may even be disruptive. Citizens may try to repel attackers, but without success. Citizens sometimes may participate and contribute, but only under the direct leadership of an exceptional leader who can correctly organize them. Baahubali (English translation: "The One with Strong Arms") has superhuman strength and the charisma to lead soldiers in defense of the kingdom. In *Tiger Zinda Hai*, Syrian girls fight their kidnappers but only after special forces commander Zoya directs them. In *Simmba, War, Uri, Dabanng,* and *Baaghi*, well-trained and skilled special forces or physically-endowed cops rescue the weak and innocent. Without much assistance, Tanhaji repels the Mongols using his wits and will. Even in the science fiction thriller, *2.0*, android robots and bots save helpless citizens. In most cases, citizens abstain, cower, or die along with unnamed soldiers fighting behind the hero. Hundreds die fighting terrorists in Iraq, Syria, Kashmir or are killed by the invading hordes from Mughal and Kalakaya. Dozens die battling crime gangs and corrupt officials. Collective action for the common good does not appear in any of these movies. Collective action poses a threat to neoliberal capitalism which favors market forces over public interests. Entertainment by TNMCs (and Indian media following their leadership) must dissuade audiences from any possibility of democratic alternatives to existing hierarchies. As former British Prime Minister Margaret Thatcher once asserted, "there is no alternative" to privatization and self-interest. Action movies present threatening villains and citizen passivity and inability as elements of the human condition. Class and community solidarity do not appear in these action films. Any attempts at citizen actions are deemed inept, comical, or tragic, but never successful without a recognized hero leading the forces. For TNMCs, democracy is unreasonable for society and will not be advocated in film.

To win consent from audiences and to establish their own legitimacy, media productions need to at least recognize social inequality and government corruption. As noted earlier, that means challenges and criticisms will occasionally be included in a film, but cleverly incorporated into the larger narrative. Having unlikeable and unsuccessful characters voice the social critique marginalizes any challenge to existing power. Having heroes or rulers make reforms benefitting the population or dispatching particularly evil bureaucrats or corrupt officials suggests that the hierarchy acts for the collective good—but leaves any possibility of direct citizen participation beyond the film's resolution.

3. *Heroes Need Special Skills*

If we are unable to defend ourselves, our family, or our society, then we need some other protection. Not just anyone will do. Even existing forces may be insufficient against terrorists, aliens, or unknown traitorous bureaucrats. Specially-trained, well-tested, skilled, and righteous heroes are needed. Such heroes can use additional technology to seek out, surveil, and monitor potential enemies. They should also be given free rein to do whatever it takes to stop evil, which does not recognize civil rights, fairness, or norms of human behavior. All of the protagonists of the top grossing action films 2017–2020 have exceptional physical attributes, several have had special training. *Baahulbali* not only has superhuman strength, he was also trained in warfare, mathematics, and administration. He easily overpowers attacking enemies and rescues his love. In four of the movies, *Tiger*, *War*, *Uri*, and *Baaghi*, the saviors are special forces operatives, with rigorous training in martial arts, weapons, and espionage. In each *Baaghi* film, for example, Ronnie defeats scores of attackers. In Syria, he fights off tanks, helicopters, and troops. Three of the protagonists, Saaho, Simmba, and Chulbul in *Dabanng*, are exceptionally athletic, aggressive, and skilled fighters from their years interacting with street gangs. They each single-handedly overcome assaults by armed thugs, rescue the innocent, and kill at will. Aakash, the pianist in *Andhadhum*, who faked blindness to hone his musical skills, had gained exceptional abilities to conquer the villains after he actually became blind. The athletic Tanhaji trained in sword fighting by his father, scaled walls, withstood torture, and still led the campaign repelling the Mughal invaders. None of these heroes are average citizens.

Each of these top action movies feature single, independent loners, which seems contrary to India's more traditional attention to community harmony and self-restraint. Yet, after 30 years of neoliberalism and the expansion of marketing and advertising-driven media, the culture can no longer be described as collectivist. There has been "a gradual shift in India from a highly group-oriented societal framework to an individual-istic one" as India is fast becoming "a society where greater importance is laid on personal autonomy, space, and privacy over maintaining" more collective traditions (Rashtra, 2020). Certainly, past cultural imperialism in the 1980s and 1990s has had some effect on the dominant cultural practices in India today, including rising commercialism and consumer-ism among all social classes. Although no direct correlation can be drawn between movie content and social behavior, movie messages and audience behavior outside the theaters proclaim an adherence to individualism and consumerism.

Action movie content at least encourages displacing collective responses to social and economic inequality (such as the mass farmer protests) with "the catharsis of spectacle and the collective sharing of individualism in action" (Artz, 2015, p. 206). Perhaps more importantly, rather than prompting reflection on social conditions or inspiring audiences to social or political action, action movies nurture politically passive audiences. Understanding both the possibilities and constraints of codes and conven-tions in entertainment helps explain the cultural limits of action movies. Codes established by appearance, lighting, camera angle, time on screen, character traits and appearances, and even physical settings set parame-ters for creative variation. Likewise, conventions in action films require spectacle, chase, confrontation, individual violence, bureaucrat incom-petence, and retribution against villainy. Such repeated frames cultivate audience tastes and understandings, providing fertile ground for repeat viewers and increased ticket sales. Economically and politically, coopera-tive collective action against economic inequality by organized citizens is more threatening to TNMCs than it would be to the invaders, thugs, and terrorists of their movies.

4. *Hero Violence is Necessary*

To assure those under attack are protected, the hero must be judged moral. Once the hero's motivations are validated, any actions that follow will more likely be accepted. Action movies set up viewers to know the villain is deceitful and dangerous. In very brief glimpses, heroes, even anti-heroes, are shown to be caring and protective. Ensuing violence is at least accepted and sometimes applauded. Visceral satisfaction accompanies much of the violence. In a survey study of 600 parents, gun violence was acceptable when it was considered justified while increased viewings of violence normalized its occurrence and justification (Romer et al, 2018).

Thus, if the movie narrative and hero's behavior establish positive motivations and character judgment, violence by the hero is accepted, perhaps even desired. Action movie conventions of spectacle, chase, and fight move so quickly that any audience consideration of civil rights or legal procedures is likely suppressed. The actions of the heroes in the ten films observed have no apparent limits on their use of extra-judicial violence. Baahubali beheads an opponent's son. Rather than arresting and jailing the brutalizers of a young woman, Simmba kills them. His partner and Home Minister lie to cover up his vigilante action. In *Uri*, India's national security advisor responding to Kashmiri attacks shells the Pakistani border and disguises assault helicopters with Pakistani Air Force emblems—in violation of international law. Chulbul assaults a prisoner during interrogation, kidnaps government ministers, forces an illegal confession from them, and finally murders the villain. The deranged Pakshi in *2.0* is led to a space station and destroyed—no civil rights for evil doers in science fiction! As an anti-hero rogue, Saaho has no pretense of legality, but the film justifies his violence avenging his father's death. Saaho double-crosses many, destroys buildings, steals money, and murders his enemy.

Within the scripts approved by TNMC producers, action heroes can ignore laws and due process given the narrative's absolute certainty that targeted enemies are evil and guilty. Any dialog or break in the action would interfere with the quick dispensing of movie justice by righteous individuals. Heroes—government agents, corrupt cops, monarchs, and tough but lovable criminals—do not need approval by any law or institution. They obey a higher authority, the authority of the TNMC script and consent of viewers that know who is bad and what they've done to deserve punishment. A solid conviction of guilt, well-established established by script and performance, leads to a logical conclusion that violence by the hero must be the most responsible action. Besides, instant justice is enjoyable, almost cathartic, especially for audiences used to the daily injustices of corrupt officials and the tedious inactions of government bureaucrats and actual authorities.

Entertainment violence is not a far remove from real military action in Kashmir, at the Pakistani border, or against protesting farmers in Delhi. Justifying hundreds of dead movie soldiers and gang members as guilty lines up nicely with the certainty that any resistance to neoliberal austerity deserves punishment.

5. *Elite Authorities and Existing Hierarchies are Best for All*

Transnational and Indian action movies are not the first films to feature individual action heroes rescuing innocents and defending law and order. Previous movie heroes relied on their own courage and obeyed laws to defend society; TNMC heroes use their special skills and ignore laws to protect authority and hierarchy. TNMC action movies end when villains have been conquered and—equally essential to the story—when the identified hierarchical authority has been reaffirmed. Glaring social problems may provide background for action movies, but the plots and narratives narrowly focus on how individuals respond to crises. For example, *2.0* raises important and fact-based concerns about the environmental impacts of industrial production, but the story never transcends the actions of the villain and the reactions of state power. The *Baaghi* films have a special forces soldier circumventing established authority, directly inflicting pain and violence on villains, and defending the hierarchy he rebelled against. *Baaghi* movies are coproduced by N. Grandson Entertainment and Fox Star, a subsidiary of Disney (one of the largest TNMCs with revenues of $69 billion in 2020 and ranked 49th on the Fortune 500). Major independent Indian media ascribe to the same conclusion: Each Baahubali movie ends with the hierarchy intact, Tanhaji dies but Shivaji's kingdom is saved; each of the special forces heroes (in *Tiger*, *Saaho*, *Uri*, and *War*) uphold the police hierarchy and India's national honor. Even the independently rebellious anti-heroes (in *Simmba* and *Dabanng*) defend police powers or return power to a criminal hierarchy. In every instance, in each action movie, TNMC and Indian productions legitimize existing social structures and the institutions of power. Disrupters and resistors to established order appear as deranged, anti-social, and dangerous—but ultimately unsuccessful. Heroes actively and successfully protect hierarchy and authority, which usually remains passive, almost invisible, as an established given, the necessary structure which constrains the entire story.

Defending the existing social order permeates action movies and most other popular entertainment. The purpose of policing, including that of movie action heroes, is to maintain the status quo, which extends to maintaining power in any nation, because it makes sense "to demonize and try to deter protests and protestors. Media images are crucial here. They help to make sure that protests are regarded (because represented) as scary, violent affairs, associated with criminality, irrationality, and danger" (Bowman, 2012, p. 56). Action movies underwrite policing actions by the nation-state warding off evil. Ronnie's rejection of authority in Baaghi (which translates as "rebel") conveniently distracts viewers from his continual defense of authority. The "corrupt" Chulbul in *Dabanng* acts outside of the constraints of legal action—to more efficiently execute murderers, gang members, and child traffickers—to protect the political establishment. Transnational media produce and market action movies avoid directly addressing wealth and structural inequality and instead provide engaging spectacles of conflict on behalf of neoliberal capitalism—personified by heroes and villains. The hegemonic pull of TNMCs is apparent in the same content themes and ideological messages produced by not yet-TNMC Indian media.

Action movies present symbolic media violence and seduction in defense of neoliberalism in India and transnational capital globally. "Action movies present protest, challenge, and political critique of capitalism and its governing norms and institutions as misguided, naïve, disruptive, and unworthy of consideration, shielding capitalist hegemony" from democratic critique on behalf of the public, the subordinate classes and castes, the working classes and their allies (Artz, 2015, p. 213).

These themes are hard to miss: (1) danger is everywhere; (2) citizens are unable to protect themselves; (3) we need heroes and special forces to protect us; (4) heroes must act unhindered and without constraint; and (5) hierarchy and authority are normal and desirable. These themes do not bring audiences to theaters or streaming services. Audiences are attracted by the spectacle, the breath-taking action, the direct action thwarting villains, and the satisfaction of seeing the good and the just succeed.

Of course, action movies do not actually secure justice. Even within the film stories, replacing corrupt officials and making mild reforms are all that is ever offered. Mashishmati, the Moghul Empire, and the Mahashrati Confederation are ancient kingdoms. RAW (Research and Analysis Wing—India's intelligence agency) exists and engages in covert operations, but action movie accounts fictionalize its activities. Meanwhile, the ruling Modi government asserts authority and police action from Kashmir to Delhi. Likewise, transnational media partnerships and JV are real and powerful. TNMCs are dedicated to neoliberalism, commercialization, austerity, and the consequent social inequality. The ability of TNMCs to merge the ideology of power with the impulses of resistance and justice demonstrates their hegemonic leadership and creativity.

Transnational Production and Indian Media

The top grossing action movies cited above include TNMC productions and Indian media movies that reflect the turn toward transnational themes and ideological content. The domestic and global box office success of each of these movies reflects the cross-cultural pollination of scripts, actors, settings, and expanding transnational collaboration that attracts and leads national media toward particular content as a path to profit. Disney's Fox Star, Viacom/CBS, and Reliance/DreamWorks led the transnational productions, with *Baaghi*, *Simmba*, and *Andhadhun*. Given India's diversity of language, culture, religion, caste and social class, co-productions among Indian media might reasonably be understood as an internal transnationalism, or at least cross-cultural collaboration. The two *Baahubali* (2015, 2017) films co-produced by Arka Media Works in Telugu partnered with Tamil media Studio Green and Sri Thenandal, Marathi media Global United, and Hindi media AA Films. The Telugu hit *Saaho* (2019) by UV Creations included distribution partners SPI

Cinemas in Tamil and Yash Raj Films in Hindi. The T-Series co-production *Tanhaji* (2020) partnered with Ajay Devgn Films which released a Marathi version. While Yash Raj productions of these particular action movies do not have transnational partners, the productions are trans-regional and trans-lingual media JV. In addition, Yash Raj consistently has had co-production deals, joint venture partnerships, and has attracted multiple transnational investors. The owners, producers, and directors of Yash Raj Films have adopted TNMC practices as evidenced in their scripts, multicultural productions, and translations—and their openness to transnational investors. Moreover, all of these action movies, both transnational and national are commodities produced for corporate profit—with scant concern about the cultural identity of their partners or their content.

Action movies are produced to attract large audiences by meeting and nurturing their entertainment expectations that have been cultivated by recognizable codes and conventions constructed by transnational media partnerships. In addition to the five themes described above, action movies produced by TNMCs and national media following their lead promote capitalism and consumerism with product placements, deals between actors and advertisers, and creating other media commodities such as television series, novels, comics, music albums, video games, and branded fashion. Audi, BMW, Coca-Cola, Air India, Tata Motors, Volvo, Canon, Tag Heuer, Nokia and many other products appear in action movies, while action stars like Salman Khan, Akshay Kumar, and Mahesh Babu appear regularly in television commercials. "Consumer goods symbolically linked to action heroes solidify the excessive individualism of the genre and allows viewers to vicariously identify with their hero through consumption" (Artz, 2015, p. 216). None of this is accidental: every character in every script knows what is expected, because as Yash Raj Film chairman and filmmaker, Aditya Chopra says, studios direct the actors "about the look and attitude" they need to cultivate, so audiences will understand the movie and its message (Jha, 2005). Millions of viewers regularly watch Yash Raj, Arka Media Works, Fox Star, Reliance, Viacom, T-Series, and dozens of other producers with their repetitive messages loud, clear, and spectacular. Importantly, the cultural values of these movies are the same, confirming the claims of this book. No one could identify significant cultural differences between TNMC and non-TNMC action movies from India in the last five years. It is unlikely that anyone could even identify the national identity of the film studios based on the content of their action movies.

Action movies ask little of the audience: villains and heroes are obvious; justifications for violence are clear; hierarchies and authorities are assumed and normalized. The narrative is secondary to the spectacle. Any national cultural values are mostly irrelevant. Immediate, powerful, and effective direct action by uncomplicated heroes delivers vicarious pleasure and some visceral satisfaction, largely explaining why audiences keep returning to the genre.

As part of the neoliberal transnational expansion, TNMC-infused action movies communicate to millions of citizens that self-interest should be their priority—anything else is beyond their capabilities and should be left to the experts and authorities of the established social order. Just come back for the next sequel. In India, as elsewhere, transnational media leads television, film, and internet production by demonstrating the structures, relations, and content that attracts audiences, cultivates them to individualism and consumerism, and delivers profit to media owners and investors while reinforcing neoliberal capitalist relations globally. Thus, resulting cultural values and practices are not imposed by Hollywood or Washington, but continue to express Indian-inflected consumerism, inequality, and entertainment conventions.

References

AnimationXpress. (2018, October 2011). DQE's "Jungle Book" and "Peter Pan" get global master toy licensee. *AnimationXpress*. https://www.animationxpress.com/latest-news/dqes-jungle-book-and-peter-pan-get-global-master-toy-licensee/

Artz, L. (2015). *Global entertainment media: A critical introduction.* Malden, MA: Wiley-Blackwell.

Barrowman, K. (2013, June). *Beyond Bruce Lee:* Or how Paul Bowman never learned to stop worrying and love the movies. *Senses of Cinema.* https://www.sensesofcinema.com/2013/book-reviews/beyond-bruce-lee-or-how-paul-bowman-never-learned-to-stop-worrying-and-love-the-movies/

Bhushan, N. (2014a, February 24). India, Canada sign co-production treaty. *Hollywood Reporter.* https://www.hollywoodreporter.com/news/india-canada-sign-production-treaty-682740

Bhushan, N. (2014b, September 18). India, China sign film co-production treaty. *Hollywood Reporter.* https://www.hollywoodreporter.com/news/jennifer-garner-to-star-in-netflix-body-switch-comedy-family-leave

Bhushan, N. (2015, June 3). Fox's Star India and Bollywood Studio Dharma Productions Announce 9 Film Deal. *Hollywood Reporter.* https://www.hollywoodreporter.com/news/fox-s-star-india-bollywood-800028

Bhushan, N., & Brzeski, P. (2020, April 22). Eros India CEO explains STX merger logic: "The bigger story is on the OTT side." *Hollywood Reporter.* https://www.hollywoodreporter.com/news/eros-india-ceo-explains-stx-merger-logic-bigger-story-is-ott-side-1290850

Binged. (2020, July 3). Top 5 most subscribed OTT in India. *bookmyshow.com.* https://in.bookmyshow.com/buzz/blog/streaming/top-5-most-subscribed-ott-platforms-in-india

Bollyspice Editors. (2019, February 25). Eros International joins hands with leading Korean production companies to make a film and series on Heo Hwang-Ok, Embrace of Gaya. *Bollyspice.* https://bollyspice.com/eros-international-joins-hands-with-leading-korean-production-companies-to-make-a-film-and-series-on-heo-hwang-ok-embrace-of-gaya/

Boston, W. (2019). At Jaguar a turnaround reverses. *Wall Street Journal B,* 1–2.

Bowman, P. (2012). *Culture and the media.* New York: Palgrave Macmillan.

BQ Desk. (2017, December 15). Disney acquires Star India, Tata Sky stake via Fox deal. *Bloomberg Quint.* https://www.bloombergquint.com/business/2017/12/14/disney-acquires-star-india-tata-sky-stake-via-fox-deal

Bright, J. (2015, June 24.) Meet Nollywood: The second-largest movie industry in the world. *Fortune.* https://fortune.com/2015/06/24/nollywood-movie-industry/

Business Today. (2019, January 30). Income inequality gets worse; India's top 1% bag 73% of the country's wealth, says Oxfam. *Business Today.* https://m.businesstoday.in/lite/story/oxfam-india-wealth-report-income-inequality-richests-poor/1/268541.html

Business Wire. (2020, February 7). Sony Pictures Networks India enters into a licensing agreement with the India Performing Rights Society Ltd. *Business Wire India.* https://www.businesswireindia.com/sony-pictures-networks-india-enters-into-a-licensing-agreement-with-the-indian-performing-right-society-ltd-66885.html

Chishti, A. H. (n.d.) Big, ever bigger business. *Media Ownership Monitor India.* https://india.mom-rsf.org/en/findings/corporateownership/

Chopra, A. (2009, March 22). Stumbling toward Bollywood. *New York Times.* https://www.nytimes.com/2009/03/22/movies/22chop.html

Curtin, M. (2003). "Media capital: Towards the study of spatial flows. *International Journal of Cultural Studies 6*(2), 202–228.

Dastidar, S. G., & Elliot, C. (2020). The Indian film industry in a changing international market. *Journal of Cultural Economics 44,* 97–116.

Dixit, I. (2021, January 10). Purse strings. *New York Times Magazine,* 7–10.

DQE Entertainment. (2010, June 15). DQE and Sun TV Networks in broadcast deal for multiple international properties. *Cision PR Newswire.* https://www.prnewswire.com/news-releases/dqe-and-sun-tv-networks-in-broadcast-deal-for-multiple-internation-al-properties-96357539.html

Elegant, N.X. (2021 January 27). Foreign investment crated in 2020, India was a surprise bright spot. *Fortune.* https://fortune.com/2021/01/27/india-fdi-foreign-investment-2020/

Frater, P. (2018, January 31). TV 18 buys control of Viacom joint ventures in India. *Variety.* https://variety.com/2018/biz/asia/tv18-viacom18-india-contol-1202683872/#!

Friedman, T. (2006). *The world is flat.* 2nd ed. New York: Farrar, Straus and Giroux.

Gramsci, A. (2000). *The Antonio Gramsci reader: Selected writings, 1916–1935.* In D. Forgacs (Ed.). New York: New York University Press.

Harrison, J. (2021, January 12). How a billion screens can turn India into a powerhouse of opportunity. *Ernst & Young ey.com.*

Hoyler, M., & Watson, A. (2019). Framing city networks through temporary projects: (Trans)national film production beyond "Global Hollywood." *Urban Studies 56*(5), 943–959.

HT Entertainment Desk. (2021, January 23). Madhu Mantena buys shares in Phantom Films. *Hindustan Times.* https://www.hindustantimes.com/entertainment/bollywood/madhu-mantena-buys-anurag-kashyap-vikramditya-motwane-vikas-bahl-s-shares-in-phantom-films-101611390211847.html

Iwabuchi, K. (2002). *Recentering globalization: Popular culture and Japanese transnationalism.* Durham, NC: Duke University Press.

Jain, K. (2007). *Gods in the bazaar: The economics of Indian calendar art.* Durham, NC: Duke University Press.

Jain, N., Soneja, T., & Ahluwalia, J. (2016). *Indywood: The Indian film industry.* Deloitte Touche Tohmatsu. https://www2.deloitte.com/content/dam/Deloitte/in/Documents/technology-media-telecommunications/in-tmt-indywood-film-festival-noexp.pdf

Jha, L. (2020, October 6). Sony's slated merger with Viacom 18 now called off. *The Mint.* https://www.livemint.com/industry/media/sony-viacom18-merger-called-off-11601888757116.html

Jha, S. K. (2005, September 26). Dhoom 2 goes on the floor. *Rediff India Abroad*. http://www.rediff.com/entertai/2005/sep/26dhoom.htm

Joshi, N. (2019, September 11). Streaming giant Netflix inks multi-year deal with Karan Johar. *The Hindu*. https://www.thehindu.com/profile/author/Namrata-Joshi-435/

Karmali, N. (2020, April 7). India's ten richest billionaires. *Forbes*. https://www.forbes.com/sites/naazneenkarmali/2020/04/07/indias-10-richest-billionaires-in-2020/?sh=217958e37c23

Keelery, S. (2020a). Highest grossing Hollywood movies India 2020. *Statista*. https://www-statista-com.pnw.idm.oclc.org/statistics/695625/highest-grossing-hollywood-movies-india/

Keelery,S.(2020b).Value of the film industry in India FY 2014-2024.*Statista*.https://www-statista-com.pnw.idm.oclc.org/statistics/235837/value-of-the-film-industry-in-india/

Keeton, P., & Scheckner, P. (2013). *American War cinema and media since Vietnam*. New York: Palgrave Macmillan.

Leena, S. B. (2016, February 2). Sun partners Yupp TV to offer content in West Asia, North Africa. *The Mint*. https://www.livemint.com/Consumer/sNUzvaaqFC2iSjsIFxE-CaP/Sun-TV-partners-YuppTV-to-offer-content-in-West-Asia-North.html

Lichtenfeld, E. (2007). *Action speaks louder: Violence, spectacle, and the American action movie*. Middletown, CN: Wesleyan University Press.

Liu, A. (2019, July 17). Top Indian drugmakers expand in China a policy changes trigger opportunity. *Fierce Pharma*. https://www.fiercepharma.com/pharma-asia/top-indian-drugmakers-expand-china-as-country-pressures-generic-costs

Lorenzen, M., & Täube, F. A. (2007). Breakout from Bollywood? Internationalization of India film industry. Druid Working Paper 07-06. *Danish Research Unit for Industrial Dynamics*. file:///Users/leeartz/Downloads/Breakout_from_Bollywood_Internationalization_of_In.pdf

Mandaiker, A. (2014). Impact of Bollywood on Indian Culture. *Desiblitz*. https://www.desiblitz.com/content/impact-bollywood-indian-culture

Mangaldas & Co. (2015). Foreign investments and the Indian media and entertainment industry. *Lexolog*. https://www.lexology.com/library/detail.aspx?g=9d3e84da-2b38-48ba-bb06-fb1601091c43

McCarthy, N. (2014, September 3). Bollywood: India's film industry by the numbers. *Forbes*. https://www.forbes.com/sites/niallmccarthy/2014/09/03/bollywood-indias-film-industry-by-the-numbers-infographic/?sh=2d5df9f72488

Media Ownership Monitor India. (2020). Media ownership matters. *Media Ownership Monitor India*. https://india.mom-rsf.org/en/

Mehta, R. B. (2011). Bollywood nation, globalization: An incomplete introduction. In B. Mehta, & R. V. Pandharipande (Eds.), *Bollywood and globalization: Indian popular culture, nation, and diaspora* (pp. 1–14). New York: Anthem

Middleton, R. (2021, February 10). TBI Kids: Unpacking animated co-productions & global potential. *TBI Vision*. https://tbivision.com/2021/02/10/tbi-kids-unpacking-animated-co-productions-global-potential/

Nagarathna,A. (2020, December 19). Latest TRP Ratings: Indian Idol out. *Filmibeat*. https://www.filmibeat.com/television/news/2020/latest-trp-ratings-indian-idol-12-out-ghum-hai-kisikey-pyaar-meiin-re-enters-top-5/articlecontent-pf319212-307698.html

Patranobis, S. (2019, January 5). Increase in number of India films released in China could lead to audience fatigue, report says. *Hindustan Times*. https://www.hindustantimes.com/bollywood/increase-in-number-of-indian-films-released-in-china-could-lead-to-audience-fatigue-says-report/story-8zxPU4GFrpaJmHVHECI9vM.html

PriceWaterhouseCoopers. (2010). *Global pharma looks to India: Prospects for growth.* https://www.pwc.com/gx/en/pharma-life-sciences/pdf/global-pharma-looks-to-india-final.pdf

Priyadarshi, S. (2015, December 21). South-south trade and its implications for the world economy. *International Banker.* https://internationalbanker.com/finance/south-south-trade-and-its-implications-for-the-world-economy/

Punathambekar, A. (2013). *From Bombay to Bollywood: The making of a global media industry.* New York: New York University Press.

Rajadhyaksha, A. (2006). The curious case of Bombay's Hindi cinema: The career of indigenous "exhibition" capital (part 1). *Journal of Moving Image.* https://www.academia.edu/42290820/The_Curious_Case_of_Bombays_Hindi_Cinema_The_Career_of_Indigenous_Exhibition_Capital_part_I

Ramachandran, N. (2019, January 25). Sony Explores Stake in Indian Powerhouse Zee Entertainment (Report). *Variety.* https://variety.com/2019/tv/news/sony-explores-stake-indian-powerhouse-zee-entertainment-1203117889/#!

Rashtra. (2020). How India is co-opting individualism with collectivism. *vocal.media.* https://vocal.media/families/how-india-is-co-opting-individualism-with-collectivism

Rasul, A., & Proffitt, J. M. (2012). An irresistible market: A critical analysis of Hollywood-Bollywood coproductions. *Communication, Culture & Critique 5,* 563–583.

Reporter, B. S. (2012, June 6). TV 18-Viacom to take on STAR-Zee in distribution. rediff.com. https://www.rediff.com/money/report/tech-tv18-viacom-to-take-on-star-zee-in-distribution/20120606.htm

Rodrigues, U. M. (2010). Glocalization of Indian television. In M. Ranganathan, & U. M. Rodrigues (Eds.), *Indian media in a globalized world* (pp. 3–25). Thousand Oaks. CA: Sage

Romer, D., Jamieson, P. E., Jamieson, K. H., Lull, R., & Adebimpe, A. (2018). Parental desensitization to gun violence in PG-13 movies. *Pediatrics 141*(6). https://www.researchgate.net/profile/Dan-Romer/publication/325129002_Parental_Desensitization_to_Gun_Violence_in_PG-13_Movies/links/5b032fe8aca-2720ba099009a/Parental-Desensitization-to-Gun-Violence-in-PG-13-Movies.pdf

Sabarwai, H. (2021, March 4). FDI rises 40 per cent to $51.47 billion in April-December 2020–21: Govt data. *Hindustan Times.* https://www.hindustantimes.com/business/fdi-rises-40-per-cent-to-51-47-billion-in-april-december-2020-21-govt-data-101614854828044.html

Schmall, C. (2020, December 5). Defiant farmers burn their own fields to protest Modi reforms. *New York Times,* A11.

Sen, M. (2011). It's all about loving your parents": Liberalization, Hindutva and Bollywood's new fathers. In R. B. Mehta, & R. V. Pandharipande (Eds.), *Bollywood and globalization: Indian popular culture, nation, and diaspora* (pp. 145–168). New York: Anthem.

Sen, R. (2015, December 10). Where are the Muslim characters on Hindi television? *Newslaundry.com.* https://www.newslaundry.com/2015/12/10/where-are-the-muslims-characters-on-hindi-television

Sethi, A. (2021, June 7). Why Amazon is confronting the richest man in India. *New York Times.* https://www.nytimes.com/2021/06/07/business/amazon-reliance-ambani-future.html

Shackleton, L. (2014, August 26). India's Eros International has struck a deal. *Screen Digest.* https://www.screendaily.com/eros-viacom18-strike-distribution-pact/5076650.article

Shashidhar, A. (2020, July 21). Sony to own 74% after merger with Viacom 18; ready for duel with Disney-Star. *Business Today India.* https://www.businesstoday.in/current/corporate/sony-pictures-to-own-74-per-cent-after-merger-with-viacom-18-brace-up-for-fight-with-disney-star/story/410500.html

Singh, M. (2020, May 21). KKR to invest $1.5 billion in India's Reliance Jio platforms. *TechCrunch*. https://techcrunch.com/2020/05/21/kkr-invests-1-5-billion-in-indias-reliance-jio-platforms/

Sinha, N. (1999). Doordarshan, public service broadcasting, and the impact of globalization. In M. E. Price, & S. G.Verhulst (Eds.), *Broadcasting reform in India: Media law from a global perspective* (pp. 22–40). London: Oxford University Press

Spencer, D. (2019, December 6). China: India pharma firms coming. *Pharma Boardroom*. https://pharmaboardroom.com/articles/china-indian-pharma-firms-incoming/

Statista. (2021). Leading free television channels across India in week 4 of 2021, by weekly viewership. *Statista.com*. https://www.statista.com/statistics/1028761/india-top-free-television-channels-by-impressions/

Suhrawardy, N. (2021, February 19). Indian farmers' protest: A strong democratic test? *Counterpunch*. https://www.counterpunch.org/2021/02/19/indian-farmers-protest-a-strong-democratic-test/

Tatna, M. (2017, March 21).The power of international markets: In India, it's Bollywood vs Hollywood. *HFPA Golden Globe Awards*. https://www.goldenglobes.com/articles/power-international-markets-india-its-bollywood-vs-hollywood

Tatna, M. (2019, August 3). Hollywood in India. *Hollywood Press Association*. https://www.goldenglobes.com/articles/hollywood-india

Thomas, T. (2019, July 31). Invesco Oppenheimer Fund to buy 11% stake in Zee Entertainment. *Mint*. https://www.livemint.com/companies/news/invesco-oppenheimer-fund-to-buy-11-in-zeel-for-rs-4-224-crore/amp-1564577772129.html

Thussu, D. (2016). The scramble for Asian soft power. *Les enjeux de l'information et de la communication* 17(2), 225–234.

TNN. (2016, June 23).Vice Media forms JV with Times Group for India foray. *Times of India*. https://timesofindia.indiatimes.com/business/india-business/VICE-Media-forms-JV-with-Times-Group-for-India-foray/articleshow/52871290.cms

Todhunter, C. (2016, November 30) What has neoliberal capitalism ever done for India? *Counterpunch*. https://www.counterpunch.org/2016/11/30/what-has-neoliberal-capitalism-ever-done-for-india/

Walsh, D. (2007, August 24).The Bourne Ultimatum: Action packed and it pays the price. *World Socialist Web Site*. https://www.wsws.org/en/articles/2007/08/bour-a24.html

Yau, E. (2018, December 11). Why Indian films like Dangal and Toilet are so popular in China. *South China Morning Post*. https://www.scmp.com/culture/film-tv/article/2177193/why-indian-films-dangal-and-toilet-are-so-popular-china-similar

Yudice, G. (2005). *The expediency of culture: Uses of culture in the global era*. Durham, NC: Duke University Press.

4

CROUCHING TIGERS

Transnational Media in and from China

Leng Feng, a special ops renegade, parties on an African beach. Attacked by mercenaries, Leng defeats all marauders, rescuing African locals and Chinese workers. Operating outside international law and Chinese and local authority, Leng Feng saves the innocent, defeats the villains, and patriotically protects China's integrity and global status. Leng Feng is a hero and the movie, *Wolf Warriors* (2017), became the highest grossing non-English film of all time, earning over $900 million. The movie pleased millions and displayed China's rising world power.

Capitalist China

Perhaps not as dramatically as in the movies, China also appears in the world's news as a rising economic, political, and military power. While Chinese military capabilities are much overstated, its economic power is likely underappreciated. In the last 15 years, China foreign direct investment (FDI) to the US totaled more than $180 B (American Enterprise Institute, 2020), including some $10 billion in media and over $17 billion in communication technologies. China's economy reached $15 trillion GDP in 2020, continuing to gain on the US GDP, which was $20 trillion (Statista, 2020). In 2020, China received $168 billion in FDI, surpassing the US. For the last 30 years, market-driven calculations have infiltrated China's "accelerated transition from a planned economy to a market economy" (Zhao, 2008, p. 179). Clearly, China is a capitalist state, with authoritarian government control exercised by the Chinese Communist Party (CCP). In the midst of the global coronavirus pandemic, when China feared inflation, it continued to "encourage foreign financial institutions to enter China for shared development" according to trade

DOI: 10.4324/9781003162452-05

commissioner Guo Shuqing (Brasher, 2021). This reorganization of the economy did not happen by accident or under pressure; Chinese authorities turned
to neoliberalism by choice and design. So now, the CCP rhetorically argues
that increased production and export is the path to progress for the Chinese
nation.

The government regulates all industrial production, but in its adoption of
neoliberalism and private enterprise the CCP government also accepts and
even invites foreign investors—always into partnerships or joint ventures
with state or private companies. The most immediately visible confirma-
tion of China's journey toward transnational capitalism appears on its con-
gested streets and highways—filled with traffic from cars sporting insignias
from around the world. The "big four" automakers in China (SAIC, Wuling,
Geely, Chang'an) have established transnational partnerships with all of the
world's leading manufacturers. Geely rivals US manufacturers in sales and
profits with over $1 billion in auto sales in 2016 (Gillespie, et al, 2018). Geely
is majority owner of joint ventures with UK's Lotus and Sweden's Volvo and
has a 10% stake in Daimler Benz. SAIC, a state-owned auto maker, has had
a joint venture with Volkswagen-Audi for 25 years. The SAIC Volkswagen
partnership has struck other deals with Spain's SEAT, Czech's Skoda, UK's
Bentley, and Italy's Lamborgini for joint operations in China. SAIC also has
major partnership with GM making Buick, Cadillac, and Chevrolet models.
In fact, GM sells more cars in China than in the US. GM also has a joint
venture with SAIC and Wuling, that each year sells some 2 million mass market cars priced under $10,000. Wuling has an additional joint venture with
Mitsubishi. China's Guangzhou Auto (GAC) has transnational partnerships
with Fiat-Chrysler, Honda, Mitsubishi, and Toyota. GAC Honda's 50:50 venture manufactures 600,000 cars annually, and GAC now has JVs with most
other Japanese automakers (Wang, 2019). State-owned Beijing Auto bought
5% of Daimler Benz 2019. Chang'an Auto, another large state-owned firm
that makes cars, vans, and light trucks has a joint venture with Ford. As the
Chinese government moves deeper into neoliberal protocols by relaxing limits on foreign ownership in 2022, BMW plans to increase its stake to 75%
in its current joint venture with Brilliance Auto—which also has a JV with
Renault making commercial vehicles. Auto production and the millions of
cars in the polluted streets and cities of China dramatically confirm the government's commitment to neoliberal, transnational capitalism, and the rule of
the market.

Whatever its socialist rhetoric, the Chinese government and its CCP
leadership actions underscore their dedication to capitalist market relations.
Trump scuttled the Transpacific Partnership (TPP), but the transnational cap-
italist class in Southeast Asia and the Pacific were committed to "free trade."
After several years of negotiations, a regional trade agreement—the Regional
Comprehensive Economic Partnership (RCEP)—was signed by 15 Asia-Pacific

nations in November 2020, including China, Australia, New Zealand, Japan and South Korea along with the Association of the South East Asian Nations — Brunei, Cambodia, Indonesia, Laos, Malaysia, Myanmar, the Philippines, Singapore, Thailand and Vietnam — in a deal that encompasses nearly one-third of the world's economy, 650 million people, and potentially $200 billion in production and trade annually. China's prime minister, Li Keqiang, said the agreement is "a victory of multilateralism and free trade" (Dolack, 2020). Although some US commentators recognize that multilateral trade favoring business over labor and the environment is not popular, they also admit that the US still has a desire for such "free market" deals (Tan, 2021). In short, economic and political pressures from both the global and Chinese capitalist class remain, because they want and need transnational production.

China also has agreed to a myriad of other trade and development agreements: a $6 billion rail line from Laos to China; a 2015 $5 billion co-production high-speed rail deal in Indonesia with state firms and several private companies; a China rail JV from Hungary to Greece completed its Serbia segment in 2021. China has made even larger investments in the Middle East, including a 2021 deal for $400 billion investment in infrastructure and energy with Iran (Fassihi & Myers, 2021). China is Iraq's biggest trading partner, and according to the *Financial Times*, China is also now the Middle East's biggest foreign investor with strategic partnerships with all the Gulf States (Anderlini, 2020). Compare this with Washington's confused foreign policy agenda in the region, its unprecedented indecisiveness, absence of a definable political doctrine and the systematic breakdown of its regional alliances (Baroud, 2021). As Trump seemed to retreat from global neoliberal practices, China embraced WTO (World Trade Organization) protocols; the US capitalist class was troubled. It's not that China directly challenges the US economically, it's that China has become a dynamic transnational operator with growing industrial and trade partnerships in Europe, Africa, and Latin America. Transnational capitalism propels forward corporations who lead the charge. Although millions of people do not benefit, market practices increase the size and wealth of the managerial classes and spurs their mass consumption. Almost every major corporation in every nation promotes open borders for capitalist investment and production.

Consumerism and Nationalism

China is no exception. Transnational partnerships are expressed as capitalism with "Chinese characteristics." The government declared that consumerism contributes to national pride. Socialism only exists as a hybrid ideology to shield the government's capitalist policies (Zhao, 1998). As noted in the book's introduction and the previous chapter on India, media globalization did not circumvent the nation-state. In Korea, for example, the government deregulated all media sectors in 1997. In China, the government also "plays a crucial role in regulating domestic cultural policies and guiding development" (Yik-Chan, 2003, p. 75)—largely to protect both government-run and private industries, including "national" media. Ironically, the ideology of neoliberal capitalism has been consistently introduced by the nationalist and pseudo-socialist rhetoric of the Chinese government. While cultural imperialism tends to romanticize non-US cultures as nationally-independent expressions of popular democracy, the national culture promoted by the Chinese nation-state is little more than economic and political agenda-setting by the CCP regime and its elite bureaucratic beneficiaries. In particular, the structures and practices of media in China cannot be understood separate from the social class structure which includes an authoritarian political system that advances and protects the burgeoning capitalist class closely affiliated with state institutions. In this case, and many others, defense of the national culture against Western influence contributes to the suppression and marginalization of working-class voices and diverse cultural interests in the name of cultural integrity for the government's undemocratic agenda (Sreberny, 2001).

A political economy perspective that recognizes social class relations of industrial, consumer, media and cultural production posits a more radical view: power is not primarily national or geographic, but social class. The question always posed is: Who owns the means of media and cultural production? When capitalist media owners champion their own commercial media independence against US cultural imperialism, neither democracy nor public interest benefit. Of course, transnational partnerships do not advance the public interest either.

Recognizing the neoliberal project of transnational capitalism does clarify what is at stake. Capitalism has enacted a global program of exploitation. The world working classes, indigenous groups, and their myriad allies likewise need to create a transnational response establishing wide public access to media production and distribution, without market norms or constraints. Nation-state governments do not exist in a social vacuum. Nor do they represent the majority. As they join the neoliberal project commercializing public resources for capital, offering consumerism for some and austerity for the majority, governments reveal their function: to serve the nation's corporate owners with whatever political means adopted. Dominant national and transnational ideologies serve the interests of both the local elite and the transnational capitalist system. In fact, "local ruling classes are capable of dominating their own societies without the aid of instruction from abroad" (Sarti, 1981, p. 327). The CCP is not reliant on or subservient to US cultural imperialism. On its own, the CCP facilitates market relations and consumerism in China. Socialist rhetoric gives "cover for policies of development inspired by capitalism" (Dirlik, 2005, p. 9) while "governing activities are recast as non-political and nonideological problems that need technical solutions" (Ong, 2006, p. 13). What little divergence of norms, structures, and practices of media production that exists in China due to multiple languages and changing cultural practices cannot be explained by cultural imperialism or the supposed flattening resulting from globalization.

China is not only an industrial society, it has become a consumer society. Since 1992, advertising revenues fund most television production, resulting in "greater commercialization in television stations" and "the transformation of China into a consumer society" (Yik-Chan, 2003). China is the second largest consumer market in the world at $6 trillion in 2018. As the Chinese government continues to adopt neoliberal policies, advertising, and retail markets, consumerism will become more habitual. As former Communist leader Deng Xiao Ping declared in the mid-1990s when China began offering tax breaks to foreign investors: "To get rich is glorious!"—even in a regimented social structure Chinese bureaucrats and professionals have become "proudly conspicuous consumers" (Doctoroff, 2005, p. 22, 25). McKinsey & Company reports that the affluent-middle class is growing rapidly, and for most social classes, spending on consumer goods has increased, including on mobile phones, gaming consoles, jewelry, clothing, shoes, and toys. Purchases of luxury goods are rising as personal consumption "has been a powerhouse for economic growth" in China (Ho, Poh, Zhou, & Zipster, 2019).

Chinese movie hits often emphasize patriotism, but popular films like *Ne Zha* and *The Wandering Earth* still prominently feature individualized stories with powerful visuals. Nationalist themes provide background, which is unsurprising, given the CCP's attempts to control capitalist market policies and background Confucian traditions that counsel respect for authority. As in India and elsewhere in the world, nationalism provides a useful coating for the expansion of neoliberal commercialization. Thus, a special report by the *The Economist* published two stories on the same day: one noting "how nationalism is shaping China's young" and the other asserting that "individualism reigns in China" (Economist, 2021a, 2021b). Thus, media serve national politics while also promoting advertising and individual consumption. Ultimately successful capitalist media must "redeploy its creative resources and reshape its operations if it is to survive competition and enhance profitability" (Curtin, 2007, p. 11). Hence, whatever the patriotic cover, media desire transnational partnerships. In the process, movie "effects are more polished. Stories are given a more traditional Western structure. They're big-budget spectacles that just happen to be Chinese" (Zeitchik, 2019). Nationalism may cloak Chinese entertainment, but the Chinese cultural body grows into consumerism.

Regional TNMC Partners

The commercialization of television production and networks and the opening to commercial film studios and foreign investment assured a surge in production that was still unable to keep up with the increased gap between consumer demand and supply in television broadcasting and feature films. Television dramas from Korea, Hong Kong, Taiwan, Japan, and the US filled the open space and illustrated models for entertainment—boosting transnational collaboration. China television has co-produced programs with Malaysia, Singapore, Hong Kong, Taiwan, and Korea. Fuji Television sold some 25 of its programs to China in the last few years and now Fuji-Chinese media co-productions are its business priority (Blair, 2019). Regional transnational production predominates because these nations share some historical and linguistic affinities. TNMC productions would likely be greater but the Chinese government has a 25% limit on imported martial arts and monarchy-based television dramas to protect its own domestic television producers (Yik-Chan, 2003).

For US media, "exploiting the developing Chinese film market is not just opportune, it is essential" (Richeri, 2016, p. 325). For China, the growth in cinema helped consolidate a social cohesion around a collective identity, while also promoting individual consumerism. Increased joint ventures and co-productions indicate that the leadership of TNMCs—its partners, organization, ideological content, commodities, cultural diversity, technology, and advertising and marketing—has attracted Chinese commercial media (with government approval) seeking to please diverse audiences and increase domestic and global revenue. In the 21st century, communication is an important site of capitalist accumulation, as well as a crucial means of social organization and class and identity formation" (Zhao, 2008, p. 17).

As Chinese private media work with transnational partners, they "appropriate and integrate" the business model through regional and international cooperation while abiding by national regulations (Yi-Chen, 2003, p. 89), even while they are "internalizing and exploiting orientalist conceptions of China to their own political and economic advantages" (Zhao, 2008, p. 142). At the same time, Chinese investors flooded into Hollywood (Garrahan & Sender, 2016). In both cases, commercial and government Chinese media willingly consent to the TNMC leadership: adapting formulas and content (especially action and animation—which feature low-risk narrative content) for regional media co-production and distribution, while incorporating symbolic and stereotypical representations of traditional Chinese culture. This is a hegemonic process, not one of domination or imposition (Artz, 2015). Chinese media expect to prosper from learning and following the TNMC production model and its individualized narrative template; US and EU media accept the government filters on content restrictions. Spectacle and cultural diversity attract and please millions. Thus, TNMCs have outpaced US cultural domination and secured global leadership for production norms and cross-cultural entertainment content.

Regional agreements in Southeast and East Asia are particularly attractive and lucrative given the cultural and linguistic similarities, the new consumption patterns, and the technological changes (i.e., cable, satellite, internet, mobile phones, streaming apps). Although Chinese regulations erect barriers to many regional media projects, pan-Asian co-productions "create new products and services that are transnational, or borderless" such as costume dramas and popular cinema (Lim, 2006). Reflecting the variety of regional transnational partnerships, "pan-Asian cinema takes various forms: talent sharing, cross-border investment, co-productions, and market consolidation through distribution and investment in foreign infrastructure" (Yeh, 2010, p. 188). Whatever the transnational pan-Asian relation, the national identity of media producers is seldom discernible in the content of the most successful films and television programs.

Among the contradictions and interactions of transnational film co-productions, two appear most significant and demonstrable: encouraging consumerism and homogenizing the cinema culture. Xu Song (2018) explains that regional transnational media create cinematic spectacles that simplify cultural differences, expand references to other countries, can be understood easily, blend cultures and nations deliberately, and utilize transnational superstars and international personnel across borders (p. 180). Transnational films for Chinese audiences must "embrace and integrate" cultural elements to attract large audiences (Xu, 2018, p. 180). At the same time, transnational movies must undergo "cultural and ideological cleansing" to attract and please audiences from many nations (Ezra & Rowden, 2006, p. 2; Iwabuchi, 2002). This double task is easiest with action, animation, and fantasy films that downplay specific cultural identifiers while providing multiple audiences with ample recognizable representations, some of which echo orientalist stereotypes.

Transnational structures of shared management with extensive vertically integrated partnerships determine the content, distribution, and exhibition essential to a film's success. Film exhibition in China mandates partnering with authorized distribution companies, The China Film Group and Huaxia Film Distribution, essentially insuring that most imported cinema in China is transnational.

The Nation-State and Corporate Interests

Transnationalism, like all previous capitalist iterations, adapts and relies on a variety of government forms. European governments instituted "Television without Borders" to enhance cross-culture media exchange; the Nigerian government allows unhindered, even pirated media production; the US government supports increased media consolidation and limits public access; the Chinese government maintains tight control over news media, regulates film content, but promotes joint ventures and partnerships with transnational producers and distributors. Chinese media regulations officially allow 34 revenue-sharing imported films annually that can only retain 25% of the box office (Lang & Frater, 2018). Imported movies without national partnerships can negotiate a flat fee for exhibition through the China Film Group or Huaxi Film Distribution (Zheng, 2018). In contrast, Chinese TNMC co-productions have no limits on the number of films that can be exhibited or profits that can be shared. In each case, the appeal of potentially massive profit prompts transnational media to accept the government's terms of production and regulation of content.

Despite lamenting the lack of democracy in China, or elsewhere, transnational media do not exist apart from capitalist social relations, which do not need and have not historically championed democracy. The tenuous connection between capitalism and democracy has been repeatedly made clear: US media applauded the Shah coup against democratically-elected Mossadegh in 1954; *Time-Life* supported Roberto Marinho and the Brazilian dictatorship in the 1960s; and most recently all major television networks trumpeted full support for US-backed coups in Venezuela (2002), Egypt (2013), and Bolivia (2019). The stable political control and low labor costs for entertainment media partners outweigh their concern for democracy and free speech. Thus, TNMCs offer action, spectacle, and cultural diversity acceptable to Chinese audiences and bureaucrats, while avoiding excessive concerns with civil or human rights. In other words, there is a political and economic convergence of transnational capitalism and "socialism with Chinese characteristics" as "transnational media and the Chinese authorities work in tandem to produce a state-global media complex" of entertainment (Fung, 2006, p. 84) featuring stories replete with spectacle and diversity with little citizen integrity or democracy.

Chinese government and corporate transnational relations are too extensive to recount fully, given the space constraints of a single book. Several examples may at least reflect the nature, breadth, and coverage of transnational capitalism with China.

When K-pop gained international popularity, and China became one of its largest markets, Chinese media and investors became some of its biggest fans. E-commerce leader Alibaba invested in Korea's cultural powerhouse SM Entertainment; China's Banana Culture managed the Korean girl groups T-Ara and EXID; and Yue Hua Entertainment represented K-pop groups that had Chinese and Korean members (Herman, 2018). And it's not just music that crosses borders. Korean drama and reality shows such as *Idol Producer* by CJ Entertainment are popular on Chinese television. Thus, there was an increased incentive for transnational co-productions by South Korean and Chinese media.

There are other Chinese TNMC arrangements that go beyond regional deals. Tencent, the internet giant that has over 1 billion users on its messaging app WeChat, is a major transnational media company, with investments or shares in over 600 companies—mostly in culture and entertainment (Chen, 2019). Tencent has substantial transnational relations, including with the South

TABLE 4.1 Tencent video game investments (partial list)

Grinding Gear Games (80 percent ownership)	New Zealand
Miniclip (majority ownership)	Switzerland
Glu Mobile (14.46 percent stake)	US
Epic Games (40 percent)	US
Activision Blizzard (5 percent)	US/French
Ubisoft (5 percent)	French/US
Paradox Interactive (5 percent)	Sweden
Supercell (84.3 percent)	Finland
Riot Games (100 percent)	US
CJ Games (minority stake)	South Korea

African internet and media giant Naspers, which with a 30% stake is Tencent's largest shareholder. Tencent bought 12% of SnapChat in 2017. The following year, Tencent bought 10% of US film studio Skydance (which also has investments from the Korean TNMC CJ Entertainment). In 2020, the India-US TNMC ErosSTX partnered with Tencent on the action thriller *Rogue*. TenCent, which already owned 10% of Universal Music group, invested $361 million for 5% of Warner Music in 2020. Tencent also has multiple partnerships in TNMC video game companies (See Table 4.1).

Alibaba, the Chinese e-commerce and internet company, owns minority shares in Lyft, TangoMe, and a $120 M investment in Canada's Kabam mobile games. In 2015, Alibaba invested $200 M in Snapchat, millions into Magic Leap, the overly hyped virtual-reality headset developer, and 6% in Groupon, which has since cratered. In 2018, Alibaba invested in Jeffery Katzenberg's NewTV making short videos for mobile phones.

2016 was the height of Chinese global media investments "in a barrage of eye-popping cash injections into Hollywood film slates and production outfits" (Brzeski, 2016). Chinese real estate and investment conglomerate Dalian Wanda bought Legendary Entertainment for $3.5 billion; Beijing-based Perfect World Pictures invested $250 million in a long-term joint venture with Universal; and Bona Film Group signed a $235 million co-production deal with 20th Century Fox, among others.

Consenting to Transnational Media Relations

There are few TNMC productions *from* China, most are TNMC joint ventures and co-productions made *for* Chinese audiences. With China Movie Channel, Panasonic Viacom co-produced *Transformers: Age of Extinction* (2014) which included heavy product placement, including China's Meters/bonwe t-shirts and milk brand Yili. *Mission Impossible: Rogue Nation* (2015) was a joint operation by Skydance, Bad Robot, and Alibaba Pictures. French TNMC Wild Bunch partnered to form the $322 million China Europe Film Fund. China's Oscar nominated best foreign language films in 2015 (The

Nightingale) and 2016 (Wolf Totem) were co-productions with French studios (Coonan, 2015). By 2016, 73 co-productions were exhibited in China. That same year Fundamental Films China purchased 28% stake in the French studio, EuropaCorp (now Mediawan), producer of the *Taken* series (2008, 2012, 2014) and a subsequent 2017 television program. Fundamental Films partnered with French filmmakers on *Valerian and the City of a Thousand Planets* (2017); *24 Hours to Live* (2017) an action film set in South Africa, *Replicas* (2018), and *Outlaws, Inc.* (2021). Tencent, iQIYI, and Youku, and theaters accounted for $10 million in sales of French co-productions in 2019.

China has many co-productions agreements with many countries, but not all have been as fruitful as the Sino-French agreement. Due to high costs of production in Britain, the *Special Couple* (2015), co-produced by UK Zephyr Films and the Shanghai Media Group, is one the very few joint ventures with British studios. The animated feature, *Kukai: Legend of the Demon Cat* (2017) was co-produced by Japan's Kadokawa Hong Kong's Emperor Motion Pictures, and Shengkai Film. India's Aeon and Moonstore (US) joined as distributors for the film which earned $100 million globally. *Ayka: My Little One*, was a Russian, Kazak, Chinese co-production entered at the Cannes Film Festival in 2018. A Kazak-Chinese co-production, *The Composer*, opened the Beijing Film Festival in 2019. Korea's active TNMC CJ Entertainment planned for several China co-productions with Wanda Film and others beginning in 2017, but then for several years, the political controversy over the deployment of a US missile system in Korea led to cancellation or postponement of Korean-Chinese joint projects. The 2021 release of the Chinese-Korean *Catman* may indicate a return to their TNMC ventures (Frater, 2021). Other joint ventures with New Zealand, India, and Japanese TNMCs are underway, including: a live action-CGI film *Shelved* with Southern Light Films (NZ); ErosSTX signed a two film deal with Huaxi Distribution; and Toei Japan is co-producing a new animated *The Monkey King* film with Bona.

Overall, "China's film industry is getting good at churning out hits with higher production values, better craftsmanship. and big-time support from the CCP, and that is squeezing out English-language blockbusters. In 2019, eight of the top 10 moneymakers in China were domestic productions" (Faughnder, 2021). It seems that Chinese filmmakers have learned from their joint ventures and partnerships with TNMCs. Many are following TNMC leadership in production practices, action content, film franchises (like *Detective Chinatown*), multicultural superstars, media product diversification, increased marketing, and more theater and streaming distribution to maximize audience size and profit (McCarthy, 2021). Chinese television has also invited corporate branding through product placement, brand sponsorships of series, the introduction of branded "mini-dramas" within the program, and cast member endorsement of brands between programs (Canaves, 2019). Cultural imperialism has been upstaged by transnational production, including its formula of film franchises with "mega-budgets, outstanding digital visual effects, and superstars [that] has been more or less adopted by Chinese film industry" (Song, 2018, p. 182).

Transnational relations are hegemonic—mutually beneficial to all participating media partners (Artz, 2015). Thus, routine TNMC productions with "Chinese characteristics" secure official approval and maximize shared box office revenues (Song, 2018, p. 181). Likewise, Chinese national media adopting transnational media practices and formats advance their own capitalist interests. The box office successes of *Wolf Warrior 2* (2017), *Operation Red Sea* (2019), and *Ne Zha* (2019) are prime examples of Chinese media emulating the transnational model, while multiple transnational partnerships continue with profits unabated as demonstrated with *Pacific Rim* (2018), *Godzilla* (2019), and *Monster Hunter* (2020). The pandemic stifled most Hollywood productions in 2020 and Chinese productions topped the domestic box office, including five action movies: *The Eight Hundred*, a war action film co-produced by Huayi Brothers, TenCent, Beijing Enlight Media, and Alibaba Pictures grossed $475 million; *Jiang Ziya* (The Legend of Deification), the follow-up to the animation fantasy *Ne Zha* brought in $250 million; the action sequel *Shock Wave 2* earned $226 million; and a war action film, *The Sacrifice,* that grossed $175 million.

Notably, while violence, nudity, and language do not dominate television or movie storylines, so-called Western values attached to advertising—privatization, individualism and consumerism—reign as elements of contemporary Chinese culture. For example, Hunan TV's *Super Girl*, a version of *American Idol* (following Germany's Fremantle show), launched its third incarnation in 2015. *Super Girl* invites contestants to audition and then perform, with audiences of 2.5 billion voting via paid text messages for their favorite singers. The show not only stresses celebrity and consumerism, it's produced by a regional government TV station embracing the capitalist free market. Chinese authorities, commercial media, and advertisers proclaimed that fan consumption and voting demonstrated citizen democratic choice. Similar messages are apparent in film. In *Kung Fu Panda 3* (2016), co-produced by India Reliance's DreamWorks and Oriental DreamWorks, a talented martial arts panda stars in his individual quest for happiness. In the last several years, Chinese audiences seemed to prefer similar dominant themes of self-interest and hierarchy in animation, action, fantasy, and historical narratives appearing in Chinese national and transnational film (Fu & Govindaraju, 2010)—echoing messages in leading transnational films, as will be discussed in the section below on dominant themes.

Even with government-run production studios and tight regulation, the commercial media industry is consolidating rapidly. Huayi Brothers, Englight Media, Huaxi Film, Bona Films, Alibaba Pictures, Tencent, and the Wanda Group acquired smaller studios and integrated many others into vertical and horizontal chains of consolidated and controlled production for commercial profit. These media giants also developed "thick tails" as they entered gaming, television, animation, toy, and internet streaming (Deloitte China, 2017, pp. 7, 10).

Meantime, the pull of transnational joint ventures and co-productions continued: Legendary Films and Guillermo Del Toro's Double Dare You Productions released *Pacific Rim: Uprising* with Universal in 2018, earning $300 million; in 2019 Legendary produced *Godzilla: King of the Monsters* with Warner Bros. and Japan's Toho making $400 million. Tencent Pictures joined with Hasbro and Paramount on *Bumblebee* (2019) reaching $468 million. The sci-fi action film *Monster Hunter* (2020), based on a Japanese video game, was a TNMC joint production by Constantin Films Germany and Canada's Impact Pictures, co-financed and distributed by Tencent Pictures, Sony, and Japan's Toho-Towa of Godzilla fame. Deloitte China (2017) noted that these export-oriented joint ventures will likely increase because "achieving success in the global market is the ultimate goal" for Chinese TNMC film co-productions (p. 4). As Zhao (2008) argues, the most significant change in the Chinese media system has been "its commercialization and its transformation into a platform for capital accumulation—regardless of the national origins of capital"—so concerns about the national identities of media producers are less important than the "patterns of integration of Chinese capital within and beyond Chinese borders" (p. 149).

Cultural Identity for Marketing

Transnational media relations clarify the capitalist class nature of globalization that has surpassed the vagaries of cultural imperialism: "there was never an essential 'Chinese culture' to begin with; foreign ideologies and communication technologies, from Buddhism to Marxism, have long shaped Chinese society" (Zhao, 2008, p. 149). Chinese culture has 56 distinct ethnic groups with multiple languages including Cantonese, Mandarin, Taiwanese/Minnan/Hokkien, and 100s of dialects that are "mutually incomprehensible," although media select certain languages because "the mixing of Chinese languages, along with English, Japanese, or any other language, may be just a vehicle for expanding the potential market" (Huat, 2012, pp. 40–41). Even the identification of Confucianism with China is a convenient social construction that has been rearticulated as the cultural substance of Korea, Japan, Taiwan, Singapore, Hong Kong, and their elusive diasporas, providing an "ideological gloss over political authoritarianism" (Huat, 2012, p. 33). In short, Chinese as a language, a culture, a tradition, is always a vague marker, an artifice needing political, historical, and social context to have meaning (Zhao, 2008). To many citizens in Hong Kong, Taiwan, and Singapore, Chinese culture means the loss of independence. We suddenly enter a theoretical morass of "cultural imperialisms"—US in China, China in Hong Kong, Hong Kong in Singapore, Singapore in Malaysia. For transnational media, however, there is no dilemma. Chinese culture is creatively articulated and presented as variations on past stereotypes of dress, demeanor, and behavior. In turn, Chinese TNMCs have revised and modernized national characteristics, but still downgrade the capabilities and integrity of average citizens. In both cases, standardized, updated cultural tropes provide codes and conventions for media content understandable to global audiences, especially in East Asia.

Transnationalism functions to lead national media systems toward other logics of accumulation: corporate takeovers of public media spaces; standardized genre and formats; promotion of spectacle over substance; doses of cultural diversity; and the use of precarious and contracted skilled labor. In the last decade, Chinese bureaucrats, private investors, and commercial media producers and exhibitors have internalized and followed transnational capitalist practices and market protocols—with and without direct US, Japanese, or EU capital and content. For example, contrary to concerns about US imposition of WTO standards, reports by Chinese government media "corresponded with the American media" coverage and promotion of transnational corporations (Hui, 2006, p. 102). In another instance, local political intrigue set the stage for broader "privatization of large sections of the railways, education, healthcare, communications, energy resources and so on" without any US, IMF, or WTO involvement (Hui, 2012). In 2019, before the pandemic, China's box office topped $9 billion. That year China produced 850 films, one-third were co-productions. In other words, the Chinese film industry is far from insular. Indeed, the Chinese film industry, private and government, has an ever-increasing transnational orientation with dozens of co-productions with South Korea, Japan, Hong Kong, France, the US, and other nations (Hoyler & Watson, 2019).

An Incomplete and Brief Overview of Chinese Media

Newspapers and Magazines

China has one of the largest newspaper markets in the world with almost 2000 papers. Although readership remains low at 300 million, 2019 advertising revenue was anticipated to top $20 billion. Most newspapers and magazines are government or party owned because state officials seek tight control over national and international news and information. One apparent exception is the Shangdong Dazhong Badao Media group of 86 companies, which publishes newspapers, a fashion magazine, and on-line, with a total readership of 5 million (Dun & Bradstreet, 2021). Commercial newspapers are published in Hong Kong, which is still nominally independent. Many

TABLE 4.2 Leading China newspapers by circulation

1. Xinhua News Agency's Reference News	3.25 million
2. People's Daily (Communist Party)	2.5 million
3. Guangzhou Daily (regional Communist)	1.85 million
4. Yangtse Evening (Xinhua affiliate)	1.75 million
5. Qili Evening (Dazhong News Group)	1.7 million

(*Statista, 2012*)

like the *South China Morning Post* hold a more critical view of the Chinese government and its media regulations. Table 4.2 lists top five newspapers in China by circulation.

In contrast to print news media, lifestyle and entertainment magazines are welcomed by government authorities as they encourage consumerism and market openness. Domestic Chinese partnerships with mass market magazines *Cosmopolitan, Esquire, Harper's Bazaar, Good Housekeeping, Elle,* and professional publications like the *Harvard Business Review* are not just sources of consumer information, they are "indispensable symbols of class distinction and identity formation"—such that the "Chinese consumer, lifestyle, and business magazine market is thus truly transnational and transcultural—transnational ideology embellished with national tastes" (Zhao, 2008, p. 156). In short, it's much more than just transnational partnerships between France's Lagardère, Hearst, Condé Nast, and Japan's Shogakukan with Chinese publishers like Shanghai Translation. After all, transnational media are not solely about product sales and profit, they also carry persuasive ideological messages of the social and cultural advantages of the market economy for the new professional middle classes in China, India, Brazil, and elsewhere.

Meanwhile, the crisis of overproduction haunts Chinese media, especially in print. Several international magazines have closed shop, while others have withdrawn from China due to competition and oversaturation of the lifestyle market. Even the successful *Vogue China*, with a circulation of 1.5 million and 370 million internet views, has surpassed the needs of the middle-class consumer market, so it has launched other income sources such as its phone app Vogue Mini, its own credit card, and partnerships with luxury brands, film producers, celebrities, and social media platforms. The interests of transnational capital and its media are clear: 900 million rural and urban workers are underserved by media, almost irrelevant to its restructuring of production and consumption. Prospering magazine joint ventures serve the millions of young, urban professionals attracted to the latest trends and consumer goods. Moreover, "a highly commercialized domestic communication system that is already skewed toward the affluent social strata in the coastal regions is facing further upmarket pressures...the pressures of global competition have forced [the Chinese government's CCTV] to prioritize services to high-end domestic audiences" (Zhao, 2008, p. 160).

Yet because capitalism "no longer seeks to incorporate all within it, but proceeds rather by marginalizing the great majority" (Dirlik, 2005, p. 311), serious social conflict will erupt. To forestall mass resistance, nation-state and corporate leaders will need to implement more than neoliberal reforms to placate millions—or resort to systematic coercion. Either way, they will need to expand their media news and entertainment enterprises to justify the marginalization of disenfranchised social groups.

Television

More than 3000 channels broadcast digitally in China, with China Central Television TV (CCTV) the largest nationwide television station. Five other government-run stations broadcast nationwide: Hunan, Zhejiang, Jiangsu, Beijing, and Shanghai Media's Dragon Television. Billions of viewers tune in to weekly dramas, variety shows, and competitive performance programs; billions also use video websites iQIYI, Youku, Tencent, and Le Vision. Television dramas and reality television are increasingly transnational regional productions to meet audience demand and compete with non-Asian TNMCs.

Most Chinese provinces and cities have their own television stations. Some stations broadcast in regional languages like Tibetan, Uighur, and Mongolian, as well as Mandarin. In 2018, television and radio revenues reached $100 billion (Thomala, 2021). Government-run CCTV has 50 channels reaching 1 billion viewers and broadcasts in six languages. CCTV has a heavy news and documentary focus. CCTV has multiple agreements with TNMCs for distribution, including with Germany's RTL Freemantle for the comedy series *Thank God You're Here* and the talent competition show *Don't Stop Me Now*.

The second most watched station is Hunan TV, owned by the provincial government. Hunan broadcasts across China and the East Asian region, including Taiwan, South Korea, Japan, and Australia. Hunan airs mostly entertainment, dramas, and talent contests like *Super Girl*, and variety shows including several based on Korean and Hong Kong formats, as well as a local adaptation of Freemantle's *World's Got Talent*. Hunan TV claims 730 million access its internet broadcast daily. Zhejiang TV (ZTV), is owned by another provincial government with a national reach and a satellite signal covering 40 countries. ZTV is an entertainment and consumerist powerhouse. Talent, reality, game shows, modeling and dating programs emphasize wealth and self-interest—selling large youth audiences to national and global advertisers. Other provincial governments have their own television stations and satellites for entertainment and profits. Hundreds of shows are released yearly and billions of viewers tune in.

For the last several years, China television studios have embarked on an assertive appeal to TNMC television producers (Roxborough, 2018). Hunan TV agreed to a major deal in 2018 to co-create new formats with Dutch/French

Banijay's Endemol Shine, the TNMC behind *Big Brother* and *MasterChef*, among other global TV hits. Endemol Shine also agreed to co-produce the UK crime drama *Broadchurch* with Chinese partners Cloudwood and Blue&White&Red Pictures, and a new docutainment series, *The Nation's Greatest Treasures* with CCTV. TNMC Viacom's Nickelodeon has a five-year deal with China's state broadcasting authority to make animation for television. Viacom's MTV operates several satellite music channels—MTV China, MTV Mandarin, MTV Taiwan, and MTV India—that also air reality shows, entertainment news, and animated TV programs. MTV Asia co-produces youth mini-programming with China's WebTVAsia. Meanwhile, Fox Networks, now part of Disney, partnered on a reality sports competition show, *The Dunk of China*, featuring NBA star Jeremy Lin as a judge. These and more ventures arose during the chill over US missile installations in South Korea that temporarily curtailed joint Chinese-Korean television productions.

TNMC Phoenix TV was originally a 1996 joint venture of 20th Century Fox and CCTV that formed a partnership with BBC for television programs and the Canada Film Board to air animation and documentaries. In 2013, Fox shares were purchased by TPG, a US-based transnational private equity firm. TPG now owns 12%, China Mobile 20%, China's s sovereign wealth fund 8%, and Today's Asia, a private Chinese company, owns 37%. As a thriving TNMC, Phoenix has satellite channels broadcasting to North America, Europe, and Southeast Asia, as well as a global pay-TV service.

To find more outlets for their dramas, ten Chinese television studios formed a distribution alliance in 2017 to increase their Asian distribution deals and deliver new shows to Europe, Africa, and the US, including new ventures with Netflix (Xinhua, 2017). Baidu/iQiyi (421 million subscribers), Alibaba/Youku (500 million subscribers) and Tencent Video (137 million subscribers) have emerged as dominant in original content production, given the tremendous increase in mobile devices and digital streaming and their global distribution partnerships with Netflix (Harson, 2018). Consequently, more TNMC digital deals developed. For example, Ireland's QYOU has a distribution agreement with China Entertainment Group for streaming on Weibo, Youku, and Tencent. Germany's TNMC Bertlesmann has investments in more than 60 Chinese digital companies and has not been charged with German cultural imperialism.

Digitally-based transnational media deals in the region are not exclusive to China: Indonesia's Go-Play teamed with US Vice Media to create content for its streaming app; Japan's LINE TV in Thailand has established partnerships with local television studios for mobile content; the $680 million streaming market in Korea is dominated by TNMC Netflix and Wavve, a joint venture of television networks KBS, SBS, and MBC. Korean television studios also have other streaming TNMC deals with France's Vivendi Dailymotion; iWonder in the Middle East and North Africa; a co-production deal with NBC Universal; and dozens of other broadcast partners and affiliates in Europe, Asia, and the Americas.

Most Chinese television networks and channel ownership are government run. Yet despite the aura of censorship, government media restructuring permits almost unlimited transnational partnerships in advertising which delivers large revenue and promotes consumer and market values. More than 125,000 ad agencies thrive in China because print and broadcasting are highly dependent on advertising (Zhao, 2008, pp. 83–84). Thus, driven by competition for advertising revenues, most provincial television broadcasters mimic successful commercial television programs with reality format shows such as *Super Girl*, *Super Boy*, and *Where Are We Going, Dad?* from Korean programs; *Who's Still Standing* based on an Israeli game show; *You Are the One* from an Australian dating game; and others. Advertisers may not determine content, but provincial television programmers have learned that apolitical commercial entertainment brings consuming audiences that can profitably be sold to advertisers. Leading advertisers in 2018 included: Guangzhou Pharmacy (a 50:50 joint venture with Walgreens); Estee Lauder; L'Oreal; GlaxoSmithKline (which has joint ventures with Jiangsu Biotech, Alibaba, and China retailer JD.com); Yum China (a transnational corporation with 7600 restaurants and revenue of $6.8 billion in 2016); and other national and transnational corporations (Thomala, 2020).

Bilibili, a leading streaming platform in China, has signed several transnational production agreements, including a documentary underwater film series with France's Arte and LGB. Bilibili attracted big investors, including Alibaba and Sony both of which contributed more than $400 million for minority stakes. Tencent paid $30 million for a 15% share in 2015. Bilibil signed a co-production agreement with Discovery Channel and a distribution partnership with National Geographic for nature documentaries (Frater, 2020a).

Other genre are more popular among youth: anime is a $21 billion business in China. Nickelodeon and Disney have already partnered with Peach Blossom Media in Singapore to make hybrid animations like "Tomato Twins" for the region. Because Japan anime producers have regularly outsourced production to Korea and Philippine media, deals with China come easily. So, Bilibili, Alibaba, and Tencent have now partnered with Japanese producers as they try to create Chinese anime or co-productions that might lure Chinese youth away from their Japan anime fan communities. In other words, TNMCs make repeated pivots in their quest for large audiences.

Film

Television and print media provide ample opportunities for advertising sales, but movie production and distribution are the most active areas for Chinese media transnational expansion and collaboration. Print and television have substantial government oversight and regulation because they are closely connected to domestic politics, whereas film entertainment provides a ready source of foreign participation as well as the potential for transnational investment and product distribution to untapped audience markets. China has more than 77,000 screens with more under construction; the US has 40,000, with many closing (Davis, 2021). The three largest cinema chains in China are Wanda Cinemas, China Film Stellar, and Dadi Theater, while Britain's TNMC Cinemark and CJ CGV, Korea's largest theater chain, each own several thousand. And mass audiences easily fill up those thousands of cinemas. During the global pandemic, China was the largest film market with $3.12 billion box office in 2020 (China Daily, 2021). In 2019, ticket revenue in China totaled $9.8 billion, while the US/Canada market was worth $11.32 billion.

The Chinese government both regulates and facilitates transnational developments in film and internet. At home, domestic filmmakers seek non-Chinese partners to access resources, expertise, and investment. Abroad, larger commercial media from China have invested and partnered with producers and distributors with expectations of increased revenue. The Chinese government attempts to guide the journey of both transnational impulses. In 2014, Chinese state and private media met with European film studios to organize an informal trade organization called "Bridging the Dragon" that meets annually to discuss current regulations, explore projects, and network transnational deals. The 2020 virtual gathering identified 15 film projects for Sino-European collaboration (Frater, 2020b).

Regulations filter when, how, and who can access the largest film audiences in the world. Yet, major movie studios have adapted in their quest for Chinese riches, and their fawning interest has been tapped by both government-run film studios and private commercial media. These interests have converged in movie production and distribution. China has signed film co-production agreements with 22 countries, including the United States, France, Russia, New Zealand, Japan, and India. Nearly 250 co-productions were made between 2000 and 2019, 49 of which surpassed the 100 million box-office mark, according to China Film Co-Production Corporation (Fan, 2020).

Even within the limits on exhibition in China, foreign films were still earning 28% of the domestic box office in 2019 when movies grossed a record $9.8 billion (Brzeski, 2020). Meanwhile, Chinese filmmakers have slowly adopted TNMC models: individual narratives, franchise-friendly formulas, and executive-dominant production norms, while also eyeing the global market—eventually securing transnational distributors, partners, and investors. Chinese film producers have channeled the ideological and structural essence of transnational media. For example, very early on in transnational media restructuring, Disney, Beijing New Pictures, and lucrative product placements released the action film *Hero* (2002). *Hero* exhibits all of the action adventure tropes reigning in TNMC and Chinese box office successes today: a public threatened, saved by a hero using violence, with hierarchy reestablished. The film portended the commercial and ideological triumph of transnational media through alliance with nation-based partners. Transnational capital clearly indicated its intent to replace cultural imperialism with class collaboration across borders. Benefits accrued to national media and national capital which profited from FDI, industry expertise, access to resources and new markets (Artz, 2015). The integration of China into transnational production and distribution flows paralleled the construction of social class hierarchies within China: the most important divisions were "not those of East or West, or Chinese and foreign, but new divisions along the lines of generation, class and region, with different access to power, wealth and knowledge, and different relationships to the forces of globalization" (Dirlik, 2005, p. 302). Thus, transnational media in China is a social class phenomenon, not an illustration of cultural imperialism or global hybridity absent class power. Yuezhi Zhao (2008) perceived a new hegemonic bloc of political and cultural consent consisting of "transnational capitalists, foreign state managers and policy makers, globalizing Chinese political, economic, and cultural elites, and the urban-based 'middle class' whose members are the preferred customers of both domestic and transnational capital" (pp. 167–168). She concluded that the Chinese communication industry partnerships with TNMCs "accelerated the expansion of transnational capitalism and facilitated potential transnational class formation" even as the neoliberal project stirred domestic opposition (p. 179).

Film Studios

Discussions of media in China usually include commentary on US media blockbuster imports, the government's stringent regulations and media ownership, Alibaba and Tencent's digital dominance, and the Wanda Group's transnational media investments and activities. A survey of film in China necessarily tackles each of these concerns. Leaving aside direct observations about US imports, this section identifies the leading government and commercial filmmakers, especially those with transnational media connections—which of course includes Alibaba, Wanda, Tencent, and importantly, the China Film Group.

China Film Group Corporation

The China Film Group Corporation (CFGC) is the largest and most influential government-owned media group in China. CFGC finances films, produces about 30 films each year, and distributes about one-third of all films released, many exhibited in its own cinema chain (Olsson, n.d.). All imported movies need approval from a China Film Group's Co-Production Corporation division. Media companies must partner with CFGC, a private studio with a co-production license, or have a China distributor like semi-private Huaxia Film Distribution. CFGC also produces television programs, animation features, film equipment, advertising, and developed DMAX, China's version of IMAX big screen projection.

In 2015, China Film formed a joint venture, Flagship Entertainment, with WarnerMedia and a Chinese private equity form to make at least 12 films. Flagship has released three action movies: *The Adventurers* (2017), *Paradox* (2017), and *The Meg* (2018). Flagship co-produced the animated *Wish Dragon* (2021) with Sony's Columbia Pictures. CFGC entered a joint venture with New Zealand and Canadian animators to co-produce 17 live action and animated features over eight years (Block, 2015). The first feature *Beasts of Burden* by China Film Group and New Zealand's Huhu Animation moved to post-production in 2018 (Arjit, 2017). In 2019, China Film backed *Skyfire*, a disaster action movie, with British director Simon West and starring Taiwanese-Australian, Chinese, and British actors (Fan, 2020). China Film is the prime entry point for transnational movie production. China Film Group also develops television programs. CFGC joined with Tencent Penguin Pictures in a 2020 co-production television series for CCTV with BBC, Germany's ZDF, and France Télévisions (Davis, 2019). Over the last two decades, several hundred film and television co-productions by French, Australian, Korean, German, American, Japanese and other TNMC studios have been made in partnership with China Film, not all have been box office successes (See Table 4.3).

Alibaba

Alibaba Pictures is one of the largest commercial film producers in China. The studio is part of Jack Ma's e-commerce Alibaba Group which had 2020 income of $28 billion from on-line shopping, movie ticket sales, internet, video streaming, and digital and print news outlets. Alibaba owns

TABLE 4.3 CFGC co-produced or co-financed transnational films 2016-2020 (partial list)

Film	Genre	Partners
Xuanzang (2016)	Historical action	Eros International (India)
The Great Wall (2017)	Sci-fi action	Atlas, Legendary/Wanda, Universal
Fate of the Furious (2017)	Action	One Race Films, Universal
Mission Impossible (2018)	Action	Tom Cruise, Paramount, Alibaba
The Meg (2018)	Action	Flagship, di Bonaventure, Warner
Detective Pikachu (2019)	Action	Legendary/Wanda, Toho, Pokemon
Wandering Earth (2019)	Sci-fi action	Alibaba, Netflix
Mosely (2019)	CGI sci-fi action	Huhu Studios (New Zealand)
Airstrike (2020)	War Action	Blue Box International (US)
Wish Dragon (2021)	Animation	Sony, Columbia, Tencent, Netflix

Hong Kong's *South China Morning Post* and has partnerships with the government's Xinhua news agencies and provincial broadcasters like Zheziang TV. The Group's Tao Piaopiao is the leading film distributor—22 films in 2018, including 8 of the top 10 (China Film Insider, 2018).

Alibaba has minority ownership in Enlight Pictures a leading commercial filmmaker. As minority partner with Huayi Brothers film studio, Alibaba financed a 10-film partnership through 2024. Huayi (with Alibaba and Tencent) also has a long-term deal with American-Indian transnational ErosSTX for "12 blockbusters, 12 big-budget films and seven medium- and small-budget films, plus 400 episodes of TV dramas" (Brzeski, 2017). In 2016, when the Bona Film Group moved from a publicly traded company to private investors, Alibaba took a minority stake. That same year Alibaba joined Amblin Pictures as a minority partner co-financing Amblin and DreamWorks films. Alibaba films partnered with India's Reliance Entertainment/DreamWorks, and Participant Media on the 2018 Oscar winning film *Green Book*, which grossed $330 million (See Table 4.4).

Although the Chinese government has facilitated privatization and consolidation in media entertainment and digital technology, it has become increasingly nervous about the economic and political influence that Alibaba might gain with its continued media expansion (Yang, 2021). In spring 2021, Alibaba was fined $2.8 million for exclusionary practices that restricted competition. The US press framed the action as Chinese attacks on democracy, but at the

TABLE 4.4 Alibaba Pictures Film Partnerships since 2017 (partial list)

Title (Year)	Genre	Partners
Real (2017) i,d	Korean action fantasy	CJ Entertainment, TMS Comics
Journey to the West (2017) p	Chinese action fantasy	Wanda Media, Chjna Film Group
Paradox (2017) p	Action	Bona Group, Warner Bros. Flagship
Mission Impossible (2018) p	Action	Tom Cruise, Paramount
Next Gen (2018) d	CGI Sci-fi action	Wanda Media, Netflix
Greenbook (2018) i, p	Buddy action	Reliance, Participant, DreamWorks
Wandering Earth (2019) p	Sci-fi action	China Film Group, Netflix
Ugly Dolls (2019) p	Animated comedy action	STX, Huaxia
A Dog's Purpose (2019) i,p	Family comedy	Amblin, Reliance, Universal, e-One
Gemini Man (2019) i,p	Action	Fosun, Skydance, Paramount
BIOS (2021) i,p	Sci-fi action	Amblin, Universal, Dutch Angle
Night at the Museum (2021) i	Action	TSG, Disney-21st Century Fox
Warriors (TBA) i, p	Animal action	STX/Eros

(i = investor, p = producer, d = distributor)

same time European and Australian regulators fined Google and Facebook for anti-trust violations and the US press raised no alarms about democracy under attack. Most importantly, anti-trust regulations do not indicate that Chinese officials veered from transnational capitalism. In fact, the *People's Daily* commented that the regulation was "a kind of love and care" to protect free market norms: "Monopoly is the great enemy of the market economy. There is no contradiction between regulating under the law and supporting development" (Zhong, 2021). The fine is less than 4% of Alibaba revenues for one year, just enough to make it more cautious about "anticompetitive" behavior but not restricting growth or dominance. As Chinese market regulator LI Qing said, we "encourage enterprises to keep innovating and to become big and strong" (Zhong, 2021). The ongoing support for the WTO, private media, and TNMC partnerships confirms China's willing participation in transnational relations.

Wanda Group

The privately-owned multinational property developer Dalian Wanda Group charged into entertainment and cultural production ten years ago with its purchase of AMC Theaters in the US for $2.6 billion. Wanda's holdings now include Open Road Films, Fathom Events, Legendary Pictures, Wanda Films, AMC/Carmike cinemas, Nordic Cinema, e-commerce partnerships with Chinese Internet platforms, Tencent and Baidu, and Infront Sports Media Switzerland which has broadcast rights for FIFA (the global football association), badminton, and cycling events. Wanda Cinema has over 2000 screens, including multiplexes, in 100 Chinese cities and frequently draws the largest box office revenues capturing 15% or more of the market. Wanda has built more than 100 IMAX theaters in the last four years. Alibaba and Cultural Investment Holdings are minority partners in Wanda Cinemas, along with transnational investors Swiss UBS AG and Hong Kong's Citic finance group. Wanda also owns Hoyt's, the second largest theater chain in Australia/New Zealand; Odeon-UCI, the largest cinema chain in Western Europe; Nordic Cinema serving seven countries in the Baltic region; and still owns a minority stake in AMC/Carmike, the largest theater chain in the US—the huge decline in attendance during the US pandemic forced Wanda to sell a large portion of its AMC stake in 2020 (Rubin, 2021). Wanda opened its 1000-acre Oriental Movie Metropolis movie studio facility in eastern China in 2018, claimed to be the largest movie production complex in the world with state-of-the-art technology and facilities. After selling its operating shares in 13 Chinese theme parks in 2017, Wanda returned to theme park developments in 2019, with plans for a "Red Tourism" park in Yan'an, the birthplace of the CCP and $20 billion more for theme parks in Gansu and Lanzhou, even as transnationals Comcast-Universal (with Beijing Tourism and YumChina) and Danish-US Legoland (with Global Zhongjun) plan theme parks by 2021 (Watanabe, 2019; Wharfe, 2020).

Wanda Pictures

Wanda Pictures is one of the largest private studios in China. Its three *Detective Chinatown* comedy action films have grossed almost $1.5 billion. Celebrity star Andy Lau is expected to lead the fourth Detective installment, projected to film in London. Fox's Tubi streaming platform partnered with Wanda in 2020 to air *Detective Chinatown 2* and *The King's Avatar: For the Glory* in US, Canada, and Mexico. The Detective franchise also launched a web series spinoff in 2020.

Wanda's co-production and investments are national and transnational, as the studio leads the way for private Chinese studios turning to TNMCs. In 2017, Tencent formed a film, television, video game, and IP partnership with Wanda. Wanda invested in the 2016 Oscar-nominated Australian-British-US film *Lion*; co-produced *The Smurfs: The Lost Village* (2017) with Sony; and coproduced two Octonaut films with Sony's UK animation studio Silvergate Media for CCTV and Netflix in 2020 (Clarke, 2018).

Legendary Pictures

As part of its diversification and transnational turn, in 2016 Dalian Wanda purchased the US-based Legendary Pictures for $3.5 billion, which included its Legendary East division that regularly co-produces films with China Film Group. Legendary Pictures has released 21 films since 2016, almost exclusively TNMC co-production or distribution deals. While Wanda Pictures continues to find willing TNMC partners, Legendary's reputation and past connections with US, Canadian, Japanese, and other transnationals positioned it to more easily form big screen production partnerships, as evident in its recent films (See Table 4.5).

TABLE 4.5 Legendary Pictures films since 2017 (partial list)

Title (Year)	Genre	TNMC Partners
Kong: Skull Island (2017)	Action	Tencent, Warner Bros.
Pacific Rim: Uprising	Sci-fi action	Double Dare You, Universal
Jurassic World (2018)	Sci-fi action	Amblin, Perfect World Pictures
Skyscraper (2018)	Action	Flynn Pictures, Universal
Mama Mia (2018)	Romantic comedy	Playtone, Perfect World, Universal
The Thinning (2018)	Sci fi action	eOne, YouTube
BlacKkKlansman (2018)	Comedy action	Blumhouse, Perfect World, Focus
Little (2019)	Fantasy	Will Packer, Perfect World, Universal
Detective Pikachu (2019)	Fantasy action	Pokemon, Warner, Toho
Godzilla (2019)	Sci-fi action	Warner, Toho
Enola Holmes (2020)	Action	Netflix
Godzilla v. Kong (2021)	Sci-fi action	Warner, Toho
Dune (2021)	Sci-fi action	Warner

Tencent and Tencent Penguin Pictures

Tencent Pictures and Tencent Penguin Pictures are subsidiaries of the Chinese internet giant Tencent, which is owned by Chinese billionaire Ma Huateng (Pony Ma). Tencent makes and markets video and mobile games, artificial intelligence, e-commerce, and owns WeChat. Tencent has holdings in more than 600 companies, including Epic Games, Activision-Blizzard, Ubisoft, Voodoo, Platinum Games, and Korea's Netmarble. Tencent has exclusive Chinese distribution rights with Sony, Universal, and Warner music companies as well as Korea's YG Entertainment. Tencent has many investors, including Huayi Brothers Media, China's largest private film producer, which is owned by Korea's Nintendo CultureWorks Media. At the same time, Tencent is a primary investor in Huayi Brothers along with Alibaba. Tencent also owns 10% of the electric car manufacturer Nio. Tencent Pictures rapidly and forcefully entered the TNMC flow as its productions since 2017 indicate (See Table 4.6).

Bona/PolyBona

PolyBona was the first private commercial studio to be licensed by China's National Radio and Television Administration in 1999, as the government just began its turn to neoliberal privatization. PolyBona Films was formed by a merger with Poly Group owned by the Chinese army. By 2015, PolyBona was a major film producer and distributor, worth over $500 million. That year Bona invested $235 million in TSG Entertainment, which finances films and has partnered with 20th Century Fox and Disney, giving Bona a permanent TNMC relationship with large US moviemakers. By 2016, when Bona went private, it was

TABLE 4.6 Tencent Pictures since 2017 (Partial list)

Title	Genre	Partners
Kong Skull Island (2017)	Sci-fi action	Legendary, Warner
Wonder Woman (2017)	Sci-fi action	Atlas, Wanda, Warner
Venom (2018)	Sci-fi action	Sony, Columbia, Marvel
Bumblebee (2018)	Sci-fi action	Hasbro, Viacom Paramount
Men in Black (2019)	Sci-fi action	Amblin, Columbia, Image Nation (Dubai)
Terminator: Dark Fate (2019)	Sci-fi action	TSG, Fox, Viacom Paramount, Skydance
Beautiful Day Nbhood (2019)	Bio drama	Sony TriStar
Monster Hunter (2020)	Sci-fi action	Constantin (Germany), Impact (Canada)
Wish Dragon (2021)	Animation	Columbia-Sony, Netflix, Base FX Malaysia
Top Gun: Maverick (2021)	Action	Skydance, Tom Cruise, Viacom Paramount

TABLE 4.7 Bona Films since 2017 (Partial list)

Title	Genre	Partners
Paradox Bangkok (2017)	Action	Alibaba (starring Thai actor Tony Jaa)
War for Planet Apes (2017)	Sci-fi action	TSG, 20th Century Fox
A Dog's Way Home (2019)	Family action	Columbia, Sony
Once Upon Time Hollywood	Action	Columbia, Sony
Ad Astra (2019)	Sci-fi action	Regency, 20th Century Fox
Midway (2019)	War action	Summit, Lionsgate, eOne
Bloodshot (2020)	Action	Columbia, Valiant Comics, Cross Creek
Enter the Fat Dragon (2020)	Comedy action	Mega Vision Pictures (Bahamas)

valued at $640 million with Fosun—a leading Chinese private finance company with over $100 billion in assets—taking 21% of the company. Fosun is a major shareholder in the Canadian Cirque de Soleil performance group and also has a stake in Studio 8—which led to Bona's investment in Sony TriStar's disappointing *Billy Lynn's Long Halftime Walk* (2016). Bona maintains its long partnership with the China Film Group, including on *Wolf Warrior 2* (2017), the block buster war action film. Since going private in 2016, Bona has made dozens of films, mostly TNMC co-productions and distributions. In keeping with the success of other TNMC movies, Bona makes mostly action movies (See Table 4.7).

Huayi Brothers

In 2009, Huayi was hailed as the largest private sector entertainment company in China. Huayi owns a film and television studio, a recording label, and a theater chain, as well as a TV studio and talent agency in Korea. Since 2016, Huayi has been owned by the Korean TNMC Nintendo CultureWorks Media. Huayi has a long-term co-production deal with ErosSTX, making mostly action movies. In 2020, Huayi partnered with the German Centropolis Entertainment to make *Moonfall* starring Halle Berry. Huayi has consistently released box offices successes in China and internationally (See Table 4.8),

TABLE 4.8 Huayi Brothers films since 2017 (partial list)

Title (Year)	Genre	Partners
Space Between Us (2017)	Sci-fi	STX, Virgin Produced (UK)
The Foreigner (2017)	Action	STX, Wanda, Global Road
Bad Mom's Christmas (2017)	Comedy	STX, Tang Media
Molly's Game (2017)	Crime action	STX, Mark Gordon
Peppermint (2018)	Action	STX, Tang Media
Mile 22 (2018)	Action	STX
Happytime Murders (2018)	Crime action	STX, Blackbear, Henson Alternative
The Eight Hundred (2020)	War action	Alibaba, Tencent, Beijing Enlight
Blazing Samurai (2021)	Comic Action	STX, Brooksfilms, Aniventure (UK)
Moonfall (2021)	Sci-fi action	Lionsgate, Centropolis (Germany)

but in 2018 its star actress Fan Bing Bing was mired in a tax evasion scandal, which forced the shelving of the highly anticipated *Cell Phone 2* (2019) while *The Eight Hundred* required multiple recuts to please China's authorities but still made almost $500 million in 2020.

There are many, many other film studios, both government and commercial, producing films in China. As they succeed, they soon look for TNMC hook-ups to continue their commercial growth inside and beyond China. There are many examples. Hunan has a joint venture with Lionsgate; Bona has selectively reached deals with Regency, Sony, and AGC Studios. LeVision Pictures, one of the larger private studios, has co-produced several TNMC hits, including *The Expendables* (2012, 2014) with Lionsgate; *The Great Wall* (2016) with Wanda's Legendary, the China Film Group, and Universal; and a dozen more co-productions. Huahua Media and Shanghai Film Group co-produced *Jack Reacher: Never Go Back* (2016) with Skydance, Tom Cruise, and Viacom Paramount. HuaHua also partnered with Paramount on the World War II action film *Allied* (2016). *Mosley* (2019) was a co-production by New Zealand's Huhu Studios and China Film Animation that won the Best Animation at the 12th Asian Pacific Screen Awards. Fosun International, one of the largest multinational companies in China, owns 60% of Studio 8, which has Sony investments (Frater, 2017). In 2018, Sony and Studio 8 released *White Boy Rick and Alpha* with modest success. Film Carnival invested $500 M in former Disney executive's Dick Cook Studios in 2016, although four years later production still had not begun on *The Ranger's Apprentice* or the *Alchemyst* (Bulbeck, 2019) One of the more active TNMCs is Perfect World which co-produced dozens of movies under its $500 million deal in 2016 with Comcast Universal—the first direct investment multi-year partnership by a Chinese company. In 2017, Perfect World co-produced *The Mummy, Pitch Perfect 3*; in 2018, *Jurassic World, Mary Queen of Scots*; *Downton Abbey* in 2019; and in 2020 *Dolittle* and *News of the World,* and more than 40 other films with multiple TNMC joint ventures in the last five years. A major Chinese private film distributor, JL Vision, has had numerous partnerships in recent years, mostly action movies, including: *Creed II* (2018) with MGM; *Knives Out* (2019) with Lionsgate and T-Street; sci-fi action film *2067* (2020) with Australia's KOJO Entertainment; and the Belarus film *Crystal Swan* (2020). Large and small, government and private, Chinese film studios have joined the TNMC movement with great enthusiasm and huge investments.

The unfolding processes of transnational reorganization of capitalism continues to be contradictory and uneven, disrupted by resistive national populations and unanticipated market contradictions, including overproduction, failed partnerships, and poorly conceived products or marketing. In this mix, each national capitalist class, and its nation-state government, aims to enlarge its own share of the wealth produced transnationally. In China's case, given its recent experience with a deformed socialism, the introduction of capitalism has been defined by contradiction and contention, rather than consensus, among its ruling elite (Zhao, 2008). Those conflicts have caused many hiccups for China media and its overtures to join TNMCs.

For several decades, the Chinese culture industry has promoted nationalism in combination with strategic alliances in international affairs while singing of a hybrid socialism that harmonized with commercial development. The rhetorical adjustment timeline is similar to India's. In fact, the trajectory echoes India's move from state planning to neoliberal privatization—albeit with Chinese characteristics. The consequences of transnational capital for the Chinese people are also the same as elsewhere: 2019 Gross Domestic Product $14 trillion; 400 billionaires; 200 million in poverty; 82 million earning less than $600 a year; 70 million earning less than $400 a year (National Public Radio, 2021). During the pandemic, China's richest increased their wealth by 62%. Jack Ma's Alibaba fortune reaching $65 billion and Tencent CEO Pony Ma made $55 billon, while e-commerce owners Colin Huang of Pinduoduo was estimated at $30 billion and Richard Liu of JD.com ranked at $20 billion (Flannery, Chen, & Mao, 2020). Of course, as social inequality worsened and the economy slowed due to overproduction, workers resisted. There were more than 1700 reported labor disputes in 2018 (Hernández, 2019).

Action to the rescue? Chinese media offered spectacular distractions to the social and political conditions of daily life. By 2017, five of top 10 movie releases in China were TNMC productions. Action also became the highest grossing movie genre with seven of the top movies (Liu & Du, 2018) (See Table 4.9). Additional action movies and co-productions also drew crowds: Paramount's *xXx: Return of Xander Cage* and Sony's German, Canadian, US co-production *Resident Evil*, both earned over $150 M gross. Even smaller imports like the Thai movie *Bad Genius* $38 M and *Contratiempo* from Spain

TABLE 4.9 Top Ten Box Office China 2017 (Liu & Du, 2018)

Title	Revenue	Production Studio
Wolf Warrior 2 a	$1 B	Beijing Culture Group
Fate of Furious* a	$408 M	China Film Group, One Race Films, Universal (dist)
Never Say Die	$334 M	Sihai, Huaxia
Kung Fu Yoga a	$250 M	Taihe, Shinework
Journey to West* a	$230 M	Wanda, Alibaba, China Film, Village Road Show (Aus)
Transformers* a	$218 M	HuaHua Media, H Collective, Hasbro, Galaxy Weying
Dangal*	$190 M	Aamir Khan, Disney Star India
Youth	$185 M	Huayi Bros
Pirates of Caribbean a	$180 M	Disney
Kong Skull Island*a	$177 M	Wanda, Legendary, Ten Cent Pictures

*Transnational film partnership

a Action Movie

$28 M were also action movies. In all, two-thirds of the movies earning more than $15 M were action (See Table 4.9).

The huge success of *Wolf Warriors 2* demonstrated that government-approved action movies would draw huge crowds, even with highly pronounced nationalist ideology. *Sky Hunter* (2017), *Operation Red Sea* (2018), and the 2020 $475 million hit *The Eight Hundred* (2020) reflected Chinese audiences continued attraction to war thrillers (Jackson, 2020). Meanwhile, although US movies remain the leading Chinese imports, heavily marketed Hollywood superhero movies like *Spiderman, Wonder Woman, Thor,* and *Guardians of the Galaxy* underperformed expectations—all below $100 M box office. Disney's big publicity push for *Mulan* (2020) only gained $36 M in China, as audiences deemed the movie patronizing (Davis, 2020) Other US movies without brand backing (like *Blade Runner, Lego Batman,* and *King Arthur*) were even less successful.

China's large movie market does not mean a profitable movie market: more movies lose money than make money. The economic risks in movie production, as well as its potential for profit and cultural influence, led the Chinese government to negotiate co-productions with 20 countries, including South Korea, India, Singapore, Belgium, France, Italy, United Kingdom, Netherlands, Australia, New Zealand, Canada, Brazil, Russia, and Greece. The government-run China Film Group had 60 co-productions in 2017 alone (Liu & Du, 2018). TNMCs large and small have found willing Chinese partners, including for big-budget films like DreamWorks/Pearl Studio's *Kung Fu Panda 3* (2016), *The Great Wall* (2016) by Legendary/China Film Group, *The Foreigner* (2017), a co-production of Wanda Pictures, ErosSTX, and Huayi Bros, and the DreamWorks/Pearl Studio animation feature, *Abominable* (2019), among others. In 2017, China also became the largest export market for European films, with 68 million moviegoers spending $36 M on EU movies (Blázques et al, 2019).

In coming years, Chinese audiences are likely to see more franchises emulating Fast and Furious and Marvel popularity. *Detective Chinatown* has already been commercially successful with a spin-off web series and new characters ready to join the stories. Producers are looking for media partners in Europe to reach additional audiences.

China's transnational media needs are different than smaller countries with limited markets that have difficulty in scaling up production. China needs the marketing and distribution infrastructure from the US and Europe (Amidi, 2015) which are on offer because film and television partnerships are not likely to be curtailed by trade conflicts. As Yue Xiang, a director of the hugely successful *Detective Chinatown* film franchise, said, "Even at the peak of the trade war, they didn't stop auto parts from flowing," Chinese media collaboration will include hiring Hollywood talent and outsourcing production to the US (Davis, 2021b). The political economy—ownership of production spaces and sets, equipment, and actors, along with skilled sound, visual, and post-pro-duction technicians—shapes the dynamics of transnational collaboration. US television and film studios want Chinese audiences; Chinese producers need Hollywood's technology and promotional infrastructure.

Dominant Themes in Chinese Cinema

For this analysis, the films that attracted the largest audiences were selected. Hundreds of millions of Chinese citizens were attracted to these movies, sug-gesting that the themes and cultural values depicted have enough resonance that large audiences will repeatedly pay for such content. In this case, the response of audiences is accepted as empirical evidence of audience acceptance and agreement with the primary messages of the leading films. Audience-based theories such as uses and gratification or polysemy argue that audiences are not directly affected by any particular content. However, if the most watched movies share similar themes and values, it is reasonable to suggest that audiences who pay to watch such themes and values must find them comfort-ing, attractive, or rewarding in some way. At any rate, a first step in illustrating China filmmakers relation to TNMC is to identify what content they produce in transnational partnerships or in their own independent creations, neither of which are coerced or imposed by some foreign power. Table 4.10 provides a

TABLE 4.10 Top Grossing Chinese movies 2017-2021

Title Year	Genre	Gross millions	Production Studios
Wolf Warrior 2 2017	War action	874	China Film Group, Bona
Hi, Mom 2021	Comedy	819	Alibaba, China Film Group, Maoyan
Ne Zha 2019	Fantasy action	745	Beijing Enlight Pictures
Wandering Earth 2019	Sci-fi action	700	China Film Group, Alibaba, Netflix★
Detective Chinatown 3 2021	Comic action	685	Wanda, China Film Group★
Avengers Endgame 2019	Fantasy action	620	Disney, Marvel
Operation Red Sea 2018	War action	580	Bona
Detective Chinatown 2 2018	Comic action	544	Wanda, Warner, CMC Australia★
The Eight Hundred 2020	War action	472	Huayi, Wanda, Alibaba, Tencent, B. Enlight
Dying to Survive 2018	Comic action	455	Huaxia, multiple co-production studios
Detective Pikachu 2019	Fantasy action	433	Legendary, Toho, Warner, Pokemon★
My People, My Country 2019	Anthology	425	Huaxia, Bona, Alibaba

★Transnational partnership

list of top grossing movies in China during the last five years. Only one is a US import, *Avengers: The End Game* (2019). Four of the top 10 movies are TNMC co-productions. The remaining five are mostly co-productions by Chinese studios that have extensive transnational partnerships, although the films on the list are not TNMC productions per se.

In addition to the *Avengers* (2019), three other films, *Fate of the Furious* (2017), *Avengers: Infinity War* (2018), and *Aquaman* (2018) were the only imported films to make the top 20 grossing films in China in the last five years. It seems the specter of US cultural imperialism has faded fast, even as neoliberal capitalism set up residence in the world's most populous nation. Chinese media (encouraged and regulated by the CCP) have either joined or followed TNMC production, distribution, and marketing practices. A brief summary of the themes of these top films—most of which are action movies—indicates that leading movie studios promote individualism, consumerism, and hierarchy (with Chinese characteristics) to responsive and paying mass audiences.

Remarkably, but perhaps not surprising given the push-and-pull of transnational media recruitment and success, dominant and recurrent themes in leading Chinese transnational and national movies fit the same template that contemporary Indian films follow as laid out in the previous chapter. Previous observations about action genre characteristics seem to be predictive of TNMC ideological tenets (Artz, 2015; Veloso & Bateman, 2013). Chinese action movies, including hundreds that drew smaller audiences, express several political and cultural evaluations: (a) the world faces continuous threats from irrational and dangerous villains; (b) average citizens concerned with their individual daily lives are unable to defend themselves, even official authorities may be incapable; so (c) we need specially skilled individual heroes; (d) to protect us from uncivilized evil, heroes should not be constrained by laws, civil rights, or even ethical norms; and (e) our best protection and the preferred social order is authority and hierarchy; all is well when elite power is restored and individual self-interest becomes the norm.

Although a more complete analysis of the hundreds of action movies exhibited in China since 2016 would be needed to conclusively demonstrate the prevalence of these components, even a cursory review of the leading box office successes provides a useful and representative sample of the movies most preferred by mass audiences. Perhaps more importantly, the repeating production and success of the genre and its components indicates the dominant political-cultural values and ideologies of TNMC adherents—which are decidedly not nation-centric, but indicative of the perspective of the transnational capitalist class and its managers.

1. *Danger Lurks Everywhere, We Are All Vulnerable*

    At a funeral, at the beach, driving home, at a birthday party, or solving how to save the earth? Anywhere, anytime, we are all on the verge of disaster and villainous assault—at least according to action adventure movies. In *Wolf Warriors 2*, a funeral is disrupted by an evil developer, a freighter is boarded by pirates in Somalia, and a pleasant beach party is invaded by terrorists. *Hi Mom* begins when the mother dies in a car crash. Ne Zha's birthday party ends in anger and he nearly kills his father. Peaceful village life is attacked and townspeople are threatened with being buried under ice. Things get even worse for humans living under ground, in *Wandering Earth*: plans to restart earth's rotation are ruined after a "gravitational spike" breaks the thrusters. As Earth moves toward collision with Jupiter, artificial intelligence interferes with human plans. The premise for *Detective Chinatown* is simple. In Bangkok, New York, Tokyo, London, and everywhere else, crime lords, murderers, and incompetent officials run rampant over good citizens. Chinese seem to always be threatened: by Japanese colonialism in the 1930s (*The Eight Hundred*), by Arab terrorists stealing uranium (*Operation Red Sea*), and even by human/ Pokémon malfeasance in Ryme City (*Detective Pikachu*).

2. *Citizens Are Unable to Defend Themselves Without Heroes*

The rash of nationalist-based action films insists that China needs its extraordinary armed forces because unprotected citizens are vulnerable to evil. *Wolf Warrior* Leng's friends, a freighter crew, Somalian citizens and armed forces, and Chinese factory workers in Africa are all helpless and vulnerable to attack—either by corrupt developers or armed terrorists. Villagers are helpless to deter the Demon Orb, Dragon King, and other powerful heavenly forces in *Ne Zha*. Mostly appearing as background extras, humans in the *Wandering Earth* live underground, dependent on scientists and astronauts. Rescue and repair parties are unsuccessful, while The heroes' actions kill entire innocent and defenseless populations. Average citizens, other crack detectives, and cops cannot solve the crime murders presented in any of the *Detective Chinatown* films. *Operation Red Sea* spectacularly recounts how special forces rescue helpless Chinese passengers and seamen from pirates and Moroccan civilians and government troops from terrorist attacks. Because no one speaks Pikachu, no one is capable of solving crime or corruption.

3. *Heroes With Magical Powers or Special Skills Will Rescure All*

Whether historical, fiction, or full-on fantasy, action movie plots revolve around heroic protagonists and their special abilities. Ne Zha not only has special powers, he learns additional fighting skills—all of which are marshalled to change his own destiny and save villagers.

The volatile Leng Feng balks at orders, but as a skilled combatant, fighter, and soldier for good he protects civilians and the Chinese state. To save the Wandering Earth, the insubordinate Liu and his son use their skills, determination, and creativity to save humanity. *Detective Chinatown* films are comedy, yet the bumbling, goofy, and physical hijinks of detectives Tang and Qin do not undermine their cleverness and ability to solve crimes no one else can figure out. The patriotic action film *Operation Red Sea* features the Jiaolong Assault Team, an eight member special forces team that deters pirates, rescues citizens, and saves the lives of innocents. Similarly, *The Eight Hundred* retells the story of a few hundred heroic, poorly armed soldiers defending China by withstanding the onslaught of 20,000 Japanese troops by land, air, and sea for three months. Even in a fantasy universe (based on Pokémon card and video games), the human Tim has the special ability to interpret Pikachu, giving him the skills needed for solving crime in a human/Pikachu world.

4. *Heroes Must Use Violence Unconstrained by Civil Rights or Legalities*

The predominance of military action movies powerfully advanced messages about the need for extra-judicial and morally questionable actions that are needed to protect society. With no Somalian permission and against Chinese orders, Wolf Warrior Leng maims, kills, and acts as needed to save workers and civilians from rebel mercenaries. With impunity and without restraint in fighting attackers, Leng saves all the crew members and leads them to UN safety—providing some justification for his illegal, unauthorized violence. To save dragon kind—a metaphor for China—the impetuous hero Ne Zha fights demons and endangers humans, who are quite secondary to the fantasy plot. Spirits answer to no civil authority or human norms. Science fiction repeats similar justifications for violence: Liu breaks out of hibernation, travels without official clearance, and repeatedly takes actions that injure crew members. His son causes magma to cover a city, killing its citizens, but he continues on his noble quest. It seems to save humanity, humans must die. In *Operation Red Sea*, fierce battles, raids, snipers, and action sequences, including a wingsuit assault on terrorists, obscure the violation of international law while justifying Chinese military actions in multiple Arab countries. These tropes for justifying violence to protect the nation now appear regularly in all TNMC action movies, whether set in the US, Europe, India, Africa, or Asia. Transnational capitalism needs mass consent to purvey violence in defense of its interests and profits. Action movies are a popular entertainment format that rely on spectacle, action, special effects, and the demonization of enemies to viscerally excite mass audiences—with the hope that such ideological justifications may influence public opinion on real world actions (Veloso & Bateman, 2013).

5. *We Can Return to Normal When Authority is Restored*

One of the more glaringly obvious frames in most action, animation, and even drama movies is their active or tacit advocacy for hierarchy and existing authority. This appears in fantasy, science fiction, historical epics, and contemporary settings. It seems media owners only employ screenwriters and directors dedicated to elite control. Military actions are premised on the admirable heroism of a nation's armed forces. In *Wolf Warriors*, after Chinese citizens are rescued, the Chinese military is honored and the Somalia government is saved. Hero Leng returns to his military squadron, legitimizing his actions and assuring viewers that legitimate authority is in control. Likewise, the comedy, *Hi, Mom* delivers and explicit message favoring family loyalty and respect for elder authority. We can all laugh, but in the end each individual should assume their proper respectful place in the traditional hierarchy. The townspeople in *Ne Zha* kneel in appreciation before the spirit forms of their superiors. The power and authority of the Spirit Pearl reigns, once properly subordinate to the Dragon world (an iconic metaphor for Chinese power) village life can return to normal. We know that *The Wandering Earth* story has concluded when Earth enters a new star system with Liu's son as part of the social order that oversees Earth's continued migration. *Detective Chinatown* movies not only acknowledge police authority in each city, equally important Qin and Tang accept the Crimaster order rankings and expectations as the hierarchical authority for their activities. *Operation Red Sea* confirms Chinese navy superiority ending with an anecdote about repelling US vessels. In fantasy action, the Pokémon character Mewtwo restores city order, police arrest the villain, and the human hero becomes a detective as the proper human/Pikachu and citizen/authority hierarchy is restored.

Action for Neoliberal Capitalism

Notably, each of these entertainment action themes underwrites China's support of the transnational neoliberal economic and political project that proposes deregulation of the public interest and emphasizes individual responsibility for all things social. As individuals we cannot avoid or ward off evil. Anyway, we should be most concerned about our family and our immediate daily lives. Individual heroes are needed. Individual heroes should decide necessary actions to ward off evil. Authorities and rulers know best, because individuals cannot understand politics or power, and should be mostly concerned with those things that we can individually control, like consumer choice, personal health and beauty, entertainment, and other self-interests. The *Monkey King: Hero Is Back* (2015) and *Ne Zha* (2019) are two of the more vivid examples of the cultural shift by Chinese media to ideologies of individualism that are essential to consumerism and private markets.

The Monkey King is a traditional figure in Chinese literature, opera, and animation. The film *Princess Iron Fan* (1941) stressed that the Monkey King's victory over the Bull Demon King was a collective victory—a metaphor for the unity of the Chinese people against the Japanese colonial invasion. Only the participation, collaboration, and active teamwork by the villagers secured their safety. In stark contrast, *Monkey King: Hero Is Back* (2015), a co-production of several Chinese government and private animation studios, the Monkey King has "transformed into one concerned with individual and personal struggles… rather than the collective socialist heroes of earlier versions" (Sun, 2018). An adaption with Sony immediately tapped the consumer video game market, illustrating China's pivot to individual consumerism.

Ne Zha, which grossed an animation record $1 billion, also rewrote a Chinese classical myth of redemption to benefit the people. The modernized Ne Zha "shouted slogans full of individualism such as 'My fate is controlled by myself rather than the heaven' and 'breaking the stereotype, I will be my own hero' as the "film adapts the plot and figures based on accurate market considerations" (Xie, 2019) to reach youth living in "a highly competitive and consumption-driven society" (Daley, 2019).

Each of the recent top movies in China emphasize individualism, as well. In both *Wolf Warrior* adventures, Leng Feng acts on his own without restraint or concern for anyone besides his friends. Leng Feng ignores the law and authorities with impunity. His individual skill and motivation conquer all. As a representative of elite power, Leng's success validates his self-centered actions. Although *Hi, Mom* is a comedy, not an action movie, Xiaoling magically returns to the past for her own selfish, self-centered interest. In *Ne Zha,* the screenwriters altered the complex fantasy myth so the spirit child is motivated primarily by self-interest. Astronaut Liu's promise to his son propels a complicated sci-fi story in the *Wandering Earth,* in which both Liu and his son violate rules, destroy lives, and have little concern for others in their individual quests. While detectives Qin and Teng mimic the humor and misbehavior of popular buddy films like *Rush Hour* and *Lethal Weapon,* the two self-centered detectives vie to upstage other crime fighters. In *Chinatown Detective,* their individual rankings on Crimaster seem to be their most important goal. *Detective Pikachu* recounts a fantasy story based on the Pokémon franchise, whose slogan is "Gotta' catch 'em all!" proposing a lifetime of consumption of the never-ending appearance of new cards to purchase. The film revolves around the individual needs of Pikachu and his human friend Tim, appealing to Pokémon fans and families linked to its consumer universe. Many other recent and current Chinese and Chinese TNMC films blatantly promote individualism and consumerism as the path to personal and national success. Of course, shuffling individualism to the top of the TNMC deck does nothing to build democracy or lead to a more humane social order.

Media production includes thousands of participants beyond the work done directly by writers, actors, set designers, costumers, carpenters and painters, and the audio, visual, and editing technicians. As the Motion Picture Association of America noted in its 2016 report: "The total economic contribution represents the impact of direct industry jobs and spending, along with indirect jobs and wages in thousands of companies with which the industry does business. This includes caterers, dry cleaners, hotels, florists, hardware and lumber suppliers, software, and digital equipment suppliers, as well as those doing business with consumers, such as home entertainment distributors, theme parks and tourist attractions" (Busch, 2017). In other words, transnational media not only concerns studio owners and their investors, the political economy of production directly impacts millions, sometimes favorably, sometimes harshly, depending on the political and economic calculations and decisions of TNMCs and cooperative neoliberal governments.

As Asia's free market economic growth increases, labor exploitation becomes more central to TNMC production, and increased consumerism will follow. Expanding multichannel satellite, cable, streaming, and mobile phone use almost requires that media producers develop regional transnational productions for the 1.4 billion Chinese and 670 million Southeast Asians desiring entertaining formats and genre. Fuji, MBC Korea, TVBI Hong Kong, and other regional TNMCs as well as the largest TNMCs from the US and Europe are already undertaking joint ventures and co-productions in and for the region. Transnational media are responding to economic pressures by making structural changes aimed at reducing their labor costs and expanding their markets. "Rivalry has given way to friendly competition and cooperation" (Lim, 2006). The information presented in this chapter confirms that Chinese media, government and private, have also discovered that transnational partnerships offer the surest means for capturing regional and global audiences that bring increased profit.

References

American Enterprise Institute. (2020). Chinese investments in the United States. *American Enterprise Institute.* https://www.aei.org/china-tracker-home/

Amidi, A. (2015, July 19). Forget "Minions," "Monster Hunt" and "Monkey King" smash Chinese box office records. *Cartoon Brew.* https://www.cartoonbrew.com/pixar/forget-minions-monster-hunt-and-monkey-king-smash-chinese-box-office-records-116287.html

Anderlini, J. (2020, September 8). China's Middle East strategy comes at a cost to the United States. *Financial Times.* https://www.ft.com/content/e20ae4b9-bc22-4cb5-aaf6-b67c885c845c

Arjit. (2017, October 4). Beasts of burden. *Animation Review.* http://animationreviews.com/beast-of-burden/

Artz, L. (2015). *Global entertainment media: A critical introduction.* New York: Wiley Blackwell.

Baroud, R. (2021, March 19). How China won the Mideast without firing a shot. https://www.mintpressnews.com/how-china-won-the-middle-east-without-firing-a-single-bullet/276269/

Blázques, F. J. C., Cappello, M., Chochan, L., Ene, L., Fontaine, G., Grece, C., Pumares, M. J., Kanzler, M., Rabie, I., Scheeberger, A., Simone, P., Talaver, J., & Valais, S. (2019). *Yearbook 2018/2019 key trends: Television, cinema, video and on-demand audiovisual services – The pan-European picture.* Strasbourg, France: European Audiovisual Observatory.

Block, A. B. (2015, May 12). China Film Group, Canadian, Kiwi partners back 17-movie slate. *Hollywood Reporter.* https://www.hollywoodreporter.com/news/china-film-group-canadian-kiwi-794968

Blair, G. (2019, June 15). Shanghai: Fuji TV exec talks growing Japan-China business. *Hollywood Reporter*. https://www.hollywoodreporter.com/news/shanghai-fuji-tv-executive-growing-china-business-terrace-house-1218377

Brasher, K. (2021, April 3). China restricts foreign banks, worrying businesses. *New York Times*, B3.

Brzeski, P. (2016, April 1). China's Film Carnival: Five things to know about Dick Cook's $500M financier. *Hollywood Reporter*. https://www.hollywoodreporter.com/news/chinas-film-carnival-5-things-879661

Brzeski, P. (2017, April 2). China's Huayi Brothers reports 17 percent profit fall for 2016. *Hollywood Reporter*. https://www.hollywoodreporter.com/business/business-news/chinas-huayi-brothers-reports-17-percent-profit-fall-2016-990694/

Brzeksi, P. (2020, January 8). China box office slow growth marks "new normal." *Hollywood Reporter*. https://www.hollywoodreporter.com/news/china-box-office-slow-growth-marks-new-normal-1267762

Bulbeck, P. (2019, October 21). Former Disney Studios chair Dick Cook to make two adventure films in Melbourne. *Hollywood Reporter*. https://www.hollywoodreporter.com/news/dick-cook-make-two-adventure-films-melbourne-1248975

Busch, A. (2017, December 15). Chinese film and TV industry is $86.3 billion business. *Deadline*. https://deadline.com/2017/12/chinese-film-tv-industry-86-3-billion-dollar-business-mpaa-china-report-1202227826/

Canaves, S. (2019, October 15). Eight ways brands are featured on Chinese dramas. *China Film Insider*. http://chinafilminsider.com/product-placement-on-Chinese-dramas/

Chen, C. (2019, January 16). Tencent plugs holes, and boosts profits, with 163 news investments. *South China Morning Post*. https://www.scmp.com/tech/big-tech/article/2182193/tencent-plugs-holes-and-boosts-profits-163-new-investments

China Daily. (2021, January 2). China movie market bounces back. *China Daily*. http://t.m.china.org.cn/convert/c_Wk3B6KJJ.html

China Film Insider. (2018, January 31). Headlines from China: Ticketing firm Tao Piao Piao dominates Chinese film distribution. *China Film Insider*. http://chinafilminsider.com/headlines-from-china-ticketing-firm-taopiaopiao-dominates-chinese-film-distribution/

Clarke, S. (2018, July 2). "Octonauts" movies set as Silvergate launches China unit, pacts with Wanda. *Variety*. https://variety.com/2018/film/news/octonauts-movies-silvergate-china-expansion-wanda-1202860344/

Coonan, C. (2015, February 8). Berlin: France setting the pace on China co-productions. *Hollywood Reporter*. https://www.hollywoodreporter.com/news/berlin-france-setting-pace-china-771226

Curtin, M. (2007). *Playing to the world's biggest audience: The globalization of Chinese film and TV*. Berkeley, CA: University of California Press.

Daley, B. (2019, October 21). Can Ne Zha, the Chinese superhero with $1B at the box office, teach us how to raise good kids? *The Conversation*. https://theconversation.com/can-ne-zha-the-chinese-superhero-with-1b-at-the-box-office-teach-us-how-to-raise-good-kids-124987

Davis, R. (2021, March 12). China built more than 2000 new screens in the first two months of 2021. *Variety*. https://variety.com/2021/film/news/china-movie-theaters-reopen-build-more-1234929177/

Davis, R. (2021b, March 16). China should outsource production to Hollywood, says "Detective Chinatown" producer. *Variety*. https://variety.com/2021/film/news/chin-should-outsource-film-production-to-hollywood-shawn-yue-1234932346/

Davis, R. (2020, September 15). China hates Disney's Mulan, but it has nothing to do with politics. *Variety*. https://variety.com/2020/film/asia/why-china-hates-disney-mulan-1234770198/

Davis, R. (2019, June 5). BBC Studios signs co-production deal for new natural history series. *Variety*. https://variety.com/2019/film/news/bbc-studios-seven-worlds-one-planet-tencent-penguin-pictures-cctv9-1203234607/

Deloitte China. (2017). China's film industry – A new era. *Deloitte.com*. https://www2.deloitte.com/cn/en/pages/technology-media-and-telecommunications/articles/chinese-culture-entertainment.html/#:~:text=China's%20Film%20Industry%20a%20New%20Era%20Deloitte%20has,research%20and%20POV%20on%20the%20Film%20Industry%20trend.

Doctoroff, T. (2005). *Billions: Selling to the new Chinese consumer*. New York: Palgrave-MacMillan.

Dolack, P. (2020, November 27). Far from a change, RCEP is more capitalism as usual. *Counterpunch*. https://www.counterpunch.org/2020/11/27/far-from-a-change-rcep-agreement-is-more-capitalism-as-usual/

Dirlik, A. (2005). *Marxism in the Chinese revolution*. Lanham, MD: Rowman & Littlefield.

Dun & Bradstreet. (2021). D & B business directory. dnb.com. https://www.dnb.com/business-directory/company-profiles.shangdong_dazhong_newspaper_group_bandao_media_co_ltd.b9bfb79fbdc93a4a4e9fc5074385d7b9.html#company-info

Economist. (2021a, January 23). Patriotism and the party: How nationalism is shaping China's young. *The Economist*. https://www.economist.com/special-report/2021/01/21/how-nationalism-is-shaping-chinas-young

Economist. (2021b, January 23). Values, identity and activism: Individualism reigns in China—and with it more social responsibility. *The Economist*. https://www.economist.com/special-report/2021/01/21/individualism-reigns-in-china-and-with-it-more-social-responsibility

Ezra, E., & Rowden, T. (2006). What is transnational cinema. In E. Ezra, & T. Rowden (Eds.), *Transnational cinema: The film reader* (pp. 1–12). New York: Routledge

Fan, X. (2020, October 29). Movie industry moving forward. *China Daily*. https://global.chinadaily.com.cn/a/202010/29/WS5f9a0235a31024ad0ba81b78_4.html

Fassihi, F., & Myers, S. l. (2021, March 27). China, with $400 billion Iran deal, could deepen influence in Mideast. *New York Times*. https://www.nytimes.com/2021/03/27/world/middleeast/china-iran-deal.html

Faughnder, R. (2021, February 9). The wide shot: Hollywood's China trouble aren't going away. *Los Angeles Times*. https://www.latimes.com/entertainment-arts/business/newsletter/2021-02-09/the-wide-shot-hollywoods-china-troubles-arent-going-away-the-wide-shot

Flannery, R., Chen, M., & Mao, E. (2020, November 4). China's 400 richest 2020: Total wealth surges amid pandemic. *Fortune*. https://www.forbes.com/sites/russellflannery/2020/11/04/chinas-400-richest-2020–total-wealth-surges-amid-pandemic/?sh=677315e23d7a

Frater, P. (2017, December 2017). China's Fosun looking at sale of Studio 8 stake. *Variety*. https://www.yahoo.com/entertainment/china-fosun-looking-sale-studio-050513083.html

Frater, P. (2020a, June 19). China's Bilibili and France's Arte strike "Deep Med" co=production deal. *Variety*. https://variety.com/2020/tv/asia/bilibili-arte-deep-med-documentary-coproduction-1234642500/

Frater, P. (2020b, December 23). Virtual edition of Bridging the Dragon keeps alive the flame of Sino-European film production. *Variety*. https://variety.com/2020/film/asia/virtual-bridging-the-dragon-china-europe-film-production-1234874046/

Frater, P. (2021, March 3). China poised to give Korean content a boost after three year boycott. *Variety*. https://variety.com/2021/film/asia/china-giving-korean-content-boost-after-boycott-1234920540/#!

Fu, W. W., & Govindaraju, A. (2010). Explaining global box office tastes in Hollywood films: Homogenization of national audiences' movie selections. *Communication Research 37*, 215–238.

Fung, A. (2006). Think globally, act locally: China's rendezvous with MTV. *Global Media and Communication 2*(1), 71–88.

Gillespie, P., Valdes-Dalpena, P., & Isodore, C. (2018, April 10). How American cars are really sold in China. *CNN Business*. https://money.cnn.com/2018/04/10/news/economy/china-cars-tariffs/index.html#:~:text=America%27s%20most%20iconic%20automakers%2C%20such%20as%20Ford%20and,for%20six%20years%20straight%2C%20according%20to%20the%20company

Garrahan, M., & Sender, H. (2016, June 8). Chinese investors flood into Hollywood. *Financial Times*. http://ft.com/content/2cb93908-2c65-11e6-bf8d-26294ad519fc

Harson, H. (2018, June 28). Television content creation in China. *Tech Crunch*. https://techcrunch.com/2018/06/28/television-content-creation-in-china-the-biggest-industry-youve-never-heard-of-until-now/

Herman, T. (2018, February 27). Korean entertainment thrives on beneficial but tense relationships with Chinese investments. *Forbes*. https://www.forbes.com/sites/tamarherman/2018/02/27/korean-entertainment-thrives-on-beneficial-but-tense-relationship-with-chinese-investments/?sh=7f21b4046364

Hernández, J. C. (2019, February 6). Worker's activism rises as China's economy slows. *New York Times*. https://www.nytimes.com/2019/02/06/world/asia/china-workers-protests.html

Ho, J., Poh, F., Zhou, J., & Zipster, D. (2019, December 18). China consumer report 2020: The many faces of the Chinese consumer. *McKinsey & Company*. https://www.mckinsey.com/featured-insights/china/china-consumer-report-2020-the-many-faces-of-the-chinese-consumer

Hoyler, M., & Watson, A. (2019). Framing city networks through temporary projects: (Trans) national film production beyond "Global Hollywood." *Urban Studies 56*(5), 943–959.

Huat, C. B. (2012). *Structure, audience, and soft power: East Asian Pop culture*. Hong Kong: Hong Kong University Press.

Hui, W. (2006). *China's new order: Society, politics, and economy in transition*. Cambridge, MA: Harvard University Press.

Hui, W. (2012, May 10). The rumor machine. *London Review of Books 34*(9). https://www.lrb.co.uk/the-paper/v34/n09/wang-hui/the-rumour-machine

Iwabuchi, K. (2002). *Recentering globalization: Popular culture and Japanese transnationalism*. Durham, NC: Duke University Press.

Jackson, J. (2020, September 21). Chinese war movie becomes 2020's top earning movie. *Newsweek*. https://www.newsweek.com/chinese-war-epic-becomes-2020s-top-earning-movie-globally-handily-defeating-mulan-china-1533355

Lang, B, & Frater, P. (2018, March 29). China film quota talks could be a casualty in Trump's trade war. *Variety*. https://variety.com/2018/film/news/china-film-quota-hollywood-trump-trade-war-1202739283/

Lim, T. (2006). The social and cultural integrative role of Asian media productions in the new Millenium: Pan-Asian and international co-productions. *Research Depository Murdoch University.* https://researchrepository.murdoch.edu.au/id/eprint/39840/1/social_cultural_integrative_role_asianmedia.pdf

Liu, J., & Du, S. (2018). *2018 The research report on Chinese film industry* (International Version). Beijing: China Film Association.

McCarthy, T. (2021, February 21). Int'l critics line: Chen Sicheng action comedy "Detective Chinatown 3." *Deadline.* https://deadline.com/2021/02/film-review-chen-sicheng-detective-chinatown-3-1234698001/

National Public Radio. (2021, March 5). What China's "Total Victory" over poverty looks like in actuality. *National Public Radio.* https://www.npr.org/2021/03/05/974173482/what-chinas-total-victory-over-extreme-poverty-looks-like-in-actuality#:~:text=China%20defines%20extreme%20poverty%20as%20earning%20less%20than,a%20day%2C%20but%20that%27s%20generally%20for%20low-income%20countries

Olsson, C. P. (n.d.). How Hollywood is aligning its films with new markets and partners: China Film Group. *Filmpulse.info.* https://filmpulse.info/china-film-group-co-production-corporation/

Ong, A. (2006). *Neoliberalism as exception: Mutations in citizenship and sovereignty.* Durham: University of North Carolina Press.

Richeri, G. (2016). Global film market, regional problems. *Global Media and China* 1(4), 312–330.

Roxborough, S. (2018, October 18). In China, Western TV companies go co-production route. *Hollywood Reporter.* https://www.hollywoodreporter.com/news/china-western-tv-companies-go-production-route-1152752

Rubin, R. (2021, March 12). Wanda Group no longer majority shareholder in AMC Theatres. *Variety.* https://variety.com/2021/film/news/china-wanda-group-amc-theatres-1234929145/

Sarti, I. (1981). Communication and cultural dependency: A misconception. In E. G. McAnany, J. Schnitman, & N. Janus (Eds.), *Communication and social structure: Critical studies in mass media research* (pp. 317–334). New York: Praeger.

Song, X. (2018). Hollywood movies and China: Analysis of Hollywood globalization and relationship management in China's cinema market. *Global Media and China* 3(3), 177–194.

Sreberny, A. (2001). The global and the local in international communications. In M. G. Durham & D. M. Kellner (eds), *Media and cultural studies: Key works* (pp. 604–626). Malden, MA: Blackwell.

Statista. (2012). Leading newspapers in China in 2012, by circulation. Statista.com. https://www-statista-com.pnw.idm.oclc.org/statistics/243688/leading-newspapers-in-china-by-circulation/

Statista. (2020). The twenty countries with the largest Gross Domestic Product (GDP) in 2020. *Statista.com.* https://www-statista-com.pnw.idm.oclc.org/statistics/268173/countries-with-the-largest-gross-domestic-product-gdp/

Sun, H. (2018, January 29). Monkey King and Chinese animation. *Association for Chinese Animation Studies.* http://acas.ust.hk/2018/01/29/monkey-king-and-chinese-animation/

Tan, W. (2021, January 11). It's a "hard sell" if Biden administration want to rejoin massive trans-Pacific trade deal, analyst says. *CNBC.com.* https://www.cnbc.com/2021/01/11/control-risks-on-biden-administration-rejoining-tpp-trade-deal.html

Thomala, L. L. (2020, December 10). Leading advertisers' ad spending growth in China 2018. *Statista.com*. https://www-statista-com.pnw.idm.oclc.org/statistics/1056785/china-ad-spending-growth-leading-companies/

Thomala, L. L. (2021, January 15). Revenue of radio and television networks in China 2008–2018. *Statista.com*. https://www-statista-com.pnw.idm.oclc.org/statistics/224631/revenue-of-radio-and-television-networks-in-china/

Veloso, F., & Bateman, N. (2013). The multimodal construction of acceptability: Marvel's Civil War comic books and the PATRIOT Act. *Critical Discourse Studies 10*(4), 427–443.

Wang, Y. (2019, October 21). China focus: Auto joint venture sets benchmark for Sino-Japanese business partnership. *Xinhua Net*. http://www.xinhuanet.com/english/2019-10/21/c_138489736.htm

Watanabe, S. (2019, May 17). Dalian Wanda to build 12n yuan theme park in Shaanxi. *NikkeiAsia*. https://asia.nikkei.com/Business/Companies/Dalian-Wanda-to-build-12bn-yuan-theme-park-in-Shaanxi

Wharfe, C. (2020, December 12). Construction of China's first LEGOLAND park underway. Brickfanatics.com. https://www.brickfanatics.com/construction-of-chinas-first-legoland-park-is-underway/

Xie, X. (2019, August 5), Refuse to accept the fate: Ne Zha and Chinese animation. *In Zhejiang*. https;//inzj.zjol.com.cn/News/201908/t20190805_10732195.shtml.

Xinhua. (2017, December 28). China tv studios form alliance to boost tv drama exports. *China Daily*. http://www.chinadaily.com.cn/a/201712/28/WS5a445f50a31008cf16da3f9b.html

Xu, S. (2018). Hollywood movies and China: Analysis of Hollywood globalization and relationship management in China's cinema market. *Global Media China 3*(3), 177–194.

Yang, J. (2021, March 15). Beijing asks Alibaba to shed its media assets. Foxbusiness.com. https://www.foxbusiness.com/technology/beijing-asks-alibaba-to-shed-its-media-assets-wsj

Yeh, E. Y. (2010). The deferral of pan-Asian: A critical appraisal of film marketization in China. In M. Curtin, & H. Shah (Eds.), *Reorienting global communication: Indian and Chinese media beyond borders* (pp. 183–200). Urbana-Champaign, IL: University of Illinois Press

Yik-Chan, C. (2003). The nation-state in a globalizing media environment: China's regulatory policies on transborder TV drama flow. *The Public 10*, 75–94.

Zeitchik, S. (2019, December 30). The Chinese film business is doing the unthinkable: Thriving without Hollywood. *Washington Post*. https://www.washingtonpost.com/business/2019/12/30/chinese-film-business-is-doing-unthinkable-thriving-without-hollywood/

Zhao, Y. (1998). *Media, market, and democracy in China: Between the party line and the bottom line*. Urbana: University of Illinois Press.

Zhao, Y. (2008). *Communication in China: Political economy, power, and conflict*. Lanham, MD: Rowman & Littlefield.

Zheng, S. (2018, October 23). China quietly opens door to more foreign films. *South China Morning Post*.https://www.scmp.com/news/china/diplomacy/article/2169837/china-quietly-opens-door-more-foreign-films

Zhong, r. (2021, April 11). China slaps Alibaba with $2.8 billion fine in a warning to big tech. *New York Times* A11.

5

LATIN AMERICA

From Telenovelas to Transnational Media

If you want four minute crying scenes, Latin American telenovelas are for you, If you want animated comedy-horror series, Latin American films may be for you. If you want to see regional transnational co-productions, Latin American media is definitely in order.

Twenty countries south of the United States comprise Latin America, which includes Central America, South America, and the Caribbean. With a total population of 625 million, Latin America is one of the largest media markets in the world, behind China with 1.5 billion and India with 1.4 billion people. Latin America's population is one-third larger than the 27 countries of the European Union which have a combined population of 445 million, but Latin America's national cultures are not as disparate as the linguistic and cultural differences in Europe. Spanish, French, and Portuguese are the dominant languages, with smaller populations speaking English. Creole and dozens of indigenous languages. On the other hand, in contrast to Europe, North America, and Japan, and with the exception of the elite capitalist class and a small managerial class, economic conditions are poor for most Latin Americans. In 2020, GDP for the region was only $900 billion compared to the much smaller European Union's GDP of $15 trillion. In Latin America, the top 10% captures 54% of the national income, making it one of the most unequal regions in the world (WIDWORLD, 2020).

All countries in Latin America share the common experience of colonization. For centuries, Britain, France, and Portugal occupied and controlled most of the Southern Hemisphere. The region has also been subjected to more recent and continued North American dominance. At least since the mid-20th century, US government interventions and US corporate activities significantly affected the (under)development of economics and politics for each of

DOI: 10.4324/9781003162452-06

the countries (Frank, 1967; Cardoso & Faletto, 1979), as well as heavily influencing media forms and norms (Fox & Waisbord, 2002). Indeed, the original recognition of cultural imperialism was drawn largely from observations about the glaring US media influence and dominance in Latin America since the 1960s (Mattelart, 1976; Schiller, 1976). Not only did US military intervention, investment, and education assure subordination across the continent, it also guaranteed the commercial character of Latin American media, including the absence of public service broadcasting.

Each of the Latin American countries has its own historical political economy of commercial media, combining highly consolidated and privatized national markets with significance foreign ownership and influence. With the global capitalist turn to neoliberalism, Latin American corporations and governments have accelerated the privatization and commercialization of media. Privatization not only provided increased wealth for capitalist owners, it also accorded more complex social divisions that included a growing professional and managerial upper middle class that became increasingly consumerist. Growth in income has been associated with growth in spending on entertainment, movies, multichannel and pay-TV, including more interest in culturally diverse foreign stories (Straubhaar, Sinta, Spence, & Higgins Joyce, 2016, p. 219). Just as occurred in China when television audiences grew, in Latin America new television networks needed more programming to compete, leading to an increase in production studios, foreign investment, and regional media partnerships. TNMCs came to the rescue.

By the 21st century, Latin American media faced an "asymmetrical industrial landscape, resulting from two decades of media deregulation, privatization, and liberalization in which global and national networks hold dominant power through processes of media consolidation while facing competition from emerging players both domestically and abroad" (Piñon, 2014). Given the spread of neoliberalism across Latin America with deregulation, privatization, and commercialization, media became more vertically and horizontally integrated in each nation and the region, even as new competitors appeared. A handful of national media reigned: in Brazil it was O Globo; in Mexico, Grupo Televisa and TV Azteca; in Argentina, the Clarin Group; Colombia was dominated by Caracol and RCN; and in Venezuela it was the Cisneros Group.

At the same time, major TNMCs were heavily involved in the region and new regional TNMCs have appeared. For instance, Disney, the majority shareholder in TeleColombia; owns 30% of Clarin's Argentine Patagonik Films; is partnered with Comcast, Viacom, and MGM in O Globo's pay-TV Rede Cine; and airs dozens of its television programs on networks across South America. The French TNMC Banijay purchased the Dutch Endemol Shine in 2021 Endemol Shine entered a joint venture for making Spanish-language programming with Boomdog, a Mexican production studio. Endemol Shine Brazil works with O Globo and advertisers making branded programming.

The Cisneros Group, which owns Venevisión in Venezuela, has partnered with Facebook, Yahoo, Claxson Interactive, and Playboy in various distribution agreements.

In 2021, CBS Viacom purchased Chilevisión and launched the streaming Paramount+ with Claro Video in Mexico; Claro, Oi, and Oi Play in Brazil; TV Cable in Ecuador; and StarTV and TotalPlay in Mexico. Chilevisión and Spanish TNMC Grupo Globomedia's Mediapro Studio developed the reality competition show, *El Discipulo del Chef* in 2020 as part of a five year deal for telenovela series and other programming. This Chilevisión/Mediapro venture is a thoroughly integrated transnational media operation: TNMC Viacom has partners across the continent; Spanish TNMC Mediapro Studio co-produces dozens of series and films with Disney, Viacom, Netflix, and multiple Latin American studios; while the Chinese private equity firm, Orient Hontai Capital, has majority ownership of Globomedia's Mediapro Studio. What is the nationality or culture of this media content? Is Spain, the US, China, Chile, or some other nation imperially influencing viewers?

As Juan Piñon's (2014) study demonstrated a while ago, "the line between the national and the foreign in US and Latin American television has blurred because of the presence of transnational capital, productions, and formats that have 'passed' as national given different arrangements with different players" (p. 213). There are multiple other partnerships that confirm how media production in Latin America has become thoroughly transnational in scope and identity. A few examples must suffice, because there are far too many to recount in one chapter.

Sony owns 50% of the Colombian television production company Teleset with a sister division in Mexico. Sony Pictures' Floresta formed a joint venture with Globo to produce two English language telenovela series, *The Angel of Hamburg* (released in 2020) and *Rio Connections*, due in 2021 (Hopewell, 2019). Sony also co-produced the telenovela *Código Implacable* with TNMC Mediapro in 2021.

Lionsgate maintains a strategic partnership with Starz and the Spanish-language streaming service Pantaya to co-produce and distribute films. Pantaya's production partner Pantelion Films is a 50:50 TNMC partnership of Lionsgate and Televisa. Pantelion co-produced dozens of films in the last several years, including a Spanish-language remake of *Overboard* (2018) with MGM. Pantelion has forged multiple exhibition agreements with AMC, Cinemax, Cinemark, and others. Meanwhile, Pantaya owners Hemisphere Media and Intermedia also operate the Cinelatino movie channel, Puerto Rico's WAPA-TV, and Colombia's Canal 1 network.

Mediapro, as a Chinese-Spanish JV, has become an emergent TNMC in Latin America with multiple co-productions, beginning in 2016 with Argentina's Burman Studio. Mediapro now has offices in Miami, Mexico, Chile, Argentina, and Colombia, where it agreed to a long-term production partnership with Caracol Television, a major exporter of telenovelas. Mediapro's active collaboration in Spanish-language content production with diverse Latin American media illustrates that transnational partnerships often occur regionally.

Transnational relations—with partnerships between more than one company from more than one nation—face tensions and dynamics in reaching cooperation. So, TNMC ventures form in a multitude of ways: shared media ownership, investments, with state regulation; co-production practices, including culturally-diverse content creation; format sales and remakes; cross-border distribution arrangements; exhibition modes and locations, including digital streaming; and shared marketing activities; among others (Piñon, 2014, p. 215). Although each Latin American country has distinct regulations on foreign ownership, some 40% of private television stations in the region already have some TNMC partnership. Many more have co-production agreements and co-financing deals.

Clearly, transnational media cross Latin American borders and cultures while regional TNMC partnerships are thriving. The following overview by country highlights several national media that lead the transnational restructuring of production and distribution across Latin America and beyond.

Brazil

Despite being one of the top 25 economies in the world with $1.4 trillion GDP in 2020, Brazil is grossly unequal economically. The six richest men have as much wealth as 100 million Brazilians; the top 5% have the same wealth as the other 95% (Oxfam International, 2021). The largest country in South America, Brazil is also one of the most multicultural and ethnically diverse. Brazil now numbers 215 million with complex racial and ethnic populations, including roughly 70% claiming European or "mixed" ancestry, 20% of African heritage, and 10% comprising many indigenous groups such as Gurani, Kaingangs, and Charrúa, among others (de Assis Poiares et al, 2010). As a developing industrial nation, Brazil was a 2009 founding member of BRICS (Brazil, Russia, India, China, and South Africa) the group of nations that represent about 40% of the world population and 25% of the world's economic output. During the 2002–2010 presidency of Luiz Inácio Lula da Silva, leader of the Worker's Party, BRICS set up an independent development bank for financing infrastructure projects in the five countries. For more than a decade the Worker's Party headed the Brazilian government and introduced several policies and reforms reducing poverty and benefitting labor, women, and indigenous nations. Following what many termed a "soft coup" against Dilma Rousseff, Lula's successor, Michel Temer and then Jair Bolsonaro launched an aggressive neoliberal program that rolled back environmental protections of the rainforest, reduced indigenous rights, and installed military officials in government posts. In short, throughout the last 60 years, print, radio, and television—largely led by O Globo—has worked on behalf of Brazil's corporate interests, dominating the mass media and entertaining millions.

Grupo Globo

Grupo Globo's success is written in its history as recipient of Time-Life underwriting its corporate infrastructure and as the prime media supporter of Brazil's military dictatorship that ruled from the 1960s until 1985. In return, the military subsidized the distribution of television receivers, pulled the broadcast licenses of competitors, and provided news exclusives, all benefitting Roberto Marinho and his Rede Globo TV network which willingly served the government's export-based developmental plans. Brazil's military junta, in power from 1964 to 1985, relied on Globo to politically and culturally integrate a socially and culturally divided society. Cultural and racial diversity has been a source of national pride and also ongoing social conflict. Media and cultural production has greatly affected both. Economically, Globo directly contributed to consumerism. Politically, its programs carried messages of optimism linked to national development and cultural diversity, which helped win some tacit acceptance of the military government (Oualalou, 2013).

Rede Globo has 4 national television networks with 118 stations regularly attracting about 40% of the viewing audience. According to Media Ownership Monitor (2017), Grupo Globo is the second largest television network in the world, behind Disney-ABC in the US. In 2017, Grupo Global was 19th in the ranking of the world's largest media companies by Zenith Media ROI, a division of the French transnational PR group, Publicis. O Globo is firmly committed to transnational media expansion and collaboration. Brazil has several other television outlets, including religious-based Record TV and the Silvio Santos SBT, each having about 15% share of the national audience—will below the reach and impact of Rede Globo.

Rede Globo's prime strategy for building audiences, reaping profits, and advancing the political and ideological interests of Brazil's capitalist class has long been telenovela production. For the working and middle classes, as well as the urban and rural poor, telenovelas became a central source of information about Brazil that wasn't already clearly apparent in news. Telenovelas provided a limited space for fabricated social entertainment but not for political conversation. Globo's telenovelas were one way the military dictatorship could assuage disaffection and opposition while popularizing a "Brazilian" national identity linked to development. Combined with Globo's news reports, telenovelas contributed to an integrated, national identity for Brazilians divided by ethnicity, class, gender, and cultural difference. Globo telenovelas consist of middle-class settings, colloquial language, and current events such as festivals and elections, all with an element of upward social mobility.

Every part of Globo's television and film production is tightly controlled: lighting, wardrobe, scenery, and attractive actors. Globo invested in technology, infrastructure, and creative talent, but by the late 1980s, like most of the world's nationally-based media, Grupo Globo had saturated its domestic market and looked abroad for more profits. Globo purchased 90% of Telemontecarlo in Italy and 15% of Portugal's SIC television channel—both since sold off as Grupo Globo found short-term TNMC partnerships and joint ventures more functional and profitable. A key to Globo's success has been its ability to industrialize the creative process so it could broadcast at least three different telenovelas every day, each with 140–180 episodes (Oualalou, 2013). Additionally, Globo implemented viewer responses, audience surveys, and social media, adjusting narratives to meet audience preferences and maximize ratings, advertising sales, and profits. Although the writing was and is simple and repetitive for audience understanding, characters and plots were and are complex enough to resonate with viewers. A more complete discussion on the telenovela genre is presented in a separate section at the end of the country overview.

Grupo Globo is a minority partner to ATT/Vrio in Sky Brasil, a pay television system with 57 channels and over 5 million subscribers. Globo also has an exclusive distribution deal with Côte Ouest, based in Mauritius and South Africa, providing telenovelas to French and English-speaking African countries. In 2017, Globo formed a joint venture with Vice Media for youth-focused programming on Globosat, which reaches 53 million viewers. Globo co-produces many telenovelas with other Brazilian studios as well as with Universal Pictures (e.g., the 2017 series "Malasartes" and "Aldo"). Globo has partnered with Endemol Shine, the Banijay-owned French TNMC, on several reality television programs, including *Big Brother Brazil*.

Shine Brazil has production and distribution agreements with all of the main broadcasters and platforms in Brazil. Shine has developed several "branded" unscripted entertainment series with Proctor & Gamble, the Belgium transnational Anheuser-Busch InBev, and Heineken, among others. In 2020, Shine Brazil formed a partnership with Chico Rei, a Brazilian e-commerce platform, to distribute *Simon's Cat* media and other products. *Simon's Cat* is an animated web cartoon, book, film, and video game enterprise from Britain having millions of fans in over 100 countries, including Brazil and the rest of Latin America.

Whether with Shine, Universal, Sky Brasil, or other TNMC, on balance, Grupo Globo straddles Latin American and exports globally not by its singular domination, but by "reaching co-production deals and programming agreements with domestic competing networks across the whole region" (Piñon, 2014, p. 226). Early on, Globo recognized the effectiveness of hegemonic leadership through regional TNMCs. Most television and film producers in Latin America have followed, establishing their own regional, cross-border co-production, format adaptation, and distribution agreements. Venivision, for instance, reduced production in Venezuela because of the US sanctions, increased its co-productions in Miami and partnered with Televisa, RCN, and Caracol on telenovela programming. In the last few years, Rede Globo has adopted the "super-series" short-telenovela genre introduced by Telemundo, producing shorter series with more sexuality, violence, and controversial topics, intending to have more appeal for men and affordably reach larger international audiences. Globo has also increased its telenovela co-production output working with Comcast Universal and several Brazilian studios (Vassallo de Lopes & Greco, 2018, pp. 99, 108).

Throughout Grupo Globo's history, Marinho and the Brazilian government have linked support for Globo's control over the Brazilian media market with nationalist pretensions. Dos Santos (2009) has argued that revival of Brazilian film production was less about defending Brazilian cultural integrity than about Globo's move to strengthen its control over the national market. In other words, Grupo Globo was not concerned about cultural imperialism, but was determined to capture greater market share by adapting to the transnational media production models of scope and scale (Donoghue, 2014)—especially with Spanish and Argentine media partners.

Mexico

Mexico is the second largest nation in Latin America with 130 million population, about one-third less than Brazil, but has almost the same GDP with $1.2 trillion in 2020. Still, in 2016, the Organization for Economic Cooperation and Development (OECD) listed Mexico among the top three nations with the highest inequality rates. One percent of the population owns half of the total wealth in the country. The insistent introduction of privatization and austerity facilitated the rise of monopolies, the appearance of a sizable middle class, and a huge increase in poverty for millions. Neoliberal practices benefitted a handful of industrialists in Mexico, notably including several media owners, including: Carlos Slim Helú, the richest person in Latin America, who owns America Movil, one of the largest corporations in the world with 230 million subscribers from Mexico to the Netherlands and Austria, and 17% of the *New York Times*; Ricardo Salinas, who owns TV Azteca; and the Azcárraga family, which owns Televisa/Univisión.

Mexico borders the United States so it's an important production location for many US companies. Additionally, over 30 million US citizens are Mexican-American, while another 10 million US residents were born in Mexico. In the US, 41 million speak Spanish as their first language. Mexico exports $360 billion to the US annually, while Brazil's US exports total just $67 billion a year. In short, Mexico has large and multiple relations with its Northern neighbor, including important cultural, economic, and media connections that contribute to the formation of TNMCs. For instance, the Spanish-language Telemundo and Univisión (now joined with Televisa) are major television networks in the US with more than 5 million primetime viewers. Mexico is Netflix's second largest market, airing several co-productions made with Argos Televisión, which provides many shows for other streaming platforms.

Televisa/Univisión

Televisa, owned by the Azcarraga family, has dominated television in Mexico since the 1950s as the first private television network in Mexico. (Televisa is still Azcarraga-owned, but investors Bill Gates, the Oppenheimer Fund, pension funds, and several private equity firms have become shareholders.) In the early 1990s, Mexican President Carlos Salinas initiated neo-liberal reforms, privatizing many national resources, including public media, and expanded commercial broadcasting. The banking and insurance conglomerate Grupo Salinas purchased several government media for $645 million and established TV Azteca. Grupo Salinas soon challenged Televisa's dominance, attracting about one-third of viewers by 2000.

Open channel television in Mexico reaches 65% of the population, some 80 million viewers. Televisa attracts more than 60% of the national audience on Las Estrellas, the most watched channel, and Canal 5. TV Azteca owns two national networks, with satellite signals reaching 13 countries in Latin America.

Television in Mexico is dominated by this duopoly of Televisa and TV Azteca. The two companies control more than 90% of the national audience. They also are the primary beneficiaries of government advertising. In 2017, Grupo Televisa received 17% of the total and TV Azteca 9.8%, trailed by two other media groups *El Universal* newspaper (2.7%) and Grupo Formula (2.7%). Overall, television companies received 35% of the government's advertising budgets.

Televisa controls 60% of pay television and owns three of the top websites in Mexico. By 2017, Televisa's cable and satellite TV providers held two-thirds of market share. As a functioning TNMC, Televisa also is majority owner of Sky Mexico, a pay television joint venture with ATT/Vrio that produces content and owns several channels in Mexico and Central America.

In April 2021, Televisa merged with Univisión, creating the largest Spanish-language media company in the world. International competition for Hispanic audiences gave way to a transnational partnership that expects to capitalize on shared talent, content, formats, production, and distribution. Televisa brings four free-to-air channels, 253 local stations, 27 pay-TV networks channels and stations, its Videocine movie studio, and the Blim TV streaming services. Televisa joins the Univision and UniMás broadcast networks with its nine Spanish-language cable networks, 61 television stations and 58 radio stations in major US Hispanic markets and Puerto Rico, and digital properties, including its streaming service, PrendeTV (Villafañe, 2021). Two US investment firms, Searchlight Capital and ForgeLight, bought 64% of Univision in 2020, with participation from Google and Sofbank, the Japanese transnational investment firm—making this merger the largest Spanish-language TNMC in the world. Several of Televisa/Univisión's investors have additional TNMC deals: Searchlight has a joint venture with TNMC Liberty Global in Choice Cable, Puerto Rico's second largest provider and owns Canadian telecom Mitel; while Sofbank has multiple investments in other media and telecom TNMCs. In short, Televisa/Univisión not only has considerable TNMC experience, it is globally well-connected with other TNMC co-producers. In Mexico, Televisa replicates proven formulas like telenovelas, reality series, and competition shows that ensure profits, and launched its streaming service Blim to 17 countries in 2016. (For more see https://www.televisainternacional.com/).

Meanwhile, TV Azteca expanded its partnerships for melodramas with Turkish studios and worked with the Turkish distributor Inter Medya for the Mexican remake of Exatlón, a sports reality competition show.

Film Production in Mexico

Rodrigo Gómez has provided a useful overview of the Mexican film industry, explaining that from 1939 to 1992, the film industry was underwritten by the Mexican government, which was an active protector, funder, producer, distributor, and exhibitor. The film industry was controlled by the government as part of the dynamic of the clientelist, centralist, authoritarian, and presidentialist Mexican political system of the second half of the 20th century. At the same time, the government defended the capitalist system and functioned as any other private investor, leading Mexico to have the most developed film industry in Latin America at the time. Film not only raised revenues for the government, it also was a primary component of popular culture, even as Hollywood imports increased in the 1980s (Gómez, 2020, pp. 59–62). When neoliberalism was fully introduced in the 1990s, the film industry was privatized; subsidies were provided to foreign producers but not national studios. The Mexican film industry was gutted as Hollywood imports increased, pay-TV was introduced, and creative labor became precarious. The Mexican government only returned to financing film production in the last two decades, although consolidated distribution and exhibition still privilege Hollywood movies and limit Mexican film releases. Unexpectedly, transnational co-productions and releases on streaming platforms have provided some venues for expanding Latin American, US, and European audiences. After surviving the initial hit from privatization, Mexican film studios such as Argos and Ánima have turned to transnational protocols as a means to stabilize and increase production (Gómez, 2020).

In the early 2000s, Mexico's undeveloped small market not only led actors and directors north to Hollywood it also prompted film studios with limited resources to find transnational partners. "A lack of federal support for project development—a key element in financing international films in the modern era—probably accounts for why so few Mexican films were completed in the early years of the decade. It may also help explain what drove Mexico's top directors to seek more consistent opportunities in the US" (Aguilar, 2016).

As government support improved, foreign investments increased, and TNMC partnerships grew, so did filmmaking. For example, the Mexican-American Esperanto Filmoj studio joined with British Heyday Films to produce the sci-fi thriller *Gravity* (2013) a $700 million hit winning many awards including a Golden Globe, six BAFTA, and several Academy Awards. By 2014, Mexican filmmakers released 130 movies.

Pantelion Films

Pantelion Films is a quintessential TNMC—a joint venture of Televisa, the largest media corporation in Mexico, and the Canadian TNMC film giant Lionsgate. Lionsgate, which includes minority partners Tele-Muchen, Liberty Global, Discovery Communications, and ATT, also has multiple holdings in several media companies in Latin America and Europe. Formed in 2010, Televisa/Lionsgate's Pantelion Films sought to produce movies attractive to Latino audiences that avoided cliched stereotypes (Wollan, 2011). One of the earliest successes was the co-production hit *Instructions Not Included* (2013) earning $100 million. Table 5.1 lists recent Pantelion films.

Ánima Studios

One of the most illustrative TNMC's is the renowned and highly-productive animation firm, Ánima Studios. Based in Mexico, Ánima also has studios in Madrid and Buenos Aires. In the last decade, the studio has produced many

TABLE 5.1 Pantelion Films Since 2017 (Partial List)

Title	Year	Coproduction partners
How to Be a Latin Lover	2017	3Pas Studios
3 Idiotas	2017	Greenlight (India), Bobo (Mexico)
Condorito: La Pelicula	2017	Arronax Animation (US), Pajarraco Films (Colombia)
La Boda de Valentina	2018	Filmadora Nacional (Mexico)
La Leyenda Charro Negro	2018	Ánima Studios (Mexico)
Overboard	2018	MGM (US)
Perfect Strangers	2019	Cinepolis (Mexico)
Rescale de Huevitos	2020	Huevocarbon (Mexico), Sky Mexico, Televisa, ATT

popular movies and television series, most have attracted large audiences and several have received international awards. The bi-lingual animation hit *Top Cat and His Gang* (2011)—a reimagining of the Hanna-Barbera cartoon— co-produced with Illusion Studios (Argentina) was a commercial success in Mexico. The movie was released in Britain and the United States in 2013. A CGI prequel, *Top Cat Begins* was co-produced in 2015 and distributed by Warner Bros. In 2016, Ánima Studios teamed with Canadian animation studio Rainmaker Entertainment to launch the Átomo Network on YouTube with some 10 million subscribers. That same year, the studio's European division, Ánima Kitchent, co-produced PINY (with Televisa and Russian broadcasters Karusel TV and Ani) which aired on Disney Spain. In 2016, Ánima with Televisa's Videocine released the fourth film in the *La Leyenda del Chupacadras* comedy horror animation series; followed by *La Leyenda del Charro Negro* (2018) distributed by TNMC Pantelion in the US; and *Las Leyendas: El Origin*, which had a delayed release due to the pandemic. Since 2017, Ánima Studios has a distribution deal for *Las Leyendas* with Netflix to air its first Latin American original series. The studio also partnered with Colombian Teravision Games to make a mobile game app for *Las Leyendas*.

Adding to its comedy-horror animation genre, Ánima released *Ana y Bruno* (2017) with India's Discreet Arts Production—aired on the TNMC streaming service Pantaya. Ánima and Discreet Arts also partnered on *Monster Island* (2017) which exhibited in theaters in Mexico, South Korea, Spain, France, the UK and the US and then aired as a Netflix movie. In 2018, Ánima Kitchent teamed with Televisa, UK-based MAI Productions, and Spain's Selecta Vision to produce the Spanish-Mexican kids television series *Cleo & Cuquin* aired on Nick Jr. and had English, Spanish, Portuguese, and Russian versions; in 2020 the TNMC series premiered on CCTV in China. Ánima joined with UK Prime Focus World on a CGI animated feature *Here Comes the Grump* (2018) for Italian theaters and was later released to more than 20 countries.

Space Chickens in Space was an Australian-Mexican-British-Irish animated television series (2018–2020) written by Norwegians and co-produced by Ánima, Studio Moshi in Australia, Dublin-based Gingerbread Animation, and Disney Europe. Ánima teamed with the Canadian Pipeline Studios to produce the Netflix series, *Legend Quest: Masters of Myth*, in 2019. In 2020, Ánima and Televisa's Videocine produced the first Spanish-language super-hero animation, *La Liga de los 5*.

As a world recognized, award-winning animation studio, Ánima continues to build transnational partnerships: *Brave Bunnies*, an animated pre-school series of shorts was co-produced by Ánima, the Ukrainian Glowberry, and Italian TNMC De Agostini Editore. Aardman Animations in Britain became the European distributor and ViacomCBS Europe bought rights to air the series beginning in 2021. In 2020, Ánima formed a partnership with Ecuadorian Touché Films to co-produce animations for EnchufeTV, the

TABLE 5.2 Anima Co-productions Since 2017 (Partial List)

Year	Film/TV series	Co-production partners
2017	*Ana y Bruno*	Discreet Arts (India)
2018	*La Leyenda Charro Negro*	Pantelion
2018	*Cleo & Cuguin*	Televisa, MAI (UK), SeleSpacta Vision (Spain)
2018	*Space Chickens*	Moshi (Australia), Gingerbread (Ireland), Disney Europe
2020	*Here Comes Grump*	Prime Focus (UK)
2021	*Brave Bunnies*	Glowberry (Ukraine), DeAgostini (Italy), Aardman (UK)

most successful YouTube channel in Latin America. It would be exceedingly difficult to identify the cultural imprint of any of Ánima Studios animation co-productions, but clearly there is no strand of cultural imperialism in this TNMC. Disney's global reach has been supplemented by multiple award-winning, audience-pleasing transnational productions that undermine past cultural dominance (See Table 5.2)

Smaller TNMC Film Studios

Videocine, Televisa's film studio which also distributes films, backed the Mexican-French co-production of *New Order* (2020). In 2019, Videocine reached a distribution deal with Amazon Latin America to carry all of its films.

Canana Films, a studio founded by Gael Garcia Bernal and telenovela star Diego Luna, has made several highly acclaimed co-productions, including *Eva No Duerme* (2015) with French studios JBA Production and Pyramide, Argentine Haddock Films, and Spain's Tornasol Production; *Mr. Pig* (2016) starring Danny Glover; the bi-lingual action film *Salt and Fire* (2016), directed by Werner Hertzog and co-produced with Arte France Cinema and the US-based Benaroya Pictures; and *Miss Bala* (2019) with Colombia Pictures and Sony.

Endemol Shine Boomdog, the Spanish-language division of French Banijay's Endemol Shine, is a joint venture with a leading independent production company, the Mexico City-based Boomdog. Endemol Shine Boomdog has produced some of the top unscripted reality shows and scripted telenovelas in the region, including: "Mira Quien Baila" (Look Who's Dancing) entering its ninth season on Univision in 2021; "MasterChef Mexico" on TV Azteca; the film *Nicky Jam* (2018) for Telemundo and Netflix; a Spanish version of South Korean talent reality show, *Quien es la Mascara?* co-produced with Televisa; and other television fare. In addition Shine Boomdog has co-production deals with Mexican studios Fabrica de Cine and Chollawood Productions. Following almost 20 years of content development, Televisa and Shine Boomdog renewed their alliance to co-produce Spanish-language series worldwide, including telenovelas and game shows (de la Fuente, 2019). (Also see http://www.endemolshine.us/esboomdog/).

A smaller studio, Argos Comunicación, has co-produced telenovelas with NBC's Telemundo network for years, and also began co-producing with TV Azteca about 15 years ago. Argos has become the most important independent series and telenovela production company for private TV networks and streaming platforms. Argos produces telenovelas for Claro Video in Mexico and Netflix, including *Ingobernable* (2017, 2018).

Colombia

In 1997, the Colombian regime joined the global capitalist push for neoliberal reform, licensing two private television stations—Caracol TV and Radio Cadena Nacional (RCN). The recurring military domination in Colombia politically and economically benefited RCN and Caracol not only by privatizing broadcastings, but also by keeping wages low and intimidating the population. The social inequality and authoritarian repression created an urgent and ongoing need for hegemonic entertainment as a social diversion. Additionally, scriptwriters in Colombia have no rights as authors, giving media owners significantly more control over the creative and distribution process, furthering corporate control over production. These social conditions are bargaining points for local firms inviting TNMC participation: Caracol co-produces telenovelas with Disney for broadcast in Argentina and Peru and has a strategic co-production alliance with NBC Telemundo and RTI Colombia. RCN also has partnerships with Telemundo and Televisa/Univisión.

Caracol

Caracol Television, one of Colombia's most internationally ambitious film and TV production companies, backed the transnational co-production and Oscar-nominated *Embrace of the Serpent* (2015). The Colombian-Argentine-Venezuelan co-production was released in ten languages, including several indigenous. Caracol co-produced Colombia's 2021 Oscar submission to the Best International Feature category, *El Olvido Que Seremos* (2020). Caracol also co-financed the Colombian-Danish-Mexican Cannes' hit *Birds of Passage* (2018) that was released in several languages; and the Brazilian-Colombia-American co-produced *Monos* (2019), a Sundance Award winner. Caracol's ambition and success has been directly related to its willingness and ability to find TNMC partners for production and distribution.

RCN

RCN, owned by the Ardila Lülle Organization is one of the largest television networks in Colombia. In the late 1990s, RCN (Radio Cadena Nacional) also exported *Café con Amora de Mujer* to 77 countries, then co-produced an adaptation with TV Azteca in 2001, Televisa in 2007, and in 2021 with NBC's Telemundo—marking 30 years of regional TNMC partnerships that have replaced US media dominance. Even more impressive was *Yo Soy Betty, la Fea* which became a global phenomenon sold directly or in format to 84 countries, with many remakes and rebroadcasts in dozens of languages, including a five year run on ABC in the US. RCN has a consistent record of TNMC co-productions and format sales. In 2020, RCN partnered again with Televisa on the audience hit *Pa' Quererte*—a remake of the 2017 controversial telenovela *Papa a Todo Madre* that included a gay kiss.

Colombia has become a center of TNMC media production for the region. Teleset is one of Colombia's largest television producers based in Bogotá and operating a studio in Mexico. In 2009, Sony bought into a 50:50 partnership. Teleset produced *La Reina Soy Yo* for Televisa in 2019 and has produced Spanish versions of several foreign shows, such as *Breaking Bad, Dancing with the Stars,* and *Survivor.* TeleColombia is a major television production studio in Bogotá that is majority owned by Disney. In recurring deals, TeleColombia produces telenovelas and other programming for RCN and Televisa/Univisión's UniMás. Another leading television production house in Colombia is RTI (Radio Televisión Interamericana). RTI co-produces many series with Telemundo in the US, Televisa in Mexico, and Caracol in Colombia.

Argentina

With a population of 45 million, Argentina is much smaller than either Brazil or Mexico, but is highly industrialized, producing autos, chemicals, metals, textiles, and agricultural products. Argentina exports more than $65 billion annually, with a GDP of $642 billion in 2017,

Argentina shares the Latin American history as a Spanish colony that created much the same social inequality inherited in Mexico, Brazil, and all other countries in the Southern Hemisphere. For a brief time, post-WWII Peronism gave voice to labor rights and equality, but a growing middle-class of managers and professionals recreated a national identity that placed them as European descendants and champions of civilization atop a social hierarchy above the working class and *cabecitas negras* (Afro-Argentinians). Subsequently, the military overthrew several elected governments. From 1976 to 1983, the military dictatorship's troops and right-wing death squads killed some 30,000, including socialists, trade unionists, students, writers and others considered left-wing. Elections have been held since then, with governments after 1994 adopting neoliberal reforms and privatizing public resources.

In 1974, the Peron government did not renew private television licenses, asserting that Argentina should adopt the European public service model. After the military coup in 1976, the armed forces ran television broadcasting until 1984 when subsequent governments began relicensing private stations. A favorite of most Argentinian governments, the *Clarin* newspaper group was awarded Canal Trece (Channel 13).

Grupo Clarin

Grupo Clarin, formed in 1999, is the largest media corporation in Argentina with annual revenues of over $2 billion. The company owns: *Clarin*, the largest circulating newspaper in Latin America; Cablevisión, the largest cable provider in Argentina, which also reaches Uruguay and Paraguay; and Artrear Canal Trece, the biggest television network in the country, with a 35% audience share. A US private equity group, Fontinalis, has a 9% stake in Grupo Clarin. In 2012, the Kirchner government ordered Clarin to reduce its majority share in Cablevision and release many of its broadcast licenses in excess of anti-trust regulations, but after the new president Mauricio Macri pushed through media deregulation in 2017, Cablevision and Telecom Argentina (owned by Telefonica Spain) merged to form a phone, cable, pay-TV, and streaming company. Artrear and Canal Trece remained intact and expanded. Artrear has two production studios, Pol-ka and Ideas del Sur and owns one-third of Patagonik, with Disney and Cinecolor Argentina each holding one-third. Pol-ka is a major producer of Argentinian telenovelas that are also exported to Uruguay and Paraguay. El Trece has partnered with Turkish studios to broadcast telenovelas in Argentina.

Patagonik

Patagonik is one of the largest film producers in Latin America, releasing over 75 films in the last 20 years—a dozen in the few years just before the CoVid pandemic, including: *Los Que Aman Odion* (In Love and Hate) (2017); the hit comedy *Mama Se Fue de Viaje* (Ten Days without Mom) (2017) that became a 2020 co-production with Canal + called *Ten Days with Dad*, which aired on Netflix; *El Amor Menos Pensado* (An Unexpected Love) (2018); and *La Misma Sangre* (Common Blood) (2019) a co-production with Netflix. (More Patagonik films are described at http://www.patagonik.com.ar/brochure/brochure_patagonik.pdf).

Telefe

Telefe, owned by CBS Viacom, operates nine stations in Argentina with another half dozen affiliate stations, regularly attracting a third of the TV

market. Telefe also owns sister channels in Britain and Australia, offices in
Russia, and exports programs and formats to Eastern Europe, the Philippines,
and Israel. Telefe co-produces telenovelas with Peru's leading television network América Televisión, as well as with Endemol Shine, the French TNMC
owned by Banijay. Telefe also airs Turkish melodramas regularly, has a strategic
partnership with Brazil's religious network Rede Record, and co-produces programs with Comcast's TNT and Telemundo's Argentine studio Underground
Producciones.

Dori Media

The Dori Media Group is a telenovela production company originally formed
in 1996 to export telenovelas to Israel, which was successful. Now Dori includes
production and distribution offices in Israel, Switzerland, Argentina, Spain,
and Singapore. Dori has two cable television stations in Israel and produces
telenovelas, action series, game shows, and kids television. Many of its telenovelas are co-produced Central Park Producciones and Grupo Clarin's studios
Pol-ka and Ideas del Sur studio, among others. *Rampensau* (*Dumb Germany*)
was co-produced with Universum Film (UFA) Germany and released on
RTL's TV station VOX in 2019. In 2020, Dori Media co-produced the telenovela *Losing Alice* with Apple + and the Israeli studio Hot, and distributed by
the Canadian Cineflix Media (which includes the TNMC Participant Media).

Filmsharks

Filmsharks has become a leading co-producer and distributor of films and film
remakes in Latin America. Filmsharks participated in producing the Korean hit
All About My Wife, a remake of the Argentina 2008 film *Un Novio para Mi Mujer*
(*A Boyfriend for My Wife*); contributed to the top Spanish film of 2019 *Padre No
Hay Mas Que Uno* (*There Is Only One Father*) with Atresmedia (a TNMC joint
venture of Bertlesmann's RTL and Spain's Grupo Planeta), Basque's Bowfinger
International, and Amazon; and assisted in the Patagonik/Canal+ 2020 remake
Ten Days with Dad. In 2021 alone, Filmsharks signed distribution deals for
Televisa's Videocine horror film *Come Play With Me*; with Paraguay's Lemon
Cine and Argentina's Pelicano Cine production of the comedy *Charlotte*; with
Spanish-German TNMC Atresmedia, Estela Films, and Warner Bros. for a
remake of the French television series *Camera Café*. Through Filmsharks, Sony
acquired broadcast remake rights to *The Adopters* (2019) and *Ten Days without
Mom* (2021). In each case, Filmsharks not only partnered for distribution but
purchased the remake rights to co-produce the movies.

Filmsharks has found a lucrative and essential spot in the TNMC chain
of production—co-producing films, distributing films, and purchasing and
exchanging rights for remakes of movies that can be reissued for multiple

audiences. Filmsharks performs a vital service to TNMCs across the continent, bringing an expertise for vetting content for cross-cultural and cross-border production and exhibition value. Transnational media have not only restructured ownership and control over content production, while outsourcing creative labor, they have also opened positions for smaller TNMCs like Filmsharks to assist in identifying, repurposing, and then distributing multicultural variations that will attract audiences and investors and produce profits.

A Few Other TNMCs in Latin America

Prisa

The Spanish TNMC Prisa is majority-owned by US private equity firm Liberty Acquisitions Holdings with French TNMC Vivendi holding a 7.6% stake. In turn, Prisa owns 17% of Mediaset España (operating two leading TV stations and a film studio) with Mediaset Italy holding 41%. Prisa represents a crossroads of TNMC partnerships in culturally diverse content production and distribution. Prisa owns Caracol Radio in Colombia; Plural Entertainment in Miami, Madrid, and Lisbon. Plural Entertainment allied with US-based 360POW WOW for the co-production of new television formats. Prisa's also has the joint venture Promofilm Argentina with Spain's Imagina Grupo Globomedia.

Globomedia

Grupo Globomedia is one of the top content producers in Europe with multiple partnerships in Latin America. Globomedia produced over 30 drama series in 2019. It also created more than 150 entertainment programs, and several co-produced feature films. Its Mediapro Group, based in Barcelona, has 13 other production studios, collaborating on productions with Disney, Viacom, Netflix, and Finland's public television network, Yle, among others. Since 2018, Orient Hontai Capital, a Chinese equity firm, has been majority owner partnered with Spain's Imagina Group.

Albavisión

Albavisión, owned by Mexican Remigio Angel González, operates in 11 countries in Latin America with a total of 63 TV channels, 114 radio stations and 2 newspapers. In 2016, Albavisión's Peruvian ATV Group joined with Argentina's Grupo América to produce and distribute television fiction for 15 countries.

Telemundo

Through Telemundo, Comcast/NBC produces primarily for the US Spanish-language audience symbolically paralleling its other programming that promotes consumerism as a preferred way of life. Telemundo owns 28 television stations in the US with some 70 affiliates. In addition to Latin America, Telemundo produces and exports telenovelas to Eastern Europe, the Middle East, Africa, and Australia with offices in Russia, Indonesia, the Philippines, Portugal, China, and Japan. Telemundo also distributes "trendy dramas" by South Korea's KBS to Latin America. Telemundo's programs (dramas, sports, and reality) are syndicated to more than 100 countries in many languages.

The majority of Telemundo's programming consists of first-run telenovelas and series produced by its own studio, many co-produced with other media such as Caracol Television Colombia and Prisa/Grupo Globomedia's Promofilm in Argentina. Telemundo also has joint ventures in production with RTI in Colombia and Argos Comunicación in Mexico. The co-production *La Reina del Sur* first broadcast in 2011 and *El Señor de los Cielos* (2013) posted some of the network's highest ratings with 3.2 million total viewers in 2014—marking a turn to what Telemundo calls "Super Series"—telenovelas with more action, more locations, edgier topics, such as narco-trafficking, in fewer episodes than a typical telenovela (Sianez, 2017).

As part of Comcast/NBC, Telemundo has the necessary resources to provide polished, audience-attractive melodrama series for any national market (while improving Comcast's horizontal integration in production and advertising). In a rebuke to contraflow (Thussu, 2006), Telemundo's use of Televisa writers and formats do not challenge transnational formulas, but "are almost identical" as Telemundo "promotes the acculturation of Latinos in American society," just as Televisa's telenovelas socialize their poor and minority characters to affluent Mexican society (Avila-Saavedra, 2006).

Telenovelas as Transnational Genre

As nations adopted neoliberal programs, cable and satellite television expanded globally. Dozens of television stations needed much more media content. Appearing on the cusp of transnational capitalist reorganization of production and distribution, expertise in telenovela production gave Latin American producers a jump on the competition in global distribution.

Television stations with limited production resources located in countries with smaller audiences had few options but to import regional and transnational telenovelas, temporarily furthering the dominance of the largest six producers: Televisa, Globo, Argentina's Telefe, RCN Colombia, TV Azteca Mexico, and Comcast/NBC's Telemundo (Artz, 2015). Yet, the global media terrain is in constant flux, as transnational media like Comcast and Disney encroach on a formerly nationally-accented telenovela market. In response, Televisa, Globo, RCN, Telefe, Fuji TV in Japan, Korea's KBS, and recently Turkish telenovela producers have adopted many of the same transnational strategies as the reigning leaders, looking for co-productions, joint ventures, and format sales to bolster reach and profit.

Univisión co-produced telenovelas with its partner Televisa on its US channels Galavisión and Unimás (formerly Telefutura). Merged with Televisa, Univisión now is the largest Spanish-language TNMC in the world. Other Latin American television producers have similar transnational owners, co-production partnerships, and distribute through transnational agreements. Thus, Rede Globo and Univisión/Televisa "do not really belong to Latin America, nor to its nations, but to the transnational family of the proponents of late capitalism market expansion (Vujnovic, 2008, p. 435). Additionally, the media market has technologically expanded in the last decade with internet platforms and mobile devices offering video-on-demand streaming services and other means for distribution. TNMC desire for greater distribution has spurred commercial innovation in digital technology as a means for selling more communication hardware and exhibiting media content. TNMC content is now delivered through multiple channels "to establish a brand around the original content and create a long-term relationship with the audience—cum—consumer" and to expand merchandising of products from the fictional world of melodrama to actual retail products (Lippert, 2013, p. 92).

Series and serialized melodramatic fiction have many variations that closely contain and construct the form with identifiable codes and conventions: the wardrobe, the décor, the slang and the music presented communicate the cultural values of consumerism and capitalist success.

A number of defining narrative characteristics can be discerned. Spain's Tele5 considers nine characteristics typical of telenovelas: sentimentalism, a happy ending for the central couple, easy-to-follow stories, simple dialog, female-centered narrative, family complications, high drama and suspense, everydayness and local color, and easily recognized archetypical characters" (Smith, 2013, p. 229). The most prevalent conventions are obviously the melodramatic style—identified by highly personalized story lines with actors emoting strong feelings and emotions. Most contemporary melodramas feature romantic narratives, frequently family-centered. Recent telenovelas present strong, independent women as business owners, matriarchs, even drug lords—although the plots have women choosing motherhood, romance, and usually marriage—reinforcing patriarchy with an entrepreneurial face. As part of TNMCs global hopes for distribution and profit, telenovelas narrate a universal story of poor and rich falling in love and overcoming obstacles to their romance. Indicative of the hegemonic need to attract non-elite audiences, melodramas recount tales of social mobility and affluence—working class, women, and ethnic minorities succeed through hard work, love and marriage, and with luck reach the desired promised land of affluence. Of course, social mobility requires internalizing dominant cultural mores and practices, as acted out by protagonists and subordinates. Most melodramas from Mexico, Colombia, Brazil, and the US exude an aspirational desire for affluence as the path to happiness, mixing economic success with romance, beautiful travel scenery, and traditional aesthetics (Siriyuvasak, 2010). Predominant novela images highlight middle-class urban families finding a happy ending, often through the ritual of romantic wedding of lead characters and some form of financial success.

Beyond these several narrative conventions, some national distinctions (reflecting the operating political economy and dominant social norms) can be discerned, again allowing for individual creative variations. US soaps depict strong, independent business women with personal family and relationship problems set in fictional locations; telenovelas by Telemundo and Univisión likewise occur in unidentifiable locales with geographically indistinct "pan-Latino" characters; Mexico's Televisa has effectively marketed more conservative ahistorical family dramas about good and evil, usually with no discernible real location; O Globo's Brazilian telenovelas are more frequently framed by contemporary social issues, local settings, and popular dialect and colloquial idioms; Colombian telenovelas are often lighter fare with more humor and irony; in Spain, "culebrones" (literally "snakes") with complex plots are referred to as "tear-jerkers" for their frequently heavy emotional dialog.

Television in general and telenovelas in particular appear magical, fulfilling the viewer's need for entertainment and emotional release, especially for populations that still have pockets of illiteracy. Melodrama characters are charismatically drawn as impassioned stereotypes, making them accessible to diverse cultural and social groups. Indeed, the dominant narratives and themes are so universal that they relate not only to local audiences, but can be exported widely. In short, telenovelas convey meanings about gender, race, class, and sexuality, as well as exuding themes of individual social mobility through personal material success. The traditional conventions and codes of RCN's global hit series *Yo Soy, Betty la Fea* traveled easily to other countries embracing consumer capitalism. Recognizable codes for unattractiveness—heavy eyebrows, stainless steel braces, thick glasses, unkempt hair, and unremarkable, unconventional dress—occurred as a prelude to Betty's transformation through romance and stylistic make-over, intimating the rewards obtained by personal effort, individual consumption, deference to authority, and romantic love. Even a casual comparison of the after images of all the Betties across dozens of countries reveals the standardization of commercial norms: everywhere a hidden beauty blossoms through designer fashion and personal make-over; everywhere the revealed standardized beauty finds love, success, and happiness by questioning but then accepting the rules and authoritative cultural norms. This is not US cultural imperialism. Colombia's *Yo Soy, Betty la fea* format was made-to-order for the TNMC consumer market and advertisers. In every country, in every variation, the multicultural narrative themes for Betty were the same: an underdog outsider achieves romantic and financial success through honest hard work and a fashion and social makeover. Feisty individualism, consumerism, and willing assimilation to dominant authority leads to happiness.

As in all series melodrama, the protagonist's happiness is a clue to the moral value of her social condition. In the Czech version, *Osklivka Katka*, Katka/ Betty is the heroine of "utopian capitalism," a post-Soviet "enchantment with the market and uncritical worship of the skills that enable a neo-liberal economy to operate" (Reifová & Sloboda, 2013, p. 200). In all cases, the heroine begins as an unrefined, unconventional less-than-perfectly-attractive female worker. In each case, her individual traits of honesty, loyalty, and integrity move her toward personal success in romance and career. Going beyond cultural imperialism, the content variations of all telenovelas follow the universal narrative structure, purpose, and effect. TNMC cultural hegemony turns personal challenges into a prop by requiring the female protagonist to either be or become beautiful according to consumerist standards, fashion, style, makeover and all. *Betty* may be the exemplary TNMC template, but many, many other telenovelas have traveled across cultures using creative local versions of thoroughly standardized formats. refuting claims of both resistive cultural contraflow and domination by cultural imperialism.

As successful examples of contemporary TNMC structures and practices, telenovelas validate the TNMC thesis that interlocks among consenting capitalist class leaderships result in similarities in the structure of production and entertainment content. TNMC telenovelas also confirm the cultural hegemony thesis that multicultural and consensual TNMC content expresses the norms, practices, and ideologies amendable to capitalist social relations—without attachment to any specific dominant national culture. Hyperindividualism and the individualization of the social world as an epistemology has no national identity, rather it is an ideological trope advanced for the capitalist class globally and locally. Telenovelas, and for that matter, most other TNMC genre from game shows and sit-coms to reality programs ceaselessly offer narratives and vocabularies restricting social and political issues to personal and familial terms. Making stories more personal may bring social issues closer, but telenovelas never traverse the return journey: societal solutions to individual problems are never broached. Poverty weighs on characters, but policies and practices contributing to social inequality such as access to education, health care, and capital resources are out of bounds.

The narratives of TNMC productions echo the ads and product merchandising as the stories themselves are morality plays about affluence and wealth being protagonist goals and markers of success, happiness, and goodness. In general, telenovelas and serial melodramas advance transnational capitalist interests through creative variations that repeat the standardized image of the cosmopolitan elite urban individual—slim, beautiful, and well groomed. A structured product perfectly suited for the marketing of a wide range of products—from cosmetics to clothing and home appliances. There is nary a melodrama that does not applaud the middle class lifestyle as the common sense social norm. Remarkably, beyond occasional background scenes, telenovelas have few depictions of actual physical, manual labor—"invisible work is made present only through its effects: wealth and social status" (Reifová & Sloboda, 2013, p. 193). Instead, television and telenovelas in particular seem preoccupied with displaying fashion, tastefully decorated apartments, sleek automobiles, and other accoutrements of affluence.

For several decades in response to critiques of cultural imperialism, Latin America telenovelas have been held up as evidence of national resistance to global media; international exports from Latin America seemingly gave proof of contraflow against that same global media regime (Straubhaar, 1991). Yet, local and global success of the genre is only part of the story. From the broader more complete perspective of cultural hegemony, telenovelas appear as TNMC productions accommodating and reinforcing global capitalism—flowing with culturally-diverse complementary themes of consumerism, individualism, and market values seeping through each storyline.

Telenovelas do not contain alternative cultural representations, nor are national cultural markers the issue. Rather, in the 21st century, telenovelas have moved to the center of transnational media strategy—complementing animation, action movies, and fantasy. It is of little significance where media content geographically originates because production and distribution occur within and through transnational media processes. Most claims of contraflow, cultural proximity, and cultural imperialism analytically stress the presence or absence of local production and reception. The successful local and national distribution of telenovelas rests on more substantive components: (1) the ability of TNMCs to profit from low wages paid to skilled workers under the existing political economy; (2) the benefits from co-productions and joint ventures that lower risks and increase audience size and corporate profits; (3) government neoliberal regulations that privilege commercial entertainment and foreign investment; and (4) dependence on advertising revenues for production, requiring apolitical audience-friendly entertainment genre, structurally and ideologically siding with market relations and individual consumerism.

Adopting the commercially-funded media model set the DNA of Latin American media (whether it is of US progeny, or not) while neoliberal deregulation on behalf of global and national capitalist interests restructured the social relations of media production that now occurs with corporate media partnered across nations. As capitalist firms large and small join transnational relations of production (through mergers, co-productions, joint ventures) they also reproduce unequal social relations by employing skilled and unskilled casual labor, contracting temporary creative workers, outsourcing post-production and distribution, and implementing other practices that alienate the men and women who do most of the work domestically or abroad in local adaptations. The issue clearly is not the national address or reified cultural identity of the media corporation, but one of capitalist social relations and transnational ownership and control of the means of producing news and entertainment.

The history of Grupo Globo's symbiotic relationship with the military regime illustrates clearly the entwining of class goals and media practices in Brazil, both of which benefitted from coercion and intimidation complemented by evening telenovela entertainment. RCN's ability to sell cheap telenovelas around the world and participate in co-productions with other TNMCs is primarily a result of the low wages and wretched working conditions enforced by the Colombian military. Moreover, admitting that commercial local media opt for the transnational media formulas of standardized entertainment themes emphasizing individualism and consumerism undermines any assertions about cultural imperialism and North American domination. What appears instead is exemplary complementary programming for *transnational* capitalist cultural hegemony. In terms of content, telenovelas exhibit an internal consistency in format and ideological themes, providing significant homogeneous multicultural ingredients. TNMCs reap the profits while winning consent for capitalist cultural hegemony. The moral of the story: individualism, self-interest, authority, and consumerism reign. These televisual texts constrain audience meanings by their conventions, codes, and ideologies, as well as by the imposed expectations accorded the dramas through constant repetition. Narratives promote self-gratifying individualism, consumerism, a faith in romantic love with affluent happiness, and adherence to the authority of status quo institutions and dominant cultural norms, laced with edgy critiques accepted or tolerated by lead characters.

In a transnational world intent on spreading consumerism, the dreams of happiness provided by telenovelas have a universal value for audience appeal and commodity sales. Significantly, TNMC producers of contemporary telenovelas have perfected their hegemonic creativity, incorporating cultural diversity, gender equality, and infrequent challenges to capitalist social relations within their narratives and images as much as possible—all in service to supporting a hierarchical, authoritarian social order, whether the family patriarch as in Bollywood movies, the military structures in Chinese action adventures, or family obligations and elite authority in telenovelas. Mimicking other genre themes, telenovela messages and the values they endorse are consistent across programs, formats, merchandising, and national or TNMC content. Audiences, whether viewing local productions, adaptations, or TNMC series, find romance, social mobility, and the comfort of affluent happy endings in every offering. Moreover, each program is replete with advertising messages that reinforce conforming individualist consent to the authority of the market, the consumer culture, the status quo (as personally modified in any particular show), and continued spectatorship.

Importantly, Univisión/Televisa, Telemundo, Caracol, or any other TNMC or national producer cannot advocate for the democratic aspirations of their viewers as citizens, because they are limited by their entanglement with capitalism and its cultural hegemony. Indeed, "telenovelas are only partly a cultural product of Latin American identity [as constructed by TNMCs], but more largely the carriers of the broader values" of transnational capitalism (Vujnovic, 2008, p. 439). Instances of TNMC relations provide evidence that the cultural hegemony of the new international division of labor flexibly accommodates contributions from aspiring TNMCs offering new and creative cultural commodities. Telenovelas represent the transnational political economy of corporate interlocked production and distribution by geographically dispersed labor. Geographically-isolated and socially-atomized workers make content promoting consumerism and reproducing capitalist social relations. The genre exemplifies how the drive for profit adjusts to the expectations and habits of particular cultures, as TNMCs incorporate experiences and challenges in the fashion most appropriate for securing hegemony and reproducing the social relations of power best suited for transnational capital including its domestic members.

While telenovelas express the cultural values of their audiences, they also make narrative accommodations within the political and economic conditions of each nation to maximize audiences for sale to advertisers—defined above all by the absence of social conflict. Social conflicts at best appear as a prompt or problem for individual actions. Thus, RCN uses more humor and avoids stirring political controversy in a repressive, militarized state like Colombia, while Rede Globo features social issues like AIDS, fertility, gender identity, and race discrimination to tap into popular concerns in the more socially open Brazilian society. In fact, Rede Globo's evocation of social issues in its telenovelas illustrates its effective cultural leadership for transnational capitalist hegemony.

TNMC telenovela production requires considerable reciprocity among producers and broadcasters. Thus, while European, North American, and Asian TNMCs export to Latin America, Latin American TNMCs have sought markets in the US, Europe, and more recently in Africa. Following the rapid neoliberalization of the African broadcasting market, there was a rapid increase in television channels in Africa, By 2015, Africa had more than 500 stations in 54 countries—immediately raising demands for more content (de la Fuente, 2015). The growing expansion of TNMCs like the French Canal+ and the South African DStv Multi-Choice, owned by global internet giant Naspers (which owns 30% of China's Tencent and 28% of Russia's Mail.ru). Within the context of neoliberal capitalism, the arrival of streaming platforms and a continued reliance on advertising drove many African producers toward transnational partnerships developing longer serialized forms like telenovelas and series melodramas. Satellite and internet distribution facilitated the export of telenovelas beyond markets defined by culture or language—indicating their appeal to diverse cultures in many nations. In this mix, "new channels entirely dedicated to Latin American telenovelas sponsored by Globo, Telemundo, and Televisa have emerged" (Jedlowski & Rêgo, 2018). In Africa, "cheap to produce and readily available 24/7 on niche channels, telenovelas have proved themselves popular for their adaptation to local cultures" (Jedlowski & Rêgo, 2018). Indeed, telenovelas are no longer under the sole control of Brazilian, Mexican, and Colombian media, as studios in the US, Turkey, Spain, Kenya, Côte d'Ivoire, Indonesia, Taiwan, South Korea, and the Philippines have begun to produce and export their own serialized dramas.

The Côte d'Ivoire company, Côte Ouest—the exclusive African distributor for Globo—has become a continental leader in dubbing and distributing telenovelas across the continent, providing content to more than 155 channels with plans to co-produce African versions of Globo's series. In 2014, Venevision and TV Azteca partnered with Africa XP to launch Romanza + Africa which reaches 4.5 million Kenyan subscribers on the digital network Bamba TV. Meanwhile, Telemundo partnered with Nasper's DStv whose signal covers the English-speaking countries of the sub-Sahara. DStv also airs the Portuguese-language Globo telenovelas to Angola and Mozambique. Nina TV, a satellite channel covering most of Africa, partnered with Globo and Côte Ouest to broadcast African and Brazilian telenovelas in French and English. The 2018 special issue of *Journal of African Cultural Studies* revealed that Mexican telenovelas still have had a major impact on popular culture in Ghana, Uganda, Kenya, Tanzania, Cameroon, Nigeria, and Côte d'Ivoire— albeit not rising to the level of cultural imperialism.

While some African viewers consider telenovelas "too white," they are nonetheless well-received by millions of Africans "not because they are able to offer a model of modernity that is 'parallel' to the western one, but rather because they represent a fantastic world of ideal modern consumerism, an ideal world that creates value out of the erasure of its cultural specificities" (Jedlowski & Rêgo, 2018). In other words, as argued throughout this book, cultural imperialism has been shoved aside as transnational media promote a multiculturally diverse world of individual consumerism. Thus, the emergence of TNMCs do not indicate the imperialist imposition by any particular nation. Instead, TNMCs produce entertainment and ideologies for a global capitalist class leadership. Above all, telenovelas are hegemonically effective in Africa and elsewhere because they bring the viewer into a magical world of consumerism and romantic love, while putting emphasis on individual self-interest, family structures, and gender roles that reinforce and tolerate existing social, racial, and ethnic inequalities. Latin American telenovelas in Africa and African serial co-productions indicate that melodramas do not belong to one particular culture or nation, rather their production and distribution reveals the powerful processes of commercialization and transnational media relations.

Serials in particular—like film franchises with prequels, sequels, and spin-offs—cultivate consuming publics for the cultural landscape of the genre, its themes, and ultimately its dominant ideologies. As Jedlowski & Rêgo (2018) noted "commercial competition provoked by the introduction of satellite and digital broadcasting in recent years pushed producers toward stronger investment in longer serials," increasing co-productions, joint ventures, and TNMC mergers. At the same time, the desire for recognition (and income) by creative producers contributed to their participation in the transnational flow of culture and capital as they strove to have their content distributed through capital-intensive TNMC channels. As telenovelas and other genre are adopted and adapted by producers and audiences from different societies and countries outside of Latin America, we can expect that their ideological influence will also spread.

Transnational relations, of course create many interactive networks, as Turkish telenovela producers discovered. With trade between Latin America and Turkey increasing to $10 billion, Latin American and Turkish media made their own lucrative connections. Kanal D TV in Turkey produced *Binbir Gece* (*One Thousand and One Nights*) that aired to large audiences on Chile's TNMC Mega TV (which is 27% owned by Discovery Network). The series was then broadcast in 14 other Latin American countries. Since 2016, Caracol TV in Colombia broadcast *Elif*, the story of a six-year old separated from her mother. *Elif* was produced by Kanal 7, a Turkish TNMC co-owned by CBS Viacom, Doğan Holding, and Koç Holding, the largest industrial conglomerate in Turkey (ttvnews, 2020). Caracol followed in 2021 with *Omer, Sueños Robados* (*Wounded Birds*) another production by Kanal D. Moreover, as an integral part of the TNMC revenue chain, Turkish telenovelas are distributed in Latin America, Sweden, the Philippines, and Spain by Eccho Rights, a division of the South Korean TNMC CJ Entertainment (which also has a joint venture with Warner for reality television production). "Turkish melodramas are a new phenomenon, only [appearing] in the last decade. They started in the Turkish republics, then to the Balkans, then to the Middle East, and now Latin America" (Asli Turç in Kaplan, 2016). Turkish melodramas are "typically slower and more drawn out than English-language shows. Men are often portrayed as exceptionally romantic and emotions are exaggerated… Similarities between the regions' shows are not a coincidence. For decades, Turks watched imported telenovelas" (Kaplan, 2016).

These days, Turkish series are designed for Latin American television to fit the shorter, daily time-slots of telenovelas. More significantly, following the initial success of Turkish imports, new transnational media alliances have emerged: TIMS&B Productions Turkey signed a co-development deal with Spain's Plano a Plano; Miami-based Somos Distribution has brokered dozens of series; Turkish distributor Inter Medya has several co-production and distribution deals, including the Turkish sports reality competition show Exatlon with new versions aired in local languages in Mexico, Colombia, Romania, Hungary, and the US (Larrea, 2019). Media in "Argentina, Chile, and Mexico made their bets strongly on Turkish telenovelas" which are very popular with audiences (Durnay, Lopes, & Neves de Sousa, 2018, p. 38). In other words, TNMCs share experiences and practices to improve audience appeal while maintaining market norms, advertising, and the consumerist ideology. "Turkish television dramas often juxtapose the lives of glamor in Istanbul's big mansions and the feudal oppression of rural lives. They feature dangerous love stories and power games with all the classic archetypes of a soap opera. The distinct class differences in most of these dramas are clear-cut, often fantasized accounts of class differences that are far from reality" (Güler, 2014). None of this was led or orchestrated by US media. In fact, as evidence that an increasingly shared transnational entertainment culture has supplanted US cultural imperialism, "millions of people across Latin America now demand Turkish soaps as their entertainment" (Tomaselli, 2019). The same is true for Hispanic audiences in the US, where Televisa/Univisión free streaming service PrendeTV now has a Turkish drama channel called Amor Turco (Turkish Love) (Vivarelli, 2021).

With the exception of Turkey's Videomite, which has partnered with Netflix and Amazon and signed a joint venture with Zillion Film in Serbia in 2020, most Turkish film studios have made very few transnational co-productions. However, Turkish melodrama exports continue to grow and co-production remakes attract TNMCs. Some critics of Turkey's Prime Minister Recep Erdogan have suggested that melodramas are part of a deliberate agenda to spread Turkish influence. Turkish dramas set viewing records in Chile and Argentina and families even began naming their children after favorite Turkish characters (Kaplan, 2016). Still, even with increased Turkish television imports, it would be irrational to claim Turkish cultural imperialism has invaded Latin America.

Clearly, whether within Latin America or with media in Europe, Asia, Africa, and the Middle East, the global flow of telenovela entertainment from production and distribution to audience reception is effectively *transnational*—multiple companies from multiple nations collaborate to maximize audiences and profits. In general, the plots and themes of melodramas, soaps,

TABLE 5.3 Recent Turkish Dramas Aired on Televisa/ Univisión (Partial List)

2018	In Between—Entre Dos Amores
2019	Eternal Love—Amor Eterno
2020	Sefirin Kizi—La Hija del Embajador
2020	Fatmagul—Qué Culpa Tiene Fatmagül?
2020	Erkenci Kus—Pájaro Soñador
2021	Forbidden Love—Amor Prohibido
2021	A Thousand and One Nights—Las Mil y Una Noches

and telenovelas share the same cultural and ideological messages fundamental to neoliberal capitalism: austerity, self-interest, and consumer choice.

In fact, in the long run, as transnational dictates increasingly lead media production to global export, series melodramas are likely to display even more universal similarities as they offer multinational casting, diverse locations, and stories to appeal to culturally diverse audiences while creatively blending working class challenges into their broadcasts. Illustrative of TNMC symbiotic economic relations with advertisers, scripts are written to have "natural" pauses at prescribed commercial breaks. Convention requires that each episode be interrupted a number of times by commercials and that scenes preceding each commercial break end with a tag line enticing enough that viewers will stay tuned. Meanwhile, product placement has become the global norm.

Broadcasting schedules are adjusted to maximize target audiences. Rede Globo moved *Betty* to a different night and ratings increased dramatically, increasing ad rates as well. Rede Globo has perfected "interaction" with their viewers to increase ratings and ad sales, adjusting scripts based on audience surveys that reveal storyline and character preference, providing on-line forums for audience feedback, and promoting telenovela-themed magazines, talk show interviews, and news about telenovela stars and characters.

Not only do TNMC and nationally-produced telenovelas in Latin America lack any cultural contraflow against receding US and European dominance, they also omit positive representations of working men and women and racial, ethnic, and indigenous groups, nor is there any advocacy for democracy. This is not by accident, but by design. TNMC producers, screenwriters, and directors marshal techniques, stylistic frames, and narrative cues that articulate meanings desired by their corporate employers. Dominant frames and cues provide recognizable codes for producers and viewers alike. For instance, camera close-ups code intensity and importance for the image framed. Reverse angle shots direct character interaction. Midrange shots set the scene for character performances. Long range shots indicate geographic location as well as features of the location that affect the storyline: overhead of an entire city in morning or evening code different events as opening an episode or moving an episode to a new time and situation. Overhead shots of a city might emphasize its vibrant energy or from a different angle and location its gritty realism. Backlighting brings an aura of beauty or sensuality. Music volume, rhythm, and beat enhance suspense, levity, or climax in a narrative. Local and staged settings (interior and exterior) and backdrops help frame the scene, spurring anticipation and expectation by viewers of what might transpire. The physical appearance, make-up, and costuming of actors also codes meaning: Betty with braces and frumpy clothes cues unsophistication; Betty without eyeglasses, in heels and stylish dress cues her transformation. Cars, clothes, furniture, appliances, and accessories help define the social class or "success" of characters in such scenes. Dialog, including the use of colloquialisms, stereotypical accents, or "neutral" Spanish and language in general encodes character familiarity or distance from viewers. Overall, directors, screenwriters, and producers have many technical devices and cultural cues that assist in encoding meaning. Unsurprisingly, messages trumpet upper middle-class values and norms.

While telenovelas use the same technical devices and cultural artifacts that are available to all televisual media production, they are used in distinct and identifiable ways. In general, melodrama employs intimate camera close ups, relies on interior scenes more than exterior shots, employs stereotypical artifacts to indicate social class, often asks actors for more emotive performances, and inserts evocative musical cues to reinforce desired viewer reaction to the narrative. Audiences get some vicarious relief from the burden of very real social conditions that telenovelas do nothing to disrupt. Social mobility storylines do not translate to actual social mobility or social change in society. Telenovelas perform their hegemonic function wonderfully—attracting and pleasing audiences looking for voices that challenge inequality—containing voices and images within the narrative and plot that effectively reinforce tacit consent for life on the ground. In essence, stories and characters in series melodramas provide texts and images that reveal selected non-specific culturally-diverse representations, preferred behavioral norms, and ideological themes important for transnational cultural hegemony. Pick almost any series from any station in any country over the last decade and similar images and narratives will appear. The following are just two representative examples.

Avenida Brasil (2012)

Rede Globo's international mini-series *Avenida Brasil* (Brazil Avenue) (2012) raised the melodrama bar even by telenovela standards. *Avendia* still holds the largest audience share ever, only approached by *Força do Querer* (*Edge of Desire*) in 2017, which addressed gender identity.

Set in a contemporary Brazilian middle-class suburb, the story follows Nina, an orphaned girl who seeks revenge on her evil stepmother. Carminha, the stepmother, revels in fashion, luxury, and consumption but because she behaves badly she is clearly undeserving of the affluence. Nina, with the help of friends and loves—including a soccer star—eventually realizes that individual happiness and her own economic success won't be served by revenge. During its six month run, weekly ratings drew 50% of the television audience. Eighty million viewers watched the final episode. The novela was successful because it respected the behavior of the new middle class, their clothes, values and aspirations. The characters were proud of their origins in *Avenida Brasil*, place that in spite of being poor was cheerful and warm. *Avenida* highlighted the new middle class and also changed the way the country saw itself (Bevins, 2013).

Avenida was an advertiser's dream, regularly reaching the 35 million new middle class consumers in Brazil. A beauty supply product line was launched based on the fictional Monalisa hair salon along with sales of jewelry and clothing based on the novela's characters. Although telenovelas typically feature rich aristocratic leads, *Avenida* breaks new ground for Globo by idealizing the semi-affluent lifestyle of a happy middle class. Apparently the reality of social inequality precludes much upward mobility, as producers have opted to settle for a narrative of the middle class comfortable in its social position. "Oi, Oi, Oi" (Hi, Hi, Hi), *Avenida*'s opening theme song and subsequent popular music track invites all to enjoy life one step out of the favela. One doesn't need to be rich in the new Brazil, just have enough to buy products appropriate for your station. The newly endowed professional middle class in Brazil benefitted from neoliberal adjustments, earning a few more rials. Rede Globo and their advertisers had ample suggestions for what could be consumed. This carefully constructed telenovela epitomizes the theme and values of transnational capitalism that exacerbates social inequality and hierarchy, while depending on TNMC mass entertainment to mollify masses of working class, women, and youth and simultaneously encourage increased individualism and consumerism.

La Reina del Sur (2011, 2019, 2020) and Queen of the South (2016–2021)

The first season of *La Reina* was co-produced by Telemundo, RTI Producciones Colombia, and the TNMC Antena 3 (now Artesmedia) owned by Spanish-Italian Grupo Planeta and Bertlesmann's RTL Germany. The following seasons were co-produced by Telemundo and Netflix. The series depicted the rise of Teresa Mendoza, a young woman from Mexico who becomes the most powerful drug trafficker in southern Spain. The second season picks up eight years after the 2011 finale when Mendoza became pregnant. Mendoza was living an isolated but idyllic life under witness protection in Tuscany Italy, but the kidnapping of her daughter forces her to go back to the narco-trafficking world. To save her daughter, Teresa returns to deal with her old enemies. In an exceedingly transnational flourish, the second season was filmed in over 300 locations including Italy, Russia, Romania, Spain, Belize, Colombia and the US. With a $10 million budget, *La Reina*'s first season of 63 episodes was the second most expensive telenovela produced by Telemundo, after the narco-telenovela, *El Señor de los Cielos* (*Lord of the Skies*) (2013–2020).

Queen of the South, an adaptation of *La Reina del Sur*, premiered on USA Network in 2016 and ran for five seasons—62 episodes in all—fewer than one season of *La Reina*. In *Queen*, Mendoza lived in a Sinaloa barrio where she fell in love with a member of a drug cartel. She tried to rise above her impoverished conditions, but her boyfriend was murdered and she fled to the United States. To get vengeance and survive, Mendoza eventually started her own drug business and became very wealthy. Her activities took her to Bolivia,

Malta, Mexico, and Texas, Arizona, and New Orleans in the US. The teleno-vela was filmed in over 200 locations, and Telemundo producers announced that season five will also feature multiple locales.

These two telenovelas, the first in Spanish, the second an English-language remake, are both based on the novel *La Reina del Sur* by Spanish author Arturo Pérez-Reverte. The telenovelas are variations that chronicle how a naïve and abused Mexican woman, Teresa Mendoza, flees violence, but using her wits, financial acumen, and sexuality rises to become an international drug lord—the Queen of the South, in Spain in the first version, in the US in the second. Consistent with other telenovelas, *Reina* and *Queen* bring characters and viewers close to peace and happiness, only to crash any tranquility with traumatic events—no one is ever allowed to be safe and happy for long in the telenovela universe. "Beneath all the drama, the characters serve as a stand-in for us…You can never live the life you want to live but, like one of television's beleaguered heroines, always have to watch your plans smashed to pieces" (Marshall, 2016).

Perhaps the most significant element of *La Reina* and *South* is the prom-inence of the strong female protagonist. With an independent, resourceful, and ultimately successful female, these telenovelas appear to unsettle the tra-ditional telenovela messages of women as subservient, virtuous, and passive— what Sanchez, Whittaker, Hamilton, and Zayas (2016) termed "marianismo" (p. 396). For decades, women appeared as crime family members, sexualized drug runners, or high class call girls. Telenovelas portrayed leading female characters as dependent on men for protection, romance, and security— conveyed by a narrative that follows a poor girl's social mobility made possible by love of a rich man. Any woman with power was depicted as ambitious, self-centered, and malevolent. Throughout, women were often subjected to sexual harassment, abuse, and coerced sex, including rape. *La Reina* and *Queen* still objectified women with continual portrayals of sexual abuse, rape, scantily-dressed women, and sex workers. In the first two episodes alone, Mendoza is raped, kidnapped, and beaten. Throughout the series, Mendoza frequently uses her sexuality, physical appearance, and sensual behavior to gain access to resources and allies. Still, unlike other telenovela females, Mendoza smoked, drank tequila, used vulgarities, intelligently expressed her views, and was a morally ambiguous anti-heroine. At the same time, her beauty, fashion, and sexuality drew the attention of other characters and viewers.

Mendoza was independent and seemingly emoted female empowerment, but at crucial moments in the series, she depended on male protection—first from her boyfriend, then from a Russian drug operative, Oleg Yasikov, and her loyal bodyguard El Pote. Moreover, her sexuality appeared as key to her empowerment. "She consistently showed her femininity and sensuality by making her presence known as she dressed elegantly and wore refined make-up and hair" (Sianez, 2017). Mendoza used sex for strategic advantage.

Additionally, *La Reina* repeats the apparent narco-telenovela ingredient of rape, exhibited in Univisión's *La Piloto* (2017–2018) and RTI/Televisa/Caracol's *La Viuda Negra* (2014, 2016). Toward the end of *La Reina* and *Queen,* Mendoza suspends her narco-career for motherhood and (according to hints from *Queen's* Telemundo producers) she may find romance fulfilled with the return of her love interest. Either way, the choice for women in telenovelas, even ones as resilient and determined as Mendoza, is between a successful career or family—both apparently dependent on physical appearance and sexuality.

In addition to the contradictory assertion of female independence, *Reina* and *Queen* demonstrate that individual skills, physical attributes, and determination can lead to power and wealth, represented by fashion, consumer goods, housing, travel, and social class. In the beginning, Mendoza was uneducated, used rough language, and had crude social attributes. Mentored by men and women with higher class status, she develops a more refined appreciation of fashion, style, and expensive acquisitions. In fact, *La Reina* unfolds a bit like the make-over in *Soy, la Fea Betty*—only with more violence and a line of cocaine. The poor girl doesn't marry a rich man, but she assimilates to the norms and behaviors of the upper crust of a hierarchical and authoritarian society nonetheless. Any audience effects from narco-telenovelas will not likely move viewers to become drug runners, but they may feel comforted by the familiar promotion of acquisition and physical appearance as the means to happiness and the not-so-subtle stereotypical disparagement of gender, class, and ethnicity.

Overall, *La Reina del Sur* and *Queen of the South* present appealing stories that incorporate elements of traditional telenovelas with contemporary and controversial challenges. However, critiques of inequality or discrimination are overcome by reimaging how gender, ethnicity, and social class can be accommodated by a few modest adjustments to existing social relations. Mendoza may use her wits and intelligence—that upends the norms for female behavior—but the scriptwriters determine she must repeatedly rely on her sexuality playing to the "male gaze." Even when expectations for female characteristics were subverted, the narrative of *La Reina* still "reified gender traits" (Dunn & Ibarra, 2015, pp. 122–123, 135). In addition, hierarchies of race and class frequently informed character attributes and potential, while the storylines privileged values associated with white, European wealth. Virtuous and sinful, intelligent and sexual, Latina and refined—the new, assimilated Queen demanded and won admittance to the very social order that created the inequalities and difficulties that defined her journey. TNMC hegemony could not find a much better hegemonic message.

From *Avenida Brasil* to *Queen of the South* in Mexico and the US, telenovelas attract viewers to highly-personalized dramatic stories of survival and fulfillment, increasingly using spectacle and cultural diversity to hold viewers attention. Unsurprisingly, these are the same melodramatic narratives that propel TNMC television in other countries: *Breaking Bad, The Sopranos,* and *Deadwood* in the US; *Peaky Blinders* and *Luther* in Britain; *Prison Playbook* and *Woman of Dignity* in South Korea; or *Tatort* in Germany; among others.

Beyond Telenovelas

While new entertainment continues to be filled with national and cultural cues, whether Brazilian telenovelas in English or Turkish telenovelas with Spanish subtitles, the widespread practice of remaking successful narratives and formats has produced a "transnational culture of certain narratives that have been produced across the globe" (Piñon, 2014, p. 221). In fact, "a generalized trend can be observed towards the appropriation of formats, styles, and products," including Turkish and Korean telenovelas, high-end "super-series," and reality programs (Burnay, Lopes, & Neves de Sousa, 2018, p. 39). The debate between cultural imperialism and cultural proximity has been overtaken by a transnational cultural hybridity that adapts formats with a neutral, middle-class pan-Latino identity and language promoting an apparently classless culture of consumerism. Transnational co-productions incorporate cultural diversity in their multinational casting of actors, the spectacle of multiple geographic locations, and versions adapted for specific countries. Hence, as an example, Televisa pursued format rights with Argentinian, Chilean, Colombian, and Brazilian studios and signed co-production agreements with Colombia's RCN and RTI, as well as Sony, Endemol Shine, Lionsgate, and others. Televisa now has direct entry to the US with its Univisión partnership. Disney has co-produced teen telenovelas with Pol-ka Producciones in Argentina and Vista Producciones in Colombia. Sony co-produces with almost every major regional telenovela producer in Latin America. Rede Globo's programming appears in Argentina, Uruguay, and Chile. RCN and Caracol shows are broadcast in Venezuela. None of that reflects or indicates any national cultural imposition, but it does powerfully demonstrate the transnational character of media in the Global South.

Overall, the production of culturally popular programming was built on TNMC structures, production agreements, and a generic "pan-Latino" cultural content. National media no longer retain the prerogative for culturally specific content; TNMC partnerships offer attractive multicultural content for every Latin American country. TNMCs now produce familiar narratives and formulas with popular actors in manufactured cultural settings laced with ample product placement. National culture is no longer the privilege of any distinctly national media. Cultural imperialism lost its footing, as TNMCs sought profits from partnerships and joint ventures with multiple, regional TNMCs advocating less "cultural aroma" in their content (Iwabuchi, 2002). Linguistic accents, subregional geographic proximity, migration, and diasporic populations, along with the transformation of specific cultural practices and identities required media producers to adapt to a new social and cultural reality resulting from the neoliberal *transnational* capitalist drive to accumulate profit. We might follow Juan Piñon (2014) and set aside the idea of "the nation and instead think about the relationships among certain corporations within the region" (p. 231)—focusing on the class nature and function of TNMCs. Recognizing the manufactured character of the local and national reveals the transnational relations and practices that underwrite media content, production, and distribution. In his analysis of the political economy of media, Nicholas Garnham proposed that distribution "is the key to cultural plurality. The cultural process is as much, if not more, about creating audiences or publics as it is about producing cultural artefacts and performances" (Garnham, 1990, p. 162). If Garnham is right, then the global distribution of transnationally co-produced cultural content promoting individualism and consumerism has effectively replaced US cultural imperialism in the Southern Hemisphere and beyond.

References

Aguilar, C. (2016, April 14). How Mexican cinema entered its second "golden age". *Americas Quarterly*. https://www.americasquarterly.org/fulltextarticle/how-mexican-cinema-entered-its-second-golden-age/

Artz, L. (2015). Telenovelas: Television stories for our global times. *Perspectives on Global Development 14*(1–2), 193–226.

Avila-Saavedra, G. (2006). New discourses and traditional genres: The adaptation of a feminist novel into an Ecuadorian telenovela. *Journal of Broadcasting & Electronic Media 50*(3), 383–399.

Bevins, V. (2013, February 2). Telenovela "Avenida Brasil" speaks to Brazilians. *Los Angeles Times*. https://www.latimes.com/entertainment/tv/la-xpm-2013-feb-02-la-et-st-brazil-tv-avenida-brasil-20130203-story.html

Burnay, C. D., Lopes, P., & Neves de Sousa, M. (2018). Comparative synthesis of Obitel countries in 2017. In L. A. Paim Gomes, & J. Guadelis Crisafulli (Eds.), *American observatory of television fiction Obitel 2018 Ibero-American TV fiction on video on demand platforms* (pp. 25–70). Porto Alegre, Brazil: Editora Sulina.

Cardoso, F. E., & Faletto, E. (1979). *Dependency and development in Latin America*. Trans. M. M. Urquidi. Berkeley, CA: University of California Press.

de Assis Poiares, L., de Sa Osorio, P., Spanhol, F. A., Largura, A., Sandrini, F., & Dornelles da Silva, C. M. (2010). Allele frequencies of 15 STRs in a representative sample of the Brazilian population. *Forensic Science International 4*(2). https://www.fsigenetics.com/article/S1872-4973(09)00086-6/fulltext#articleInformation

de la Fuente, A. M. (2015, March 27). Telenovela channels Romanza + Africa and Telemundo capture new auds in Africa. *Variety*. https://variety.com/2015/tv/global/telenovela-channels-romanzaafrica-and-telemundo-capture-new-auds-in-africa-1201461791/

de la Fuente, A. M. (2019, January 22). Televisa sets development pact with Mexico's Endemol Shine Boomdog. *Variety*. https://variety.com/2019/tv/news/televisa-endemol-shine-boomdog-content-pact-mexico-1203113540/#!

Donoghue, C. B. (2014). The rise of the Brazilian blockbuster: How ideas of exceptionality and scale shape a booming cinema. *Media, Culture & Society 36*(4), 536–555.

Dos Santos, S. (2009). The central role of broadcast television in Brazil's film industry: The economic, political, and social implications of global markets and national concentration. *International Journal of Communication 3*, 695–721.

Dunn, J. C., & Ibarra, R. L. (2015). Becoming "boss" in *La Reina del Sur*: Negotiating gender in narcotelenovelas. *Popular Cultural Studies Journal 3*(1–2), 113–138.

Durnay, C. D., Lopes, R., & Neves de Sousa, M. (2018). Comparative synthesis of Obitel countries in 2017. In P. Gomes, & L. A. Guadelis Crisafulli (Eds.), *Ibero American observatory of television fiction. Orbitel 2018. Ibero-American tv fiction on video on demand platforms* (pp. 25–70). Puerto Allegre, Brazil: Editora Meridional Ltda.

Fox, E., & Waisbord, S. (Eds.). (2002). *Latin politics, global media*. Austin: University of Texas Press.

Frank, A. G. (1967). *Capitalism and the underdevelopment of Latin America*. New York: Monthly Review Press.

Garnham, N. (1990). *Capitalism and communication: Global culture and the economics of information*. London: Sage.

Gómez, R. (2020). The Mexican film industry 2000–2018 resurgence or assimilation. In R. Nichols, & G. Martinez (Eds.), *Political economy of media industries: Global transformations and challenges* (pp. 57–82). New York: Routledge

Güler, E. (2014, November 10). Turkey's biggest export: TV dramas. *Hurriyet Daily News*. https://www.hurriyetdailynews.com/turkeys-biggest-export-tv-dramas-74070

Hopewell, J. (2019, May 17). Globo, Sony Pictures TV seal milestone English-language series alliance. *Variety*. https://variety.com/2019/tv/global/globo-sony-pictures-tv-milestone-english-language-series-alliance-1203218594/#!

Iwabuchi, K. (2002). *Recentering globalization: Popular culture and Japanese transnationalism*. Durham, NC: Duke University Press.

Jedlowski, A., & Rêgo, C. (2018). Latin American telenovelas and African screen media: From reception to production. *Journal of African Cultural Studies 31*(2), 135–150.

Kaplan, M. (2016, February 9). From telenovelas to Turkish dramas: Why Turkey's soap operas are captivating Latin America. *Internatonal Business Times*. https://www.ibtimes.com/telenovelas-turkish-dramas-why-turkeys-soap-operas-are-captivating-latin-america-2296321

Larrea, G. (2019, June 11). Inter Medya aims at being the middleman for Turkey and LatAm co-production. *Todo TV News*. https://www.todotvnews.com/en/inter-medya-aims-at-being-the-middleman-for-turkey-and-latam-co-production/

Lippert, B. (2013). Betty and Lisa: Alternating between sameness and uniqueness, in J. McCabe and K. Akass (Eds.), *TV's Betty goes global from telenovela to international brand* (pp. 83–98). New York: I.B. Tauris.

Marshall, S. (2016, December 26) The rise of the telenovela. *New Republic*. https://newrepublic.com/article/138918/rise-telenovela

Mattelart, A. (1976). Cultural imperialism in the multinational's age. *Instant Research on Peace and Violence 6*(4), 160–174.

Media Ownership Monitor. (2017). Brazil: Grupo Globo. https://brazil.mom-rsf.org/en/owners/companies/detail/company/company/show/grupo-globo/

Oualalou, L. (2013, August). Brazil's telenovelas celebrate 50 years of success: The story so far. *Le Monde Diplomatique*. https://mondediplo.com/2013/08/12telebovelas

Oxfam International. (2021). Brazil: Extreme inequality in numbers. *Oxfam International*. https://www.oxfam.org/en/brazil-extreme-inequality-numbers

Piñon, J. (2014). A multilayered transnational broadcasting television industry: The case of Latin America. *International Communication Gazette 76*(3), 211–236.

Reifová, I., & Sloboda, Z. (2013). Czech Ugly Katka: Global homogenization and local invention. In J. McCabe, & K. Akass (Eds.), *TV's Betty Goes Global: From telenovela to international brand* (pp. 189–205). New York: I. B. Tauris

Sanchez, D., Whittaker, T. A., Hamilton, E., & Zayas, L. H. (2016). Perceived discrimination and sexual precursor behaviors in Mexican American preadolescent girls: The role of psychological distress, sexual attitudes, and marianismo beliefs. *Cultural Diversity & Ethnic Minority Psychology 22*(3), 395–407.

Schiller, H. I. (1976). *Communication and cultural domination.* White Plains, NY: International Arts and Sciences Press.

Sianez, D. G. (2017). *Examining perceptions on women's issues including intersectionality of class, misogyny, and stereotypes of Mexican and Latin American women within the telenovela La Reina del Sur.* Master's Thesis. University of Texas El Paso. https://scholarworks.utep. edu/cgi/viewcontent.cgi?article=1554&context=open_etd

Siriyuvasak, U. (2010). Cultural industry and Asianization: The new 'imagined' inter-Asia economy. In D. Shim, A. Heryanto, & U. Siriyuvasak (Eds.), *Pop culture formations across East Asia* (pp. 1–27). Seoul: Jimoondang Publishing

Slade, C., & Beckenham, A. (2005). Introduction: Telenovelas and soap operas: Negotiating reality. *Television and New Media 6*(4), 337–341.

Smith, P. J. (2013). Travelling narratives and transitional life strategies: Yo soy Bea and Ugly Betty. In J. McCabe, & K. Akass (Eds.), *TV's Betty Goes Global: From telenovela to international brand* (pp. 222–239). New York: I. B Tauris.

Straubhaar, J. (1991), Beyond media imperialism: Assymetrical interdependence and cultural proximity. *Critical Studies in Media Communication 8*(1):39–59.

Straubhaar, J., Sinta, V., Spence, J., & Higgins Joyce, V. M. (2016). Changing class formations and changing television viewing: The new middle class, television and pay television in Brazil and Mexico, 2003–2013. *Les enjeux de l'Information et de la Communication 17*(2), 208–223.

Thussu, D. K. (Ed.). (2006). *Media on the move: Global flow and contra-flow.* New York: Routledge.

Tomaselli, W. (2019, February 23). Erdogan is sowing a Turkish obsession in Latin America. *OZY.* https://www.ozy.com/around-the-world/erdogan-is-sowing-a-turkish-obsession-in-latin-america/92616/

ttvnews. (2020, Janaury 20). Wounded Birds to take over for Elif on Caracol. *Todo TV News.* https://www.todotvnews.com/en/wounded-birds-to-take-over-for-elif-on-caracol/

Vassallo de Lopes, M. I., & Greco, C. (2018). Dynamics of television fiction in the multichannel transition. In P. Gomes, & L. A. Guadelis Crisafulli (Eds.), *Ibero American observatory of television fiction. Orbitel 2018. Ibero-American tv fiction on video on demand platforms* (pp. 99–128). Puerto Allegre, Brazil: Editora Meridional Ltda.

Villafañe, V. (2021, April 13). Televisa And Univision to merge In $4.8 billion transaction. *Forbes.* https://www.forbes.com/sites/veronicavillafane/2021/04/13/televisa-and-univision-to-merge-in-48-billion-transaction/?sh=6de38c2974d6

Vivarelli, N. (2021, May 21). Why Turkish dramas are conquering Hispanic audiences in the US on Univisión. *Variety.* https://variety.com/2021/tv/news/turkish-dramas-u-s-hispanic-audiences-univision-1234978398/

Vujnovic, M. (2008). The political economy of Croatian television: Exploring the impact of Latin American telenovelas. *Communications 33*, 431–454.

Wollan, M. (2011, January 12). How Pantelion Films lures Latinos to the box office. *Fast Company*. https://www.fastcompany.com/1715103/how-pantelion-films-lures-latinos-box-office?cid=search

WIDWORLD. (2020, November 10). What's new about income inequality in Latin America? *World Inequality Database*. https://wid.world/news-article/inequality-in-latin-america/

Zenith. (2017). Google and Facebook now control 20% of global adspend. *Zenith Media ROI*. https://www.zenithmedia.com/google-facebook-now-control-20-global-adspend/

6

THE NEW FRONTIERS OF EUROPE

Transnational Media Partnerships

"It almost feels like Hollywood. Hungary's studios and streets are populated year-round with film crews these days as, increasingly, international partners team with local producers on ambitious series and film projects" (Tizard, 2017). Korda Studios, Cinemon Entertainment, Laokoon Film, and other Hungarian production firms have joined the European surge toward transnational media partnerships, as film production appears more open than Hungarian television which panders to Viktor Orban's authoritarian rule (Kingsley, 2018). Hungarian filmmakers followed the rest of European media's search for investors, audiences, and profits. Under the European Union's co-production rules, regional co-productions bring multiple national subsidies and credits, while the co-production creative process contributes to the cultural dynamic. As co-productions increase, lessons are learned and media partners financially benefit. Transnational media formations awkwardly culminate several decades of efforts to build a diverse but unified European culture.

The European Union: twenty-eight countries, 24 official languages (and 80 more identified as still extant), with some 160 distinct cultures within or near its borders, the enduring collective almost defies cooperative explanation. Beyond the national and linguistic differences, European social classes also have unresolved contradictions. While Europe's economic conditions appear favorable compared to many countries in the world, a more sobering picture emerges when incomes and quality of life are aggregated for the region. Clearly, the middle classes have the "political and economic power... to defend their income position against competition from below and exploitation from above" (Dauderstat, 2019), but those middle classes consist largely of the populations of the richer countries such as Germany, Denmark, and the Nordic states. Southern Europe, Eastern Europe, and sizable working class and

DOI: 10.4324/9781003162452-07

immigrant populations in France, Italy, Spain, Portugal and the UK have suffered from the neoliberal commercialization of the last 40 years. Nonetheless, corporate leaders and government politicians are determined to maintain and expand transnational production for market distribution across Europe and beyond, whatever resistance that democratic movements or populist nationalism present.

Following the devastation of WWII, Belgium, France, Germany, Italy, Luxembourg and the Netherlands agreed to collaborative political and economic relations in 1957—removing customs barriers and sharing regulations on food production. Denmark, Iceland, and the UK joined this early group in 1973. In 1993, the European Union was official formed with a parliament and adoption of the Euro as a multinational European currency. The EU now comprises 28 countries with a combined population of 327 million and a GDP of $16 trillion (2019). Despite its inequalities, the EU's economy compares well with the US ($21 trillion) China ($14 trillion) and is almost triple the GDP of Latin America ($6 trillion). Remarkably, the US media market is 50% bigger than EU's combined media market.

From the onset of neoliberal proposals in the late 1980s, European capitalists were all in. Collectively the EU—in collaboration with other transnational formations like the International Monetary Fund, the World Bank, and the 37-nation Organization for Economic Co-operation and Development—decided that deregulated free markets were necessary to further accumulate wealth for their national capitalist classes, which have become transnational in their social and economic relations and identities (van der Pijl, 1998; Sklair, 2001). Accordingly, most European industries have forged extensive transnational relations.

Auto manufacturing exemplifies transnational industrial relations and European auto companies participate fully. Fiat bought Chrysler, then merged with Puegeot—an Italian, US, French company called Stellantis, which also owns Citroën, Alfa Romeo, Lancia, Maserati, Opel, and Vauxhall. BMW partnered with Puegeot, Citroén, Benz, and Toyota in co-production joint ventures. In 2020, BMW formed a joint venture with Tata Motors India to produce the electric I-Pace Jaguar. Renault (owning 43%) merged with Nissan, then Renault-Nissan bought a controlling stake in Mitsubishi in 2016. Benz has multiple joint ventures with Chinese automakers. VW has a joint venture with SAIC in China. In 2020, VW entered a joint venture with Ford to produce electric cars. These changed relations of production reflect the new world of neoliberal global capitalism that seems to have triumphed over alternative possibilities. This same transnational trajectory appears in media, albeit with fewer major global partnerships. Media collaboration in Europe, for example, followed a more convoluted path, reflecting the historical and material conditions of national and linguistic boundaries. Nonetheless, the transnational "trading of creative content, capital, and talent bridges the physical gaps" between media owners and audiences (Hoyler & Watson, 2017, p. 945)—thereby dismantling the conditions favorable to US cultural imperialism in Europe.

For decades Europe was caught up in the Cold War against "communism" but since the fall of the Berlin Wall and the collapse of Soviet Union, the EU has been working for increased economic and political integration among its diverse capitalist-dominated nation-states. Hegemonically, the capitalist classes across Europe have promoted pan-European, cross-cultural appeals as it removed national barriers to investment and movement of goods and people. To help construct European unity and identity, the EU budgets about $200 million annually for its Creative Europe MEDIA program which supports co-productions of non-national television, films, and cultural festivals across country borders. MEDIA purposefully provides incentives for co-productions "that transcend national and cultural boundaries" (Jones & Higson, 2014).

The 1989 "Television Without Frontiers" Directive became the cornerstone of the European Union's audiovisual policy. Updated in 2007, the Directive "rests on two basic principles: the free movement of European television programmes within the internal market and the requirement for TV channels to reserve, whenever possible, more than half of their transmission time for European works" (EUR-Lex, 2008). The EU policy protects the public interest in cultural diversity, the protection of minors, and the right of reply. At the same time, in its zeal to introduce commercial and pay-TV, the European Union's liberalization of audiovisual regulatory policies gutted public broadcasting. In 2019, the European Audiovisual Observatory reported that the main producers of television fiction were commercial media based in Germany, France, Italy, Spain, and the UK, with German media corporations leading in film production (Cabrera Blázquez et al, 2019). Although neoliberal privatization by investors and governments was already in progress, satellite, cable, and internet technologies, including streaming platforms made national-cultural protections difficult to enforce. American-based, vertically-integrated TNMCs used their European subsidiaries to occasionally invest in localizing their brands—where economically advantageous—to meet market and national regulatory conditions, which often provided subsidies and tax incentives (D'Arma & Steemers, 2012).

Television reaches into almost every European home and one might think that developing national media content would provide some defense against foreign encroachment. Such an approach, however, misses the history and practice of European television. Even including public service networks, television never produced "truly native, autochthonous storytelling, in actual fact it [was] almost never totally indigenous" but was shaped by "the presence and influence of sources, partners, concepts, and products from Europe" (Buonanno, 2010, pp. 203, 210). In other words, cultural identities have never been uniquely national or separable from historic social interactions. Unless one wanted to argue for French or British or German cultural imperialism imposing their values on Spanish, Italian, and Swedish culture, deferring to an abstract European heritage provides even less clarity about cultural production and identity. More usefully, Armand Mattelart (1976) explained that *national* culture has been "elaborated and administrated by the national dominant class" intent on reproducing their national "class hegemony" and keeping themselves in power (p. 161). Even when the specific characteristics of a national culture can be identified, the more important concern should be: who determined those values and beliefs and whose interests are served? Besides US film and television dominance in Europe is not what it was 40 years ago.

In 2018, only 15% of European television channels were US brands (e.g., Discovery, Disney, Warner, Viacom, A&E) but streaming services such as Amazon and Netflix held 38% of subscribers in Europe. Thus, national media monopolies united in their own streaming joint ventures: Salto in France; 7TV in Germany; and a transnational streaming platform planned by Italy's Mediaset with Spain's Artesmedia. Competition for viewers also confronts uneven television viewing across the continent, with previously underserved countries such as Slovakia, Bulgaria, and Slovenia spurring a vibrant market, while France, Italy, Sweden, Belgium, and Britain have an over-saturated market due to over-production of content as major national media and TNMCs vie for viewers with more channels and more media platforms (Cabrera Blázquez et al, 2019, p. 44). In film production, collectively European media produce more than the US. The top five countries released 1230 films in 2018—France 300, Italy 272, Spain 246, Germany 247, and the UK 247—compared to 576 US productions (Stoll, 2020).

Meanwhile, market forces propelled further consolidation of European media so the Directive by itself became largely unnecessary beyond its ideological value (Middleton, 2020, p. 610). Attempts to restrict US media incursions evolved into partnerships and joint ventures among European media, often even including agreements with US media. Sixty four different languages are broadcast across the EU, 35 in France, 27 in Sweden, and more than 20 in Germany, Poland, Slovenia, Britain, Denmark, Estonia, and Slovakia. It follows that given the incredible linguistic diversity with limited audience size, co-productions follow a "language pattern"—German with Austria; France with Belgium and Luxembourg; and the UK with the US, while Sweden has a larger diversity of co-production partners (Cabrera Blázquez et al, 2019, pp. 14, 16).

As leading domestic media and their governments implemented neoliberal commercialized adjustments, television and film content underwent a radical transformation such that civic-oriented values and practices of public service drifted to consumerist and individualistic forms (Giomi, 2010). Across Europe, rising production costs and declining public funding arrested the development of programming, while simultaneously increasing the import of foreign content: cartoons from Japan, telenovelas from Latin America, and soaps, sit-coms, and cop shows from the US. Imports influenced both public and private broadcasters competing for viewers. Historically, France, the Netherlands, and other EU countries developed national cultural spaces that were "relatively porous and open to the influence of foreign art forms and media products from the very beginning" (Buonanno, 2010, p. 195). The prominence of American media during the late 20th century should not be overstated in comparison to the discreet European regional influences on media content.

By the 21st century, European media were not imitating imports but adapting and reconfiguring successful commercial models for the profits of their own privatized media. In many cases, national frameworks at the level of the story overshadowed any "foreign elements" (Buonanno, 2010, p. 211). Media in every European nation produced television series and formats that included codes and conventions capable of capturing large audiences and maximizing advertising revenues in their country and others. In particular, they created localized mini-series focused on highly personalized action, "emphasizing visual spectacle… set in an almost atemporal dimension, with historical references only serving the dramatic and universal appeal of the individual's inner feelings and private conflicts" (Giomi, 2010, p. 85).

Television Mini-Series: High-End Fiction

Mini-series became the format of choice for both public and private broadcasters because the mini-series short format is less expensive and more adaptable to diverse cultural tastes. Mini-series, termed "high-end fiction" by the European Audiovisual Observatory, can be understood as cinema-like television series of short duration (4–12 episodes). Public and private media in Italy, France, Germany, Spain, and the UK, began producing mini-series about 20 years ago. The UK is the overall leader in both production and distribution in the region. Of the over 1000 mini-series exported from the EU in 2019, 67% were UK productions or co-productions (Fontaine & Jiménez Pumares, 2020, p. 1). Private broadcasters, RTL, ITV, TF1, and Mediaset have integrated production processes to retain their rights to future profits and to combine production with distribution—often working for third-party TV channels. Independent production groups like Banijay/Endemol Shine and Lagardére also consolidated their production chains that included more transnational co-productions. In a parallel transnational move, Netflix's European offerings feature 44% non-English productions. In 2021, Netflix co-produced *Criminal* with writers, directors, and cast from four EU countries creating three episodes each. As Endemol Shine's executive producer Lars Blomgren said, "when all streamers have global reach" using subtitles and dubbing, then "content can originate anywhere" (in Fontaine & Jiménez Pumares, 2020, p. 43).

Telefónica, the Spanish telecom giant that dominates phone service in a dozen Latin American countries with joint ventures in Britain, France, and China, now produces a dozen original mini-series each year for its Movistar+ international broadband and streaming platforms. The Spanish/Chinese TNMC Grupo Globomedia operates Mediapro Studios, one of the biggest production-distribution companies in Europe, producing more than 30 mini-series each year, including co-productions by its studios in 36 countries. Mediapro partners with everyone: Netflix, Amazon, Disney, Canal+, Sky, Sony, smaller European studios, and more, with over 200 projects in development in 2019. Meanwhile, Netflix co-produced mini-series with Mediapro, ProSieben's German Red Arrow Studio, Sweden's SF Studio, and the RTL/Grupo Planeta TNMC Atresmedia, among others. Mediapro, Netflix and others co-produce the genre because, as the European Audiovisual Observatory reported in 2020: "European co-productions travel better because there is a solid dramatic reason behind the mix of international elements; and a good local-universal series sells everywhere" (Fontaine & Jiménez Pumares, 2020, p. 75). The days of American cultural domination are gone: transnational productions that reconfigure cultural products for multiple audiences have replaced past cultural imperialism.

In all EU countries, neoliberal projects mandated media privatization, which soon affected television and film narratives, shifting content from public television adaptations of cosmopolitan European masterpieces and epics (Buonanno, 2010, p. 196) to culturally-indistinct narratives about daily life preoccupied with "an inner-oriented perspective, paying special attention to the representation of the characters' feelings, passions, and emotional life" (Giomi, 2010, p. 82). As part of the TNMC drive to attract audiences and to narratively promote individualism, the plots, themes, and protagonists in EU mini-series reflect an ideological frame similar to action movies, telenovelas, and police procedurals in India, China, Latin America, and elsewhere. Individual heroes act due to the corruption or ineffectiveness of official institutions and the public, while the bracketing of historical or social context is surrounded by self-interest expressed through spectacular action. Writers and producers set no limit on the vigilante justice meted out by the singular hero.

These narratives parallel the decline of collective forms of belonging and other social values. "Underneath the patina of consumerist consensus and hedonism, stands an increasingly atomized, individualistic and anomic" social order (Giomi, 2010, p. 89). For viewers with real anxieties, fears, and resentments resulting from dealing with corrupt and unresponsive bureaucracies similar to those that confront the mini-series hero, direct action against villains offers a "symbolic compensation, one of the most important cultural functions of TV drama" (Giomi, 2010, pp. 89–90).

The symbolic release through entertainment effectively reinforces the hegemonic construction of dominant values of wealth, success, and individual pleasure. Critiques of the social order and its villains in dramatic stories are resolved when protagonists act in their own self-interest while defending or tolerating the status quo hierarchy and authority. Such entertainment offers catharsis without challenge. No cultural imperialism exists or is needed here. Italian, French, German, Swedish, and other media corporations reconfigure their entertainment content with available cultural markers: location, language, actors, and a few culturally-familiar interactions. Most importantly, the modest cultural adjustments made by national media and their regional partners feature themes and values to attract audiences that can be sold to advertisers. Narrative, dialog, and action advance individualism, while the advertisements encourage consumerism. In short, whether the mini-series were national or transnational productions, "dominant global motifs were creatively combined with local preferences, cultural forms were transfigured, foreign was rendered indigenous" (Giomi, 2010, p. 94). Thus, ITV, RTL, and other regional TNMCs produce game shows, sit-coms, and drama mini-series to attract audiences and increase profits, while distributing representations and messages that underwrite the global capitalist culture of consumerism.

At this point, most European television fiction productions are mini-series. These television dramas have the added benefit of recovering audience share from US imports: in 2019, 39% of all mini-series on EU television schedules were American, 29% were European productions; on streaming platforms, European mini-series dominated with 34% compared to 26% US. Significantly, 70% of the top streaming videos were also regional transnational co-productions (Fontaine & Jiménez Pumares, 2020). At least for the most popular television fiction in Europe, its seems US cultural imperialism has faltered under the rise of regional transnational media productions.

Technological changes combined with the small, fragmented linguistic and economic divisions in Europe have pushed large and small European commercial media producers and distributors toward more multicultural co-productions just to survive. In 2018, EU media co-produced 85 mini-series (See Table 6.1 and Table 6.2). Cable, satellite, and most recently internet streaming platforms presented European co-productions with new distribution opportunities. As

TABLE 6.1 Top EU Mini-Series (2016–2020, Partial List)

Title	Year	Producers	Cost per episode
The Young Pope	2016	Sky, Canal+, HBO	$5.6
Babylon Berlin	2017	Sky, ARD	$4.6 M
Das Boot	2018	Sky, ARD	$4.3 M
Le Tour le Monde	2020	FTV, RAI, ZDF	$4.2 M
Deutschland 68	2018	RTL	$3.3 M
La Bazar de Charité	2020	TF1, Netflix	$2.9 M
Occupied	2016	TV2 Norge, Arte, Viaplay	$1.6 M
Truth Will Out	2018	Kanal 5, TV Norge, Viaplay	$1 M

(European Audiovisual Observatory 2020, in Fontaine & Jiménez Pumares, 2020, pp. 62–63)

TABLE 6.2 Top EU Mini-Series Producers (2015–2019)

TNMC group	Number of mini-series
Banijay/Endemol Shine (FR)	157
ITV (UK)	123
RTL (Germany)	113
Warner (US)	97
BBC (UK)	78
Mediawan (FR)	77
ARD (Germany)	76
Discovery (US)	73
Lagardére (FR)	69
ZDF (Germany)	57
Vivendi (FR)	53

(European Audiovisual Observatory 2020, in Fontaine & Jiménez Pumares, 2020, p. 70)

Buonanno noted in 2010, the multi-modal entertainment environment established by satellite and the internet "created the conditions for a growing presence of Euro-drama" (p. 207). Meanwhile, the largest media groups in each country continued to consolidate, accounting for more than 69% of domestic TV audiences. Several of these national media monopolies (Bertelsmann/RTL, Vivendi, ITV, Nordic, Mediaset) became leading European TNMCs as well.

Cinema Europe

For film, data indicate that European co-productions also bring larger audiences and profits than nation-specific movies. For instance, UK/European co-productions "sell eight times more cinema tickets on mainland Europe than UK domestic features" (Jones & Higson, 2014).The European Audiovisual Observatory reported that more than 20% of films released in Europe through 2016 had European media as majority co-production partners with media from 150 countries (EAO, 2018). If minority partnerships are included, over 30% of movies in 2020 were transnational projects.

The move to transnational media is facilitated by governments and extra-governmental agencies. In 2017, the Council of Europe's Eurimages funding association brought together Danish, German, French, and Swedish public and private producers on *The Square*, which won the Palme d'Or at Cannes and several other best film awards. Eurimages also backed the animated drama, *The Breadwinner* (2017) which was co-produced by studios from Canada, Ireland, and Luxembourg. The movie was nominated for an Academy Award. In 2019, French movie exports reached a record 145 co-productions with large audiences in Italy, Germany, and Spain, as well as Latin America (UniFrance, 2020). Several of these regionally co-produced transnational films registered over 1 million spectators in 2019, including *Anna*, a thriller co-produced by Canal+,

EuropaCorp, and TF1; *Mia and the White Lion* by Studio Canal, Bertelsmann RTL's M6 Films, Germany's Pandora Film, and Film Afrika; the Belgian-France *Serial Bad Weddings 2*, which was the highest grossing French film of 2019; and *Asterix: Le Secret de la Potion Magique,* another sequel to the series co-produced by French CGI studio Mikros Image and M6 Films.

Despite the continued presence of Hollywood block-busters, the European film industry has remained vibrant with some 75,000 companies raising over $10 billion in revenue in 2019. To assist their private media, most European governments signed multiple co-production treaties with countries in Asia, Latin America, Africa, the Middle East, and across Europe. Many governments also offered additional financial incentives to attract filmmakers. For example, in 2016, Iceland increased its cash rebate for international productions from 20% to 25%, while Norway spent $5.3 million on its first incentive program. One of the first results was *The Snowman* (2017) filmed in Norway with a Swedish director and co-produced by UK's Working Title (an independent studio partnered with Comcast's Universal), Hollywood's Universal Pictures, and China's Perfect World Pictures. Finland established its Tekes-Finnish Fund for Innovation with an initial $10.6 million budget to assist transnational co-productions (Jensen, 2017).

European transnational co-productions incorporate cultural content, post-production decisions, and local labor from cross-border media partners. European media and their transnational partners pool their resources and tap into the national and pan-European subsidies and tax credits which greatly increase the co-production and marketing budgets for successful action, animation, fantasy, and sci-fi movies and television series. Notably, "such partnerships are an attractive way for producers to raise funds in situations where domestic channels alone aren't enough" (Marsh, 2017). Thus, of the top 400 films produced annually by France and Germany, over 100 are transnational co-productions with other European media (Hoyler & Watson, 2017, p. 958)

TNMC relations also improved distribution across Europe and internationally. China became the largest export market for European films in 2017 with 36 million ticket sales, compared to 24 million in Latin America and 27 million in the US (Cabrera Blázquez et al, 2019, p. 20). (See Table 6.3)

TABLE 6.3 Top European Film Exports 2017 (Partial List)

Title	Box office	Country of film studio
Valerian City of 1000 Planets	$226 M	France, China, US, Germany, UAE
47 Meters Down	$62 M	UK, US, Dominican Republic
Paddington 2	$228 M	France, UK
Ballerina	$106 M	France, Canada
Loving Vincent	$45 M	Poland, UK, China, Netherlands
Contratiempo (Invisible Guest)	$30 M	Spain

At the same time, US film imports still capture about half of theater admissions, with four of the top ten films being other TNMC co-productions. European media have had modest success with regional joint ventures; seven of the top ten films in 2017 were co-productions. Still, "hundreds of small and medium-sized enterprises only operate at the national level, and the national markets for most European films are too small to make big-budget productions worthwhile" (Richeri, 2016, p. 318). Thus, given the linguistically-fragmented European market, limited resources, and little experience in producing blockbuster films, few European media have had partnerships in India or China.

Spanish media and their European partners have arranged collaborative projects in Latin America, given its shared language and historical connections. France has successfully marketed French language films to Canada, Europe, and African communities. Otherwise, transnational ventures by European media are mostly regional—which still have market difficulties given the multiple languages. Swiss scholar, Giuseppe Richeri (2016) has suggested that leading consolidated European media should produce "fewer films with larger budgets in a unified language, in order to compete on the global market" (p. 327).

Meanwhile, commercial media and their friendly governments push neoliberal deregulation while they publicly stress their interest in European cultural integration. For example, the Council of the European Union, one of three of the EU's legislative bodies, states that "cultural and linguistic diversity represent an important asset" and "reflect the richness and diversity of European cultures and constitute a heritage which needs to be promoted and preserved for and by future generations" (Council of the European Union, 2019). The Council's advocacy and funding of co-productions to "build bridges between different geographic and linguistic areas and contexts, having positive effects on both majority and minority co-production partners" prioritizes the benefits to media companies (Council of the European Union, 2019). The EU works to "make cinema an important vehicle for European cultural integration," in order to "strengthen European cinema's industrial and commercial structure" (Richeri, 2016, p. 317). Thus, EU funders Eurimages and Europa Cinemas Networks back regional and international co-productions including scriptwriting, distribution, and subtitling/dubbing primarily to enhance "circulation potential." In other words, the EU is dedicated to commercial media profits without regard to national identities.

Although the relationships between domestic and foreign are often structured through the "visible or quantifiable import and export of programmes" and formats, there is much more to consider (Buonanno, 2010, p. 199). Indeed, the data and numbers presented here no substitute for the richness and color of the real world, which contains many complex nuances and variations necessary to gain a full understanding. The power of transnational media relations goes beyond statistics that demonstrate the extent of the new shared structures, practices, and content produced by multiple media partners.

Whatever the actual numbers, in policy and practice, transnational collaborations in and from Europe have transcended direct American dominance. Consolidated national media have opted to reconfigure their nation-centered productions according to transnational and transcultural entertainment forms and content. We can ask the questions: do "culturally European" films (Jones & Higson, 2014) express Europe's "common heritage" (Berting, 2006, p. 4) or reflect a more transnational culture of consumption and individualism? Do European productions parallel transnational entertainment media content in India, China, Latin America, and elsewhere? Do dominant themes and narratives in transnational productions suggest that a non-national, multilingual, multicultural consumerism has become the global norm?

The answers to these questions appear through a review of predominant transnational media practices in Europe. Space does not permit a thorough unpacking of the thousands of transnational media projects from the 28 EU countries. The following can only provide a representative sample of some of the consolidated media in each country that have found multiple TNMC partners in Europe and beyond.

Britain

The sun never sets on the British Empire! The expression was common belief by the middle of the 19th century, indicating the reach of British colonialism from the Americas to China, India, and Africa. From occupation and enslavement to resource exploitation, trade, and cultural domination, the UK maintained its position until after WWII when colonies everywhere fought for and won their independence. Subsequently, British neo-colonialism relied on indigenous comprador classes that established European political, economic, and cultural norms. The US climbed to international dominance by the 1950s, replacing Britain in economic, military, and political power. Capitalist classes in Britain and other past colonial powers became dependent on US armed forces and trade. However, by the 1970s, capitalist classes everywhere confronted overproduction and limited growth. They collectively sought a new global economic regime based on open markets, privatizations, and deregulation of public interests—as discussed in Chapter 1—transnational production was seen as solution to more accumulation of wealth in every industry: machinery, auto, agriculture, pharmaceutical, textiles, and more, including media production which quickly became consolidated across nations.

Indicative of the continuing consolidation of national and transnational media, corporate media ownership, audience share, and revenues in the UK are highly concentrated. For example, just three media dominate the British press: News UK (*Sun* and *Times*) with 13 million circulation, DMG (*Daily Mail*) 8.4 million, and Reach (*Daily Mirror*) 8 million (Ramsay, 2019). Other media forms feature similar monopolies.

Britain has the largest television and streaming market in Europe, dominated by highly concentrated media groups. The UK is home to Sky, BBC, and ITV—three of the top European media groups—and has multiple subsidiaries of US media, as well. The revered public broadcasting network, BBC (British Broadcasting Corporation) attracts more than 30% of viewers, private broadcaster ITV has about 25%, and Channel 4 has 10%. Comcast's Sky and CBS Viacom's Channel 5 regularly draw less than 10% of viewers. British Telecom, with revenues of $30 billion in 2020, is not a television producer or network, but delivers news and entertainment content to its 18 million phone, broadband, and satellite subscribers. In comparison, Netflix has only 9 million subscribers in the UK. Notably, although US television is widely available in Britain, the ITV/BBC series *The Bodyguard* was the most watched show in 2018 and BBC's *Line of Duty* (2012–2021) had the most viewers in 2019 (Fontaine & Jiménez Pumares, 2020, p. 58). Neither Netflix or Amazon can compete with the volume of original productions by BBC, ITV, and other UK broadcasters.

Of note, about 40% of UK television channels target other European countries and in 2017 over 35% of UK films were co-productions by major British media partnering with media from France, Germany, Ireland, and Sweden. Importantly, under the terms of the Council of Europe's trans-border directive even Britain's exit from the EU will not adversely affect its television and film exports or partnerships.

BBC

BBC (British Broadcasting Corporation) is the world's oldest public broadcaster and by many accounts the world's largest. BBC began as radio and added television channels after WWII. Like most public media in Europe, BBC's funding comes largely from media user license fees. In the UK, like everywhere that private media interests and government politicians turned to neoliberalism, multiple public industries were privatized. However, although the BBC was forced to sell off several of its divisions to private owners, as a nationally revered institution, the BBC was wounded primarily through attrition. From 2007 through 2016, government cuts forced reductions in staff and programming. In 2018, the commercial subsidiary BBC Studios was formed to sell programs internationally. BBC Studios now contributes about a quarter of BBC's annual revenue.

From its early years as a radio network to current television broadcasting, the BBC has established the standards for news and entertainment. Currently the BBC operates many national and international radio channels and several television channels, including regional stations (Ireland, Scotland, and Wales), two children's channels, and multiple international cable and satellite channels.

In addition to continuing popular mini-series such as *Death in Paradise* (2011–2021), *Call the Midwife* (2011–2021), *Shetland* (2015–2021), and *Line of Duty* (2015–2021), BBC continues to produce top quality, popular dramas. Most recently, these include *Mallorca Files*, *Gentleman Jack*, *Staged*, and *Serpent*. Through international agreements with other public service networks, many BBC shows are seen by millions. With Netflix and other streaming platforms, BBC's reach has grown even more. To remain the leading broadcaster in Britain, the BBC has repeatedly created multiple popular reality and competition game shows, as well as new variations on mini-series tropes—from the fifty-year recurring sci-fi series *Dr. Who*, to the more contemporary black comedy *Killing Eve* (2018–2020) and the crime thrillers *Luther* and *Peaky Blinders* (2013–2019). BBC frequently and regularly partners with television and film producers across Europe and has joint ventures for broadcasting on five continents.

ITV

ITV (Independent Television) is the oldest and largest commercial television in UK. Liberty Global has owned 6% of ITV since 2014. ITV has more than 60 production and co-production labels with local studios across Europe. ITV produces programs for BBC and UK's Channel 4, has a 40% stake in Blumhouse Television US, and signed a partnership with BMG Music in 2020. ITV also has several other transnational partnerships, including: a majority share in the Welsh Boom Group; a controlling stake in Germany's Imago TV; 51% of Monument Pictures which produces television series with and for Hulu, Netflix, and CBC; and a majority stake in Tetra Media Studio in France.

Sky

Comcast's Sky is the largest satellite broadcaster in Europe with 23 million subscribers. Sky owns Sky Italia, Deutschland, and Ireland and has several joint ventures with ITV, BBC, CBS/Viacom, and a few others. In 2019, Sky partnered with Italian production studio Lux Vide and the French Orange Studio on the hit thriller series *Devils* (2020–2022)—aired in Canada, France, Italy, and the US. While not a major TV channel in the UK or a primary producer of films, Sky maintains its operations due to Comcast's economies of scale. NBC and Universal rely on the large American market and they produce a wide range of entertainment content for Sky and other Comcast subsidiaries.

Cinema Britain

Britain has the second highest theater admissions in Europe with 176 million. The highest earning films are mostly American and British-American co-productions. Sequels, remakes, and adaptations predominate—comprising 36 of 41 films earning over $75 million. Top films include seven in the Harry Potter franchise (Heyday Films-UK), five Star Wars, the first four Tolkien adaptations (Wingnut Films—New Zealand), four Marvel, and four James Bond films (Eon Productions—UK). Although film production in Britain does not rival the scale of Hollywood or Bollywood, British films worldwide generated $6.5 billion in ticket sales in 2016, and UK media revenues reached $40 billion in 2020 (Statista, Statista, 2019; 2020). British transnational film co-productions have increased and been quite successful in recent years. In 2017, Working Title Films joined with China's TNMC Perfect World and the BBC producing *Victoria & Abdul* in English, Hindi, and Urdu. Working Title partnered with Perfect World again in 2019—this time including Japan's transnational advertising group Dentsu—to produce *Yesterday*, which earned $150 million. Zephyr Films co-produced *Special Couple* (2019) with China's Shanghai Media Group, although Chinese-British ventures produced in the UK are often difficult given its high labor costs and smaller audiences.

Recent British film co-production successes include: *The Gentlemen* (2020), a co-production grossing $115 million by UK's Longcross Studios and Miramax (co-owned by Qatar's beIN Media and Viacom/CBS) distributed by the Indian-American ErosSTX and Britain's Entertainment Film; *Emma*, a 2020 co-production by UK's Working Title Films, Blueprint Pictures (a British studio with minority Sony investment), and China's Perfect World Pictures; and *The Secret Garden* (2020), a fantasy film by UK's Heyday Films and Studio Canal. Strangely, under English law, many American-identified movies are considered co-productions due to the nationality of cast and crew, where the production takes place, or if the work is based on a British creation (See Table 6.4).

Certainly, Britain's accommodating designations of co-productions do not rise to the level of transnational partnerships collaborating fully on movie content. Such productions do however provide considerable employment opportunities for creative labor and production crews. It also demonstrates how major media cannot just imperially impose their will but must adapt to national regulations to get licenses and earn subsidies and tax credits. Moreover, creative labor and crews learn from each production and carry those practices and

TABLE 6.4 Top Ten Films in the UK Since 2017

Film	Year	Gross	UK designated co-production
Avengers: Endgame	2019	$125M	Yes
Star Wars: Jedi	2017	$115M	Yes
The Gentlemen	2020	$115M	Yes
Lion King (live)	2019	$105M	Yes
Beauty & Beast	2017	$100M	Yes
Avengers: Infinity	2018	$98M	Yes
Toy Story 4	2019	$92M	No
Mamma Mia!	2018	$90M	Yes
Star Wars: Skywalker	2019	$88M	Yes
Joker	2019	$78M	No
Dunkirk	2017	$76M	Yes

norms to less global, more regional transnational co-productions with more equitable partnerships. It is also clear from both national and transnational movie productions from Britain that the links between production, content, distribution, marketing, and exhibition follow TNMC protocols that are most profitable to studios and most comforting to mass audiences.

Leading British Film Companies

The most successful UK film and television studios have shed their national armor for the more cosmopolitan fashion of transnational media relations. Aardman Animations, famous for *Wallace & Gromit* and *Chicken Run*, recently produced *Shaun the Sheep* (2019) and a second *Chicken Run* (2021) feature. Aardman, one of the largest independent studios in the world, has gone farther. In 2018, founders Peter Lord and David Sproxton transferred ownership to Aardman's 300 employees to assure continuation of its independence (Hughes, 2018). Eon Productions has made 25 James Bond films and will likely continue the franchise format. Heyday Films has co-produced Harry Potter, Paddington, and the Fantastic Beasts films, and continues its collaborative success with *Sometimes, Always, Never* (2018) and *Once Upon a Time in Hollywood* (2019). Working Title may be the largest film studio in the UK and has a great track record of successful co-productions. Its latest releases include *Mary Queen of Scots* (2018) and in 2019, *The Kid Who Would Be King, Cats,* and *Yesterday III*. Films from these and other UK media abide by a transnational perspective in production and content.

France

France has been considered the artistic origin of cinema since Lumiére's first movie projection in 1895—notwithstanding the absurdity and silliness of the almost twenty *Asterix* animation and live action feature films (1967–2021). France zealously protects its artistic culture past and present, resisting the classification of cinema and culture as commodities in WTO trade negotiations—as have many other countries (Voon, 2007). France is also the largest producer of films and has the largest box office in Europe with over 200 million admissions in 2018—in large part because dominant media in France have fully joined the transnational movement toward mergers, joint ventures, and partnerships.

US films captured 35% of admissions in 2019, other imports drew 10%, while French movies attracted over 55% of moviegoers in 2019. During the 2020 pandemic year, US films fared better. Notably, French media comprise the leading TNMCs in Europe with multiple joint ventures and co-productions in Europe, Latin America, North America, Asia, and Africa. For more than a decade, French media have co-produced films each year in Colombia, Mexico, Chile, and Argentina. French-Argentine co-productions attract more than 1 million spectators annually (Lachaussée & Martin-Winkel, 2015). Remarkably, of the 200 French productions selected at major international film festivals, 145 were co-productions, mainly with Belgium and German media partners (UniFrance, 2020).

Meanwhile, French television expanded its reach beyond national borders. Driven by animation and documentaries, the foreign investment and international sales of French TV programs earned $384 million in 2019. The biggest increase came from international co-productions which skyrocketed by 44% to break a 10-year record, especially for animated programs and documentaries (Kessalasy, 2020). French animation surpassed $90 million (Kessasly, 2020) with popular cartoon series such as: the French/Korean *Molang* (2015–2021) (available on Netflix); the flash-animation *Simon* (2015) released to 15 countries; the award-winning *Miraculous Ladybug* series (2015–2021) co-produced by French and Korean animation studios with participation by Disney and aired in 10 countries; and the French-British CGI-animated super-hero series *PJ Masks* (2015–2020), co-produced by Hasbro's Entertainment One, Disney, and France Télévisions.

The French language and historic relations with communities in Canada, Africa, and Europe provide more external markets for French media than most European media that have a smaller linguistic reach. At the same time, the largest France-based TNMCs have gone well-beyond the region in their partnerships, productions, and distribution. In 2019, $10 million in export sales of animation co-productions went to Tencent Video, iQIYI, and Youku, major streaming platforms in China.

Banijay/Endemol Shine

Endemol Shine, is a leading transnational media company, owned by the French transnational Banijay since 2020. Banijay is 66% owned by the Japanese media and investment group LDH and 34% by another French TNMC, Vivendi (Szalai, 2020). These transnational relations extend even further: LDH itself is a transnational partnership of Financiere LOV (52%), French equity firm Fimilac (12%), and the Italian De Agostini (36%), which has a joint venture, Artesmedia, with Spanish Grupo Planeta and the German TNMC Bertelsmann RTL. Thus, as the largest international television content creator and distributor, with 120 companies in 22 nations, Banijay is completely transnational in ownership, management, and content production. (For more see https://www.banijay.com/). This French, Italian, German, Spanish, and Japanese TNMC also has co-production ventures with media in Mexico, Argentina, Brazil, and more.

Banijay/Endemol Shine has a production library that dwarfs all others, including those of Fremantle, BBC, Televisa, and Comcast Universal. This TNMC produced *Survivor, Big Brother, Peaky Blinders, Temptation Island, MasterChef, Wallander, The Kardashians, Mr Bean, The Wall, Hunted, Black Mirror, Extreme*

Makeover: Home Edition, Deal or No Deal, The Bridge, and *Broadchurch.* Moreover, these diverse formats and their remakes have no specific national culture that imposes itself on others. Most are seen by British, American, Swedish, Chinese and other viewers as creations by their own national media. In each case, these *transnational* co-productions contribute fabricated spectacles and multicultural variations for competition, melodrama, and infotainment suitable for normalizing self-interest and consumerism worldwide. With Endemol Shine, Banijay has many subsidiaries around the world (See Table 6.5)

Yellow Bird

While Banijay/Endemol primarily produces television programming, its Yellow Bird film production company, with studios in Sweden, Germany, the UK, and US creates, co-produces, and distributes successful movies for theater and streaming. In addition to Stieg Larsson's *Millennium* (2010) TV series and the 2009 feature films, *The Girl with the Dragon Tattoo, The Girl Who Played with Fire,* and the *Girl Who Kicked the Hornet's Nest*—all coproduced with Nordisk Film, Yellow Bird teamed with MGM for US co-productions of *The Girl with the Dragon Tattoo* (2011) and *The Girl in the Spider's Web* (2018). DC Comics issued graphic novels of the book and film series from 2012 to 2015. Yellow Bird also produced nine films based on Henning Mankell's *Wallander* novels and released three series for Swedish television (2006, 2010, 2013). Yellow Bird and Left Bank Films in Britain co-produced 12 *Wallander* television films for BBC, aired 2008–2013. The journalist mystery, *A Case for Annika Bengston,* was produced by Yellow Bird for Swedish and German TV in 2012 and 2013. Over the last decade, the studio continued its success with

TABLE 6.5 Banijay/Endemol Shine Subsidiaries and Partnerships (Partial List)

Division	Countries of operation
Adventure Line	UK, Sweden, Russia, Lebanon distributor
Aurora TV	Italy
B & B Endemol Shine	Switzerland joint venture
Cuarzo Productions	Spain
Endemol Shine	France, Germany, Israel, Nederland, Finland, UK, Australia New Zealand, North America, Portugal, India, Poland
Endemol Shine Asia	East Asia countries
Endemol Shine Brasil	Brazil joint venture
Endemol Shine Boomdog	Mexico joint venture
Nordisk Film	Denmark, Norway, Sweden
Raab TV	Germany joint venture
Reshet, Hadashot	Israeli partnerships
Totem Media	Belgium joint venture
Yellowbird Film	Sweden, Germany, UK, US
Zodiak Media	Europe, Eastern Europe, Russia, Nordic countries

other Nordic-noir films based on best-selling mysteries by Helene Tursten, Jo Nesbø, and Lief Persson. In 2021, Banijay's Yellow Bird joined with the streaming Acorn TV to release the six-part series *Bäckström* based on Persson's novels. The studio also produced *Snöänglar* (Snow Angels) in 2021, a six-part Swedish crime drama about motherhood.

Vivendi/Groupe Canal Plus

Vivendi, part owner of Banijay, is one of the largest TNMCs in Europe with $18 billion in annual revenue. Vivendi jumped into media ownership, production, and distribution in the late 1990s—acquiring large stakes in Havas, the global advertising agency; Maroc Telecom; and merging with the historic Pathé Films, which owned a major theater chain in France, Belgium, the Netherlands, Switzerland, and Tunisia; shares in British Sky; and Canal Satellite. After many acquisition and mergers, Vivendi became overextended and divested many of its holdings. In fact, Vivendi's recurring deals make it difficult to confidently list its operations.

As of 2021, Vivendi owned one of France's largest film and television studio Groupe Canal+, which includes: Studio Canal, and its many subsidiary production studios; the M7 network with stations in Austria, the Netherlands, Belgium, Czech Republic, Slovakia, and Romania. Canal+ has channels in Spain, Belgium, the Netherlands, Poland, Vietnam, Myanmar, and an African channel. Groupe Canal+ owns one-third of the subscription TV service of Orange, the largest telecom company in France. Studio Canal also entered a joint venture with Telecom Italia in 2017 for co-production of television and film for streaming. In 2019, Canal+ acquired Nigeria's largest production studio ROK to create content for Nollywood TV, its French-language African channel. Vivendi also owns the Canal Olympia cinema with theaters across the African continent. Studio Canal signed another transnational joint venture with Lionsgate in 2021 to distribute Paramount films. Studio Canal has also co-produced many popular films, including European and other co-productions (See Table 6.6).

In addition, Vivendi separately owns: Editis, one of the largest publishers in France; minority stakes in videogame studios Activision Blizzard, Gameloft,

TABLE 6.6 Studio Canal Productions Since 2017 (Partial List) (Partial List)

Title	Year	Gross	Co-production partners
Paddington 2	2017	$238 M	Heyday Films (UK)
The Commuter	2017	$120 M	Ombra (US), Lionsgate
Early Man	2018	$55 M	Aardman Animation, BFI (UK)
Johnny English	2018	$160 M	Working Title (UK), Perfect World (China)
Cold Pursuit	2019	$76 M	Summit (US), Mas (UK)
Radioactive	2020	Streaming	Working Title (UK), Amazon

and Ubisoft, the creator of *Assassin's Creed*; 25% of Telecom Italia; and 12% of Gruppo Mediaset, Silvio Berlusconi's media company in Italy. Vivendi also opened its Universal Music Group (one of the world's big three record labels) to a 10% investment by China's Tencent. In 2020, Vivendi doubled its stake to 24% in Lagardére, another large media group that publishes books and owns shares in the international magazine publisher Hatchette. In 2020, Lagardére sold its film studio to another growing French media group, Mediawan.

Vivendi itself partners with many, including private banks, public financial groups, and shareholders, including the multinational Bolloré transportation group which owns 26% of Vivendi and 60% of Havas. (For more see https://www.vivendi.com/en/). Bolloré controls the second most watched news network in France, CNews. CNews, described as the French version of the US-based Fox News, has been criticized for airing conspiracy theories and extreme right perspectives (Gontier & Sénéjoux, 2020).

TF1 Groupe

TF1 television is the most popular French television networks attracting 24% of the viewing audience. In addition to airing British competition shows like *The Voice, Danse avec les Stars*, and *Who Wants to Be a Millionaire*, it carries French reality and mini-series programs and several French animations such as *Ladybug* and the French/US/Canadian co-production *Monster Buster Club*. TF1 dubs the US dramas *Law & Order, CSI, Young and the Restless*, along with popular, long-running French dramas *Josephine, Ange Gardien,* and *Demain Nous Appartient*. TF1 also broadcasts FIFA soccer and other sports programs.

TF1 is an active TNMC. It owns TMC (Monte Carlo TV); a large share in the WB Television Network; 80% of joint pay-TV ventures with Discovery—Breizh, Histoire, and Ushuaia TV; and 34% of the Swedish Metro International publishing and advertising group. The TF1 Groupe produces television programming for many networks and stations in France and its neighbors. Since restructuring in 2016, the TF1 Studio has produced dozens of feature films, including recent hits: *Way Down* (2019) with Mediaset's Telecinco; released the co-production *Erna at War* (2020) with Denmark's Nimbus Film and Estonia's Nafta Films; and *Forte (Ballsy Girl)* (2021), co-produced with Belgium's Panache Productions; among a dozen other movies. TF1 is part of Lionsgate's Globalgate consortium and has partnered with many other TNMC entertainment producers.

Additional French Transnational Media Co-Productions

EuropaCorp, the TNMC producer of the *Taken* film series, partnered with Studio Babelsburg to make the German, French, US thriller, *American Renegades* (2017). In 2018, EuropaCorp was purchased by Mediawan (France), which has become a primary producer-distributor-financer of regional co-productions.

EuropaCorp/Mediawan, jointly owned by China-based Fundamental Films, has a partnership with Sony/ATV music, and also distributes films in Japan through a joint venture with Sumitomo, Kadokawa, and Asmik Ace.

Smaller film studios in France have also found transnational partners. For example, Splash Entertainment, a French/US joint venture with Draugard's Elipsanime Studio, co-produced several animation series with India's DQ Entertainment, including *Benjamin Bear* and *Lyoko*. Geko Films co-produced the award-winning *Gente de Bien* (*Decent People*) with Colombia's Evidencia Films in 2014.

Reflecting the continuing transnational impulse among French media, 2020 featured more than a dozen co-productions, including: French studio Agav Films partnership with Israel"s United King Films on *Laila in Haifi* (2020); in 2020, Palestinian, French, German, Portuguese, US, and Qatar studios collaborated on *Gaza Mon Amour* (*Gaza My Love*), which won the best Asian Film Award at the Toronto Film Festival; and *La Nuit de Rois* (*Night of Kings*) co-produced by studios from France, Côte d'Ivoire, Canada, and Senegal, which was recognized with the NAACP Best International Film Award 2021.

The most expansive transnational project involving French media was Germany's Films Boutique leading nine co-producers on *The Story Of My Wife*. The 2020 romantic drama is truly a transnational operation: Germany and Austria (Alamode), Benelux (September Films), Israel (Lev Cinema), Italy (RAI Cinema), Hungary (Mozinet), Greece (Strada), Russia (Russian Report), Czech Slovak (Film Europe), Portugal (Leopardo), and France's Pyramide. (Films Boutique also co-produced the Arabic language *Abou Leila* (2019) with Algerian studio Thala Films and Qatar financing.)

Pyramide joined with Colombian studio Burning Blue on *La Tierra y la Sombra* (*The Earth and the Shadow*) winning a Cannes Festival award in 2015. Pyramide also co-produced *The Gravedigger* (2019), filmed in Djibouti, Somalia, with Bufo Oy (Finland) and TwentyTwenty Vision (Germany).

Gaumont was the first film studio in the world and still is a mid-major French filmmaker. Its *Intouchables* (2011) remains the most successful non-English film ever, with a $450 box office. Gaumont coproduced *Rogue City* (2020) with Umedia, a Belgium/France/UK/US TNMC film studio. Meanwhile, the studio has co-produced many US serials, including *Hannibal* (2013–2015) and *Hemlock Grove* (2013–2015) with a 4th season rumored for 2021.

Germany

It's been a long time since Leni Riefenstahl's *Triumph of the Will* (1935) and other propaganda films of Nazi Germany. In the aftermath of the war, US film studios dominated. Billy Wilder, Howard Hawks, Cary Grant, and Marlene Dietrich went to Germany to make movies "amid the rubble of a country in ruins" (Thrift, 2017) making films that either avoided recent history or offered a "narrative powerlessness" (Bliersbach in Kürten, 2016). Movies that presented Germans as victims of fascism were cathartic and successful. For decades, popular television and movies often featured stories and satirical takes on Native Americans and other victims of oppression. For instance, ProSieben TV's *Bullyparade* (1997–2002) had weekly skits with Native American characters that were adapted into the film, *Der Schuh di Manitu* (*The Shoe of Manitu*) (2001)—one of Germany's most successful postwar movies drawing $72 million at the box office. Comedies and parodies remain popular film genre in Germany, as shown by the hit franchise *Fack Ju Gohte* (2013, 2015, 2017) that grossed $240 million in ticket sales. Public television continues to present comedy along with its more recent drama mini-series productions.

Until successive governments opened Germany to commercial media in the 1990s, public media received consistent and substantial support from licensing fees and state and national budgets, especially for its public service broadcasters ARD (Arbeitsgemeinschaft der öffentlich-rechtlichen Rundfunkanstalten der Bundesrepublik Deutschland—Regional Public Broadcasters) and ZDF (Zweites Deutsches Fernsehen—Second German Television). ARD, in collaboration with Austrian and Swiss public television, still produces the longest-running TV series ever: *Tatort,* a police drama, that has been aired continuously since 1970, several feature films based on the series have been made, including *Tschiller: Off Duty* (2017).

Currently there are some 400 TV channels in Germany—the two public stations have over a fourth of the national audience, with RTL receiving 8% and ProSiebenSat.1 having less than 6%. The dominant position of public television and advertising-funded commercial TV has limited the pay-TV market in Germany, although Sky Deutschland has aired some popular series, such as *Babylon Berlin* (2017–2021). In recent years, German media have co-produced mini-series dramas with media from Sweden *Bron/Broen* and *The Killing Before We Die*; with France, *Ride Upon the* Storm; with Spain *The Paradise*; and even with Chile *Invisible Heroes* (Fontaine & Jiménez Pumares, 2020, p. 72).

Traditionally, German cinema was also heavily financed by public funds. In the 1990s, however, under pressure from satellite broadcasting, cable providers, and World Trade Organization (WTO) neoliberal agreements, German film largely shifted from a state-subsidized system to market-based popular entertainment. At first, neoliberal reforms quickly opened Germany to imports and investments—from US media in particular.

Commercial media and successive German governments pointed to the benefits other industries gained from deregulation. In fact, the world's three biggest exporters, Germany, China and the United States, have been the biggest beneficiaries of WTO trade terms (Deutsche Welle, 2019). Under free trade protocols, the US gained $87 billion extra in 2016, China $86 billion, while Germany reaped $66 billion in additional financial rewards attributed to

WTO protocols. However, market deregulation in television and film translated into increased US imports.

With 90 million admissions in 2018, Germany ties with Spain as the 3rd largest market in Europe—almost 9000 German film companies with 45,000 employees garnered $10 billion in 2020 film revenue (Statista, 2020). And Hollywood films are plentiful—140 imports in 2018. Still, German studios released 153 films that year and EU media imported more than 150 productions/co-productions. Warner Bros. which co-produces films in German made $4.2 M at the box office in 2019, while two German studios Constantin Films and Studio Hamburg had over $4 M each the same year. Discovery's All3Media is the largest single producer of TV, film, and video media in Germany, but German productions combined release more than twice as much entertainment content and more than a third of top tickets sales are German productions or co-productions. Moreover, recently only a few US films topped the German box office: *Star Wars: The Force Awakens* (2015) is the only US movie to draw more than 9 million viewers in the last decade, while German media found multiple transnational partners for its own film productions (See Table 6.7).

RTL Bertelsmann

Bertelsmann, a major transnational media corporation with holdings in television, radio, books, magazines, and music, is owned largely by the Mohn family. Bertelsmann's RTL Group operates 68 television channels and 31 radio

TABLE 6.7 German Film Co-Productions (2016–2020) (Partial List)

Title	Year	Co-production country
Resident Evil: Final	2016	Canada, French, Australian, US
55 Steps	2017	Belgium
Maze	2017	UK, Irish, Swedish
Richard the Stork	2017	Belgium, Norway, Luxembourg, US
Young Karl Marx	2017	Belgium, France
High Life	2018	France, UK
Mia & White Lion	2018	France, South Africa
Pope Francis	2018	France, Italy, Switzerland
Styx	2018	Austria
Aftermath	2019	UK, US
Kindness of Strangers	2019	Canada, France, Sweden, UK, US
Little Joe	2019	UK, Austria
Polar	2019	Canada, US
Roads	2019	UK, France
Gaza Mon Amour	2020	France, Palestine, Portugal, Qatar
Monster Hunter	2020	Canada, China, Japan, US
Persian Lessons	2020	Belarus, Russia
Tochter	2020	Greece, Italy

stations in Germany, France, and other European countries. RTL has channels in the Netherlands, Belgium, Luxembourg, Croatia, Hungary, and on Antena 3 in Spain. It owns streaming platforms, production studios, and operates a number of digital services. RTL owns BMG, a major music producer which owns rights to many top recording artists. RTL Group also has a joint venture in Groupe M6, the 2nd largest French TV network, which launched the Salto streaming service in a 2020 partnership with France Télévisions and TF1 to compete with Netflix, Disney+, and other VOD platforms. M6 Films has co-produced several big hits including the *Taken* series with EuropaCorp (2009, 2012, 2015) which earned over $1 billion; *Ballerina* (2017) a French, Canadian animation co-production with $100 million box office; and *Mia e le Lion Blanc* (Mia and the White Lion) (2019) with Studio Canal.

Freemantle

A large and important division of RTL is Fremantle, which owns Penguin Random House and Simon & Schuster publishing. Fremantle also creates, produces, and markets popular reality show formats such as *Idol, Got Talent*, and the *X Factor*. Versions of the *Idol* or its *Super Singer* format have been broadcast in 150 countries to more than 3 billion viewers.

Fremantle has the largest catalog of game shows in the world, while it also has successfully produced melodramas like the Australian soap *Neighbors*, running for 35 years, and the Italian *Un Posto Al Sole* appearing on RAI 3 for more than 15 years. Fremantle began investing in high-end drama productions starting in 2014 and quickly benefitted from its existing TNMC networks. Fremantle and the Spanish TNMC Mediapro co-produced the hits *The Young Pope* (2016) and *The New Pope* (2020) that aired on Canal+, Sky Italia, and HBO. Fremantle's telenovela series, *La Jauria* (2019, 2020) co-produced with Chile's TVN and Fabula Studio, Argentina's Kapow Films, and Amazon was aired across Latin America, Europe, the Middle East, and Africa (Lang, 2020) (For more see https://www.bertelsmann.com/divisions/rtl-group/#st-1).

As a leading division within a division of a successful TNMC, Fremantle (and its Wildside Film studio) continues to transnationally co-produce series that cross presumed cultural barriers. Fremantle demonstrates that from Australia and Italy to Chile and Russia, transnational media attract multicultural audiences to a culture of individualism and consumerism that does not belong to any particular nation or culture, but does express the values and practices of global capitalism. Notably, Fremantle's most successful productions like the leading US cinema imports to Germany (80% of which are franchise sequels) emphasize heroic self-interest and deference to hierarchies and authorities. In other words, neoliberalism comes dressed in multicultural entertainment spectacle.

ProSiebenSat.1

ProSiebenSat.1, although drawing small television audiences in Germany, remains one of the larger satellite and cable broadcasters in Europe. ProSieben owns some 50 free-to-air and pay TV channels in Germany, Austria, and Switzerland. With $5 billion in revenue, it became the 2nd largest broadcaster in Europe after merging in 2007 with SBS (Scandinavian Broadcasting System). ProSieben owns Studio 71, Gravitas Ventures, and co-owns a production studio Red Arrow—with TNMCs Mediaset Italia (30%) and France's TF1 (30%). By 2020, Mediaset also owned 20% of ProSiebenSat.1. Red Arrow Studios comprises film offices in seven countries and has produced series for Amazon, *Bosch* (2017–2021); for Netflix, *Love is Blind* (2020–2022); and Lifetime's *Married at First Sight* (2014–2021); among others released in Australia, Germany, and the UK. ProSieben also maintains a strategic partnership for broadcasting rights with Constantin Film based in Germany that is part of the Swiss TNMC Highlight Communications. (For more see: https://www.mediadb.eu/en/data-base/int-medienkonzerne-2015/prosiebensat-1.html).

Constantin Films

Constantin has successfully adopted the TNMC model of film sequels with its five successful zombie-horror *Resident Evil* movies (2004–2016); its *Fack Ju Göhte* series (2013, 2015, 2017), co-produced with Lionsgate/Televisa's Pantelion Films; as well as making many of TNMC's favorite genre: action films. Constantin partnered on the Canadian co-production *Polar* (2019) for Netflix; *Monster Hunter* (2020), a transnational partnership with Tencent, Toho-Towa, and Sony; and the co-productions of 2021 action thrillers *Tides* and *The Walk*. Constantin also has a joint venture in Mister Smith Entertainment with Broad Green Pictures US to distribute films by Amblin/DreamWorks, Hasbro/eOne, and Nordisk Films.

Italy

Sixty million people live in Italy and neoliberalism has not been kind to most. Although Italy is the fourth largest economy in the EU, the benefits have not been shared equally as privatization and austerity have taken their toll. The $2 trillion GDP has not trickled down. Since neoliberalism took off in the 1990s, the poorest 50% have seen an 80% reduction in their net wealth, while the top 1% have increased their wealth by 50% (Acciari, Alvaredo, & Morelli, 2021). The unemployment rate was over 10% in 2021 with job losses concentrated among service-sector workers. Youth unemployment reached 30%. Regional inequalities between the highly industrialized North and the poorer, rural southern "Mezzogiorno" areas are also still high, with organized crime still active.

Despite the inequalities, Italy has a vibrant and diverse economy. It is Europe's biggest producer of rice, vegetables, and wine. It is also an industrialized country and the largest global exporter of luxury goods in fashion and vehicles, with more than a quarter of the population active in manufacturing.

Italy has a rich cultural heritage of literature, music, and fine art. Michelangelo, Botticelli, Raphael, and da Vinci embody the Renaissance. Fellini, Bertolucci, and Pontecorvo's *Battle of Algiers* delighted audiences and influenced filmmakers around the world. Versace, Gucci, Armani and other Italian designs have defined fashion for decades, while Maserati, Alfa Romeo, and Lamborghini set the standards for luxury automobiles. Moreover, Italian politics and history have inspired theorists from Machiavelli to Croce and Gramsci. If any country earned a cultural identity it is Italy, but as Milly Buonanno (2010) has argued Italian culture is marked mostly by its openness to and adaptations of non-national influences.

Not surprisingly, Italian media reflect both cultural openness and the hybridization of European and North American cultural content. Television provides the primary entertainment means for most Italians. Television viewing in Italy is fully digitized and only about one quarter of Italian homes subscribe to pay-TV. While RAI (Radiotelevisione italiana), the public service station funded by license fees, attracts 37% of viewers, Berlusconi's commercial Gruppo Mediaset, the largest commercial network, has 31% of the TV audience. Both RAI and Mediaset air programming from the US and Europe, especially content from France and Spain. They both also produce and co-produce with other European media their own original programming and versions of globally popular formats.

In 2018, three of the top six shows on Italian television were Italian crime dramas: *Montalbano*, the 20 year running series, had 33% of viewers; *Gomorra* (2014–2021) drew 23%, and another 20 year hit, *Don Matteo* received 22%; while the Warner Bros. comedy *Big Bang Theory* was watched by 28% (Stoll, 2020). Three years later, US offerings had slipped further. The top television programs in Italy according to IMDb (2021) were predominately regional TNMC co-productions, including: *DaVinci* (2021–2022), a mini-series co-produced by public TV networks from France, Spain, and Italy, along with Sony and a small British studio; the BBC thriller, *Killing Eve* (2018–2022); *Zero Zero Zero* (2020) an Italian thriller from Comcast's Sky Italia and Canal+; *Zero* (2021), a Netflix Italian sci-fi drama with a black cast; *Fate: The Winx Saga*, a teen drama co-produced with Ireland's Archery Pictures, Italian studio Rainbow S. p. A., and Viacom; and *Medici* (2016–2019), an Italian co-production by RAI and Lux Video with the British-French studio, Big Light Productions. *Medici* aired in 190 countries and is still playing on streaming platforms globally.

Although Italy is home to the largest movie studio in Europe, Cinecittà in Rome, theater attendance has been declining. Domestic productions, including co-productions, only took 30% of total theater admissions in 2017. Italian studios have turned to transnational joint ventures to bolster their output. For example, in 2018, RAI Cinema, the leading public filmmaker, joined with Lionsgate and two smaller US studios, to co-produce the action thriller, *Sicario: Day of Soldado,* making $75 million at the box office.

Gruppo Mediaset

Mediaset is the largest commercial broadcaster in Italy; its stations have a large viewing audience, second only to RAI, the public broadcaster, which attracts about 35%. Mediaset is controlled by former prime minister Silvio Berlusconi owning a 38% share, with Vivendi owning 12%. Mediaset owns two dozen broadcast stations; 13 pay-TV stations; 25% of Nessma TV which airs in Morocco, Algeria, Libya, and Tunisia; and a majority stake in Mediaset España, which includes Telecinco, one of the most popular Spanish stations, a half dozen others, a film studio, and Boing TV, a 50:50 venture with Warner's Turner Broadcasting.

Mediaset's production studio, Taodue, produced two of the five top grossing movies in Italy since 2016, both comedies: *Quo Vado?* (2016) with $90 M gross and *Tolo Tolo* (2020) with $52 M—both surpassing Disney's *Avengers* (2019) and Warner's *Joker* (2019) which drew only $4 M each. Taodue has also produced several television mini-series for Mediaset and other Italian broadcasters, including the cop thriller *Squadra Antimafia* (2009–2016) and its spinoff *Rosy Abate 2* (2017–2019). In 2020, Taodue also co-produced an Amazon series, *Made in Italy.*

Mediaset España's Telecinco Cinema received CineEurope's Independent Producer of the Year Award in 2017. Telecinco Cinema has co-produced six of the top 10 Spanish movie hits of all time in Spain, beating out Hollywood competition. The films include the *The Impossible* (2012), *Spanish Affair* (2014), *Spanish Affair 2* (2015) and *A Monster Calls* (2016). 2014's chart-topper, *Spanish Affair* grossed $77.5 million, four times the take of its nearest Hollywood rival, *Dawn of the Planet of the Apes,* moving Spanish films to a 24% domestic market share. *Es Por Tu Bien* (*It's For Your Own Good*) was co-produced with Disney's Buena Vista in 2017, then Telecinco partnered with Basque's Bowfinger International to make *Ola de Crímenes* (*Crime Wave*) in 2018. That year Telecinco also completed *Sara's Notebook* with Uganda director Norberto Lopez Amado which was produced in Spanish, Swahili, English and French. In 2019, the studio also partnered with Think Studio, Movistar+, and TF1 on the thriller *Way Down.*

Telecinco Cinema followed with another TF1 co-production, the heist movie, *The Vault,* in 2021.

As an Italian owned Spanish TNMC, Mediaset España, produces Spanish language films and forges multicultural co-productions in other languages that attract more viewers than Hollywood productions and their latent cultural imperialist ambitions. Each of these Telecinco movies center their stories on an individual family drama or comedy with little concern for the rest of humanity. It seems Italian, Spanish, French, and other European TNMCs cooperatively book profits while effectively entertaining millions with self-centered stories that are apropos for individual consumerism.

Other European Regional TNMCs

The Bonnier Group is a Swedish TNMC with 175 companies operating in 15 countries, mostly publishing books and magazines. Bonnier also owns SF Studios, the largest film production company in Sweden. SF Studios has partnered with Warner, MGM, ErosSTX, Sony, Comcast Universal and Canal+ in France. Deals give SF distribution rights for TNMC films in the Nordic region and TNMCs access to distribution and streaming of SF films. In 2020, SF signed a distribution deal with Netflix to air Nordic films. In 2021, Netflix/ SF Studios released the thrillers *Red Dot* and *Snabba Cash*. The studio also distributed *Margrete-Queen of the North* (2021), co-produced by Filmkameratene (Norway), Truenorth (Iceland), Sirena Film (Czech Republic) and Film i Väst (Sweden), with support from their nation's film institutes.

Egmont Group, the leading Danish media company, publishes magazines, books, comics, operates TV2 and other stations in Denmark, owns movie theaters, and produces video games. Egmont owns Nordisk Film which produces animation and feature films. Nordisk Film also operates the largest cinema chain in Scandinavia. Nordisk co-produced the Norwegian hit, *The Tunnel* in 2019 and distributed the Danish-Irish-British animation co-production *Checkered Ninja* in 2018.

Another smaller TNMC, Pandora Film Productions in Germany, has allied with many transnational film producers, including on the award-winning masterpiece *High Life* (2018), co-produced with Apocalypse Company UK, Madants Poland, ZDF/Arte Germany, and Canal+ France; on the Sundance award-winning war drama *Monos* (2019) with Stela Cine Colombia, Campo Cine Argentina, Lemming Film Netherlands, Snowglobe Denmark, Film I Väst Sweden; and the previously mentioned transnational co-production *Mia and the White Lion* (2017). Pandora may not command the recognition of major Hollywood studios, but it does contribute to the vibrant environment of transnational media alliances.

Dozens of other regional transnationals produce and distribute films across Europe and internationally, elbowing their way into global entertainment and culture. In 2017, studios from Norway, Belgium, Germany, and Luxembourg co-produced the animation hit *A Stork's Journey* to a $17 million international box office. Germany's ZDF, Match Factory, Komplizan Studios, and Films Boutique; France's Pyramide Films, Gaumont, and Wildbunch; Spain's

Mediapro; Sweden's SF Studios and Film I Väst; Topkapi in the Netherlands; Belgium's Scope Pictures; Working Title in the UK; and many, many others are co-producing multicultural and multi-lingual television series and films. (For more see https://en.unifrance.org/).

Recently, East European media have entered the transnational current as well. Poland's G7 Films enlarged the TNMC club with its first Indian co-production *No Means No* (2021) with Indian directors, cast, and music in Polish and Hindi. Poland's Studio Filmowe TOR joined with Ukraine's Interfilm Production Studio, Lithuania's Studio Uljana Kim, and the Hungarian Laokoon Films to co-produce the thriller *Eter* (Ether) (2018). Korda Studios in Hungary co-produced two seasons of *Ransom* (2018–2019) with the Canadian TNMC, Hasbro/eOne. The 2017 *The Legend of Solomon*, an animated feature by Cinemon Entertainment, was the first Hungarian/Israeli co-production. Several other Hungarian studios have joint ventures with Canadian, British, German, and other European media. In one of the first transnational deals by Russian filmmakers, Bubble Studios co-produced the super-hero animation feature, *Major Grom*, with Disney in 2021, earning $4 M.

In 2016, several European media joined Lionsgate's Globalgate Entertainment consortium to co-produce regional language entertainment. Belga (Benelux), Gaumont (France), Kadokawa (Japan), Lotte (Korea), Nordisk Film (Scandinavia), Televisa/Videocine (Mexico), TME (Turkey) Tobis (Germany), RAI Films (Italy), TF1 (France), Lionsgate and several other studios intend to produce local language films. As of 2021, films have been released in Korea, Mexico, and Europe with many more projects in pre-production.

Taken together these partnerships highlight how transnational momentum has disrupted the globalization of American cultural imperialism. Hollywood studios, Amazon, Netflix, and other transnationals are signing up transnational partners because the themes, narratives, and ideologies that are domestically and regionally created fit the economic and ideological interests of all their *transnational* capitalist owners and investors.

Frontiers for Democracy

European media are producing and co-producing feature film and television fiction that function as an integral part of transnational media relations. While partnerships with US TNMCs continue, regional TNMCs have also constructed multi-lingual and multicultural entertainment that pleases audiences and gains profits. At the same time, these regionally-operating transnational media express a neoliberal ideology and advance justifications for inequality, austerity, and state violence. Of course, these two apparently contradictory tasks cannot always be overcome. TNMCs may be tasked with building a functioning cultural hegemony for the global capitalist class, but their profit-oriented perspective often curbs the creativity necessary. Rather than writers, directors, or actors determining story features, TNMC owners, investors, and managers insist that formulas, templates, and marketing will deliver audiences. Multiple co-productions failures have been the consequence. For example, both of the over-hyped 2017 TNMC co-productions *Great Wall* and *Valerian: The City of One Thousand Planets* were considered box office bombs. Other epic "pan-European" failures trying to blend financial, infrastructural, and artistic collaboration earned the nickname "Europuddings" for their uninspired mish-mash that lacked compelling stories, characters, and dialog (Buonanno, 2010, p. 202)—in large part the result of the marginalization of creative workers.

Entertainment provides a highly effective means for popularizing norms and behaviors because it seamlessly incorporates critiques of inequality, hierarchy and authority, and race, gender, and ethnic discrimination. Hegemonic entertainment includes criticism and resistance—which is always voiced by marginalized or troublesome characters who have little power, are villainous, or provide comic relief. By including but dismissing all challenges, the reigning authority in the narrative appears as the best option. The hierarchy and rule of existing power triumphs over irrational challengers. With a few minor reforms or the removal of corrupt individuals, the social order remains intact. All of this occurs while the focus is on the hero's individual travails. Romance, success, family, happiness—all comes down to individual capability and determination. The hero from whatever culture spectacularly embodies neoliberalism: individual responsibility and self-interested action determines everything.

Understanding transnational cultural hegemony as a process of winning mass consent for the global capitalist class and its nationally-distributed members point to how reifying culture and nation by geography distorts the actual social relations and practices at work. The diffusion of neoliberal values—market dominance, consumerism, deference to authority, individual self-interest, austerity—does not need American or European imposition. It needs national capitalist classes organizing mass consent. Dedicated to the accumulation of wealth through dispossession and wage exploitation, neoliberalism needs national governments to run interference. It also relies on national media to form transnational partnerships—collaborating across borders and cultures—creating entertainment that appeals and persuades mass audiences to stay individually atomized as self-interested consumers. Attracted to and influenced by the transnational culture industry, national media either turn to regional co-productions or at least enthusiastically adopt the same codes and conventions of transnational media content. As Antonio Gramsci observed about the Italian culture of the 1930s, hegemony does not prefer coercion nor even need actual dominance. Leadership works best with consensual participation. Across Europe in the 21st century, leading media have willingly joined the transnational surge.

References

Acciari, P., Alvaredo, F., & Morelli, S. (2021, April 24). The growing concentration of wealth in Italy: Evidence from a new source of data. *VOX EU/CEPR.* https://voxeu.org/article/growing-concentration-wealth-italy

Berting, J. (2006). *Europe: A heritage, a challenge, a promise.* Delft: Eubaron Academic Publishers.

Buonanno, M. (2010). Italian TV drama: The multiple forms of European influence. In I. Bondebjerg, E. N. Redvall, & A. Higson (Eds.), *European cinema and television: Cultural policy and everyday life* (pp. 195–213). Hampshire, UK: Palgrave MacMillan.

Cabrera Blázquez, F. J., F. J., Cappello, M., Chochon, L., Ene, L., Fontaine, G., Grece, C., Jiménez Pumares, M., Kanzler, M., Rabie, I., Schneeberger, A. I., Simone, P., Talavera, J., & Valais, S. (2019). *Yearbook 2018/2019 key trends: Television, cinema, cinema, video and on-demand audiovisual services—the pan-European picture.* Strasbourg, France: European Audiovisual Observatory.

Council of the European Union (2019). Council conclusions on improving the cross-border circulation of European audiovisual works, with an emphasis on co-productions. *Official Journal of the European Union.* https://eur-lex.europa.eu/legal-content/EN/TXT/?uri=CELEX:52019XG0607(02)

D'Arma, A., & Steemers, J. (2012). Localisation strategies of US owned children's television networks in five European markets. *Journal of Children and Media 6*(2), 147–163.

Dauderstat, M. (2019, September 3). Inequality in Europe—wider than it looks. *Social Europe.* https://www.socialeurope.eu/inequality-in-europe-wider-than-it-looks

Deutsche Welle. (2019, December 30). US, China and Germany profit most from global free trade, says WTO. *Deutsche Welle.com.* https://www.dw.com/en/us-china-and-germany-profit-most-from-global-free-trade-says-wto/a-51831108

EAO (European Audiovisual Observatory). (2018). Film production in Europe: Production volume, co-production, and worldwide circulation. *European Audiovisual Observatory.* https://www.obs.coe.int/en/web/observatoire/home/-/asset_publisher/9iKCxBYgiO6S/content/film-production-booming-in-europe-up-by-47-over-the-last-10-years

EUR-Lex. (2008). Television broadcasting activities: "Television without Frontiers" directive. *EUR-Lex Access to European Law.* https://eur-lex.europa.eu/legal-content/EN/TXT/?uri=LEGISSUM%3Al24101#:~:text=The%20%22Television%20Without%20Frontiers%22%20Directive%20%28TVWF%20Directive%29%20is,their%20transmission%20time%20for%20European%20works%20%28%22broadcasting%20quotas%22%29.

Fontaine, G., & Jiménez Pumares, M. (2020). European high-end fiction series: State of play and trends. *European Audiovisual Observatory.* https://rm.coe.int/european-high-end-fiction-series-state-of-play-and-trends-g-fontaine-a/16809f80cd

Giomi, E. (2010). Public and private: Global and local in Italian crime drama: The case of La Pivra *la pivra.* In M. Ardizzoni, & C. Ferrari (Eds.), *Beyond monopoly: Globalization and contemporary Italian media* (pp. 79–100). Plymouth, UK: Lexington Books

Gontier, S., & Sénéjoux, R. (2020, October 10). Comment CNews est devenue la Fox News francaise. *Télérama.* https://www.telerama.fr/television/comment-cnews-est-devenue-la-fox-news-francaise-6716083.php

Hoyler, M., & Watson, A. (2017). Framing city networks through temporary projects: (Trans)national film production beyond 'Global Hollywood.' *Urban Studies 56*(5), 943–959.

Hughes, W. (2018, November 10). Cracking toast, comrade: Aardman belongs to the workers now. *AV Club*. https://www.avclub.com/cracking-toast-comrade-aardman-animations-belong-to-t-1830359455

IMDb. (2021). TV series, Italy (sorted by popularity). *IMDb TV*. https://www.imdb.com/search/title/?countries=it&sort=moviemeter&title_type=tv_series

Jensen, J. R. (2017, February 5). Goteborg: Finland readies incentives for international shoots. *Variety*. https://variety.com/2017/film/festivals/finland-readies-incentives-international-shoots-2017-1201978518/

Jones, H. D., & Higson, A. (2014). UK/European film co-productions: A model for creativity? Paper presented at European Network for Cinema and Media Studies. Milan, 2014. http://mecetes.com.uk/outputs/conference-papers/

Kessalasy, E. (2020, September 9). French TV exports up 18%, driven by increase in animation, doc sales. *Variety*. https://variety.com/2020/tv/global/french-tv-exports-up-18-in-2019-driven-by-increase-in-animation-docu-sales-1234763265/#:~:text=French%20TV%20exports%20were%20up%2018%25%20to%20%E2%82%AC325,second%20highest%20score%20ever%20thanks%20to%20animation%2C%20documentaries

Kingsley, P. (2018, December 19). In Hungary, airing clashing vimersions of reality. *New York Times*, A6.

Kürten, J. (2016, February 8). How film helped Germany deal with WWII. *Deutsch Welle*. https://www.dw.com/en/how-film-helped-germany-deal-with-world-war-ii/a-19442476

Lachaussée, S., & Martin-Winkel, E. (2015, October 15). Coproductions between France and Latin America. *L'actualité*. https://avocatl.com/news/coproductions-between-france-and-latin-america/#:~:text=Coproductions%20between%20France%20and%20Latin%20America%2015%2F10%2F2015%20The,widely%20the%20relationships%20between%20France%20and%20Latin%20America

Lang, J. (2020, November 25). HBO Max snags US streaming rights for Fremantle, Fabula's "La Jauria." *Variety*. https://variety.com/2020/tv/global/hbo-max-snags-u-s-streaming-rights-for-fremantle-fabulas-la-jauria-1234839885/#!

Marsh, C. (2017, May 10). Crews cash in bigtime with international co-productions. *Variety*. https://variety.com/2017/artisans/production/international-co-productions-1202421374/

Marsh, C. (2017, May 10). Crews cash in bigtime with international co-productions. *Variety*. https://variety.com/2017/artisans/production/international-co-productions-1202421374/

Mattelart, A. (1976). Cultural imperialism in the multinational's age. *Instant Research on Peace and Violence 6*(4), 160–174.

Middleton, J. (2020). The effectiveness of audiovisual regulation inside the European Union: The television without frontiers directive and cultural protectionism. *Denver Journal of International Law and Policy 31*(4), 607–627.

Jiménez Pumares, M. (2020). Audiovisual fiction production in the European Union. 2020 Edition. *European Audiovisual Observatory*. https://search.coe.int/observatory/Pages/result_details.aspx?ObjectId=0900001680a206c4

Ramsay, G. (2019). *Who owns the UK media?* London: Media Reform Coalition. https://www.mediareform.org.uk/media-ownership/who-owns-the-uk-media

Richeri, G. (2016). Global film market, regional problems. *Global Media and China 1*(4), 312–330.

Sklair, L. (2001). *The transnational capitalist class*. New York: Wiley.

Statista. (2019). The UK film industry—statistics and facts. Statista.com. https://www-statista-com.pnw.idm.oclc.org/topics/1854/the-uk-film-industry/

Statista. (2020, October). Motion pictures & television & music industry. Statista industry report—Germany. Statista.com.

Stoll, J. (2020). Leading film markets worldwide 2007–2018, by number of films produced. Statista.com. https://www.statista.com/statistics/252727/leading-film-markets-worldwide-by-number-of-films-produced/

Stoll, J. (2021). Italy: Most popular TV series 2018. Statista.com. https://www.statista.com/statistics/913759/most-popular-tv-series-in-italy/

Szalai, G. (2020, July 3). Banijay closes Endemol Shine acquisition, forming global production giant. *Hollywood Reporter.* https://www.msn.com/en-us/tv/news/banijay-closes-endemol-shine-acquisition-forming-global-production-giant/ar-BB16hBgv

Thrift, M. (2017, April 10). Cinema in the rubble: Movies made in the ruins of postwar Germany. *British Film Institute.* https://www2.bfi.org.uk/news-opinion/news-bfi/features/cinema-rubble-movies-made-ruins-postwar-berlin

Tizard, W. (2017, November 2). Hungarian co-productions spread film and TV work throughout Central Europe. *Variety.* https://variety.com/2017/artisans/news/jupiters-moon-hungarian-co-productions-spread-film-and-tv-work-throughout-central-europe-1202605016/#!

UniFrance. (2020). 2019 Report: French films at the international box office. *UniFrance CNC (Centre National du Cinéma et de l'Image Animée).* https://en.unifrance.org/news/15949/2019-report-french-films-at-the-international-box-office

van der Pijl, K. (1998). *Transnational classes and international relations.* New York: Routledge.

Voon, T. (2007). Cultural products and the World Trade Organization World Trade Organization. *Legal Studies Research Studies Research Paper No. 342.* University of Melbourne Law School. http://ssrn.com/abstract=1211605

7

THE HEGEMONIC APPEAL OF SPECTACLE AND DIVERSITY

The information and analysis presented in this book has been concerned almost exclusively with regional transnational media in recognition of the latest reconfigurations of the political economies of media in countries around the world. The changed behavior and operation of national media has been enthusiastically consensual, as domestic media owners desired increased audiences and profits through co-productions and joint ventures with regional and non-regional media. The actions and practices recounted here are the result of the intentional global restructuring of capitalism, especially its insistence on neoliberalism and the privatization of everything. However, the continuing leadership of US, UK, and French media no longer exert imperialist dominance. While their ability to produce defining entertainment and cultural conventions rests on their historic and current benefits of size and scale, the participation by less global regional media indicates the hegemonic pull of structures, practices, forms, and content. Regional transnational media are creating their own entertainment content that benefits the local and regional capitalist order, which cannot be geographically linked to some nation-state because the preferences for self-centered individualism, consumerism, and support for hierarchy and authority are essential to the continued dominance of capitalist classes in every country. Media are instrumental in this process, not just for accumulating wealth, but for popularizing norms and ideologies necessary for expanding neoliberalism and market rule. This is true across borders and cultures, across media structures, forms, and genres.

The entertainment industry contains a broad range of companies in businesses such as telecommunications, television, streaming, music, video games, and live concerts. Many of the leading US media are well-positioned to

DOI: 10.4324/9781003162452-08

globally distribute content either singularly or in partnership with media in other countries. Most of the leading companies are well-known.

Warner Bros. produces several global iconic brands, including Batman, DC Comics, and the transnationally co-produced Monsterverse of King Kong and Godzilla. ATT bought Warner Bros. in 2018 to provide content to its huge telecommunications network. Together ATT and Warner collected $200 billion in revenue during 2020. In 2021, ATT announced a merger of its Warner Bros. assets with Discovery; ATT holds 71% of the partnership (Lee & Hirsch, 2021). Discovery brings popular reality television and pseudo-science show to the merger, along with $10 billion in yearly revenue. The Warner Bros. organization includes CNN, Cartoon Network, TBS, TNT, HBO, and the streaming service HBO Max. Warner is partnered with Viacom CBS on the CW television channel. Warner has multiple transnational joint ventures in Europe, Asia, and Latin America.

Comcast generated $105 billion in revenue in 2020. Comcast owns NBC Universal, Xfinity Stream, and movie producer DreamWorks Animation. Comcast operates broadband, cable and network television, streaming internet, phone, and television and film production, and theme parks. NBC, one of the leading US television networks with 200 affiliate stations, has licensing agreements and joint ventures with media in Germany, Korea, Mexico, and Canada. Comcast's Universal Studios produced the successful blockbusters series *Jurassic Park*, *Fast and Furious*, and *Despicable Me*, in addition to many other popular movies.

Disney is the world's best known entertainment brand. In 2020, its revenues were almost $70 billion. As the leading global entertainment company Disney produces the Marvel superhero movies, as well as popular animation TV and films and Pixar's CGI features. Disney operates theme parks, resorts, a cruise line, broadcast television networks, and now a streaming service, Disney+. Disney has subsidiaries in Europe, Latin America, and India. In 2019, Disney bought most of 21st Century Fox expanding its national and transnational production and distribution.

Vivendi is the leading French mass media conglomerate that produces and distributes entertainment content through its digital and pay television services. Vivendi develops and distributes interactive entertainment and telecommunications services. Vivendi's Groupe Canal+ is a major transnational European filmmaker and television producer. One of Vivendi's largest operations is Universal Music Group, one of the world's biggest music companies with dozens of music labels. With Bolloré, Vivendi's major investor, the two companies took in $44 billion in 2019.

Following the merger of Viacom and CBS in 2019, the merged company's revenues reached $33 billion. Viacom CBS owns Paramount Pictures and the Paramount+ streaming platform. CBS owns MTV, Comedy Central, Nickelodeon, and the free streaming service Pluto TV. Viacom has international affiliates and joint ventures to distribute its television programs and co-produce films in many languages, including the TNMC joint venture Viacom 18 in India. In the US and globally, Viacom CBS operates cable networks, content production and distribution, television stations, and other internet-based businesses and consumer publishing.

Netflix, the global leader in streaming services, garnered $23 billion in 2019 from its over 200 million subscribers. Disrupting the studio to theater distribution norms, Netflix now produces original movie programming, often with transnational partners, that are released straight to streaming. Several of it films have won Academy Awards. US media and transnational media partnerships in Europe, Asia, Latin America, and Africa have launched additional streaming platforms in response to changing technology and audience access. Meanwhile, other transnational media such as Sony have joined with Netflix to produce and distribute first-run films globally (Gonzalez, 2021).

So, Hollywood clearly remains the leading model for film and TV production. However, new culture industry partnerships have also arisen across the world revealing the global development of TNMC joint ventures and co-productions that cannot be simply understood as cultural imperialism. While not global in themselves, these new TNMC formations do not transcend the "long-established historical patterns" of development that reflect the inherited "dispersal of economic, cultural, and political functions across national territories" or "the organizational logics of film production" (Hoyler & Watson, 2017, p. 951). Yet, new co-production infrastructures now include Munich, Vancouver, Beijing, Hong Kong, Sydney, Mumbai, Paris, Babelsberg, and many smaller TNMC operations. Co-production projects may be temporary, involving a range of media, creative artists, actors, and technical workers that are part of more stable systems of social relations. Co-productions have market objectives; they occur within local and national networks of skills and resources that exist before and after each particular joint venture. "Co-productions create transnational film project networks as mechanisms for managing resource interdependencies, within and across countries and national contexts" (Hoyler & Watson, 2017, p. 945) that accumulate through dominant neoliberal capitalist social relations of production.

Overall, these new social relations of production link capitalist owners, investors, and shareholders across nations, as well as organize management and labor within transnational class relations that are neither nation-based nor culturally-specific. Joint ventures exist for a limited time and purpose with temporary organizational configurations, but joint ventures and co-productions have recurring normative practices that establish a new transnational mode of production based on temporary and precarious labor. Transnational media also appropriate cultural diversity whenever and wherever possible to maximize audiences and profits.

The diversity of cultural images and icons presented are artificial, constructed in service to the media owners, their shareholders, and capitalist investors within each country and transnationally. Most countries exhibit the same complexity of culture and class—from the US and its mingling of African-American, Latin American, Asian-American, and all the immigrant nationalities of the 20th century to France with is large population of migrants from its former colonies to those fleeing war in the Middle East. Former colonial countries have even more ethnic and cultural variations. Ethiopia, in the north east of Africa, is a sharp example. Like most African countries after colonialism, Ethiopia never established a unified national cultural identity. At the same time, a landholding elite is being transformed into industrial capitalists with the privatization of textile, energy, and mining. Ethiopians are mostly a concoction peasants consisting of some 80 ethnic groupings. The Oroma account for a third, the Amhara 27 per cent, and the Tigrayans just six per cent of the population, others have smaller populations. Like many other post-colonial countries, the cultural values and practices dominant at any particular moment result from which ethnicity holds economic, political, and military power.

Governments, militaries, and capitalist classes regularly foment ethnic conflict. On the other side of the globe, Myanmar suffers from an oppressive capitalist class that has been unable to win consent for its leadership, instead resorting to ethnic cleansing and mass repression. Notably, Myanmar is a crossroads culture, squeezed between India and China. More than a third of Myanmar's population are ethnic minorities, but not clearly distinct. The British, who colonized Burma, called it a zone of racial instability. "Mayanmar was never a place of neatly packaged racial and ethnic categories," says historian That Myint-U (Beech, 2021). Even for the majority group, the Bamar, ethnic purity is contested. What would a Burmese or Myanmar cultural identity look like? As in most contemporary societies, cultural identities are an amalgamation of colonial impositions, social interaction, appropriation, and construction by the nation's capitalist class and its media.

From Nigeria, to Myanmar, to Mexico and Brazil, following colonialism, cultural identities have been constructed by and for national capitalist classes, in collaboration with capitalist interests from their former imperial power. There has never been a distinct Ethiopian, Myanmar, Nigerian, Brazilian, or Indian unified culture that could present a collective, resistant identity against cultural imperialism.

Capitalist classes in each nation accommodated their former colonial powers and then whole heartedly introduced neoliberal policies with little regard for whatever cultures might still have purchase in their countries. And capitalist classes prospered through privatization and deregulation. In India the top 1% income share was 6% in 1980. Now it stands at 21%. Transnational capitalism has created the same social and economic inequality in every participating neoliberal country—leading to the recurring dramatic protests in India, Myanmar, Colombia, France, and elsewhere.

For media, transnational relations have not improved democratic access to communication either. And despite the abundance of culturally diverse characters, locations, and languages, transnational media has not opened opportunities for more diverse cultural participation. Transnational joint ventures and partnerships have however contributed to media consolidation in most countries, as commercial media producers appropriated cultural diversity as a means to increase the accumulation of wealth by domestic capitalists and their transnational partners.

The transnational capitalist class has no allegiance to any nation or any culture. Governments that do their bidding may coincide with their geographic residence, but that is of secondary importance. TNMCs guarantee that the national governments of each media partner involved will work to facilitate and enforce neoliberal market regulations without regard to any culture or nation. In other words, cultural imperialism has been materially discarded by the transnational capitalist class's collaborative drive for increased accumulation of profit and wealth. Competition among media remains, but it cannot be reduced or reified as a national competition. Media competition resides among vertically and horizontally consolidated transnational formations. In terms of the relations of production and entertainment content there are no US media, French media, or Chinese media.

Commercial media today are a transnational industry; transnational media are owned by a social class consisting of capitalists, their investors, banks, equity funds, and shareholders, which have no particular national loyalty. Any significance attached to national identity refers primarily to the political machinations of government and corporate public relations that occasionally finds short-term strategic use for instigating nationalist sentiments among the public.

As media consolidated and partnered across national and cultural boundaries, the structures and practices that construct global culture no longer expressed strict national identities. Joint ventures, mergers, and partnerships are creating a new transnational media industry, universal in its operation, function, and social impact. Hybrid, local media content further enhances a shared transnational culture of consumerism, authoritarianism, cultural diversity, and spectacle. Emerging transnational media from India, China, Africa, Latin America, and Europe have forged partnerships for the production and distribution of media content amenable to the emerging transnational capitalist order. Reliance, Wanda, Banijay, Naspers, Filmsharks, and other "little giants" of transnational media may not be widely known. However, through shared ventures among themselves and in combination with more recognizable media corporations these TNMCs comprise major components of transnational media and the new global culture industry. As illustrated in the preceding chapters, joint operations of transnational media are not only systematically different, the thematic and ideological content produced clearly appears in film, television, and the larger global culture.

From previous examples, it should be clear that the impulses for collaboration and global expansion by both national/domestic media and existing transnational media, such as Disney and Warner, are largely economic. Of course, profit-seeking corporations need parallel political and ideological systems and supports. The overarching need to find audiences encourages larger TNMCs to rely on franchises, sequels, and reboots that have proven to attract audiences and revenues. At the same time, saturated domestic media markets push both national and TNMCs to find new audiences, new markets. Culturally-diverse, PG-13, fantasy-based action-adventure and animations have emerged as the most successful genre, yet TNMCs need national partners to chart the political pitfalls, the regulatory hurdles, and the variations of cultural preferences from diverse audiences. In tandem, national media need the expertise, resources, and global reach of TNMCs to expand their own operations. Once governments permit transnational partnerships and joint ventures within the nation, transnational operations expand wherever paying audiences can be found.

Nollywood, the Nigerian videofilm industry, and Naspers, a growing South African-based TNMC, provide a final illustration of transnational entertainment production. Naspers, through its M-Net African Magic digital and terrestrial platforms shepherded production and distribution arrangements with national media across southern Africa into its video, cable, and digital operations. Profiting from their TNMC activities in Africa provided Naspers with resources for joint ventures in Europe, including Russia and elsewhere. The "chain" of transnational production, from national regulations to investment and production, including the division of labor for production, the associated content intended to limit cost and maximize audience revenues, the distribution partnerships, and the many, many smaller creative subcontractors are each components of the larger transnational chain of production. Nigerian videos produced in just a few days and then sold quickly before being pirated represent the most extreme example of market-based media with thousands of individual producers hoping to get rich quick from their products, or be "discovered" by some larger media enterprise. The quality, quantity, and ephemeral existence of these entertainment forms did not lack creativity, but they were caught within the borders of global capitalism—eking out an existence on the edge, until those who did nothing to create the form showed up to exploit the best and discard the rest.

Nollywood and Naspers

Africa deserves a full treatment that cannot be delivered here. Until Nollywood became a hot topic for *Variety*, *The Hollywood Reporter*, and the *New York Times*, African media had been marginalized in media research and international communication. Largely this was due to the commercial impulses of much communication research that matches the interests of the media and culture industry. Because the "market" for media entertainment in Africa has been relatively small, major media have not attended to the continent until very recently. Now, combined with the apparent success of Nollywood and the appearance of small but eager middle classes in Nigeria, Ghana, Kenya, and South Africa, TNMCs from Asia, Europe, and the Americas show interest. Indeed, TNMCs are searching for African media partners that can help identify and attract consumers of movie tickets, pay-TV, streaming services, and smartphone entertainment. The field is wide open because across Africa, media entrepreneurs are eager for investors, partners, and distributors—and neoliberal governments have deregulated protections of public resources. A few TNMCs have gained experience and already made transnational deals with Nigerian producers.

The issue of cultural imperialism has some residual meaning when addressing post-colonial countries like Nigeria, Ghana, Ethiopia, and others because "Africa has a huge hinterland of culture not yet exploited by capitalism" (Haynes, 2018, p. 26). Precisely how these cultures can be incorporated into neoliberal capitalism remains to be determined. In the process, South African media, which some may see as a proxy for Western cultural imperialism, are primed to offer incentives to emerging media producers in sub-Saharan Africa. Of course, as presented throughout this book, the boundaries between domestic and foreign cultural influences are not always clearly demarcated (Kraidy, 2006, p. 6). Uchenna Onuzulike (2009) has suggested that cultural hybridity is a synthesis of distinct cultural identities (p. 177)—but even that distinctiveness is elusive.

In the case of Nigeria, for instance, in addition to the major Yoruba, Hausa, and Igbo groups, hundreds of other ethnicities speak their own languages and practice their own religions and rituals, while sharing similar values toward nature, family, community, and the cosmos. The UNESCO Convention on cultural diversity recognized variations among humanity, noting that one's cultural heritage can be "expressed, augmented, and transmitted through a variety of cultural expressions" (UNESCO, 2005). Yet, the Convention offered only a vague conception of cultural diversity that conveniently left aside diversity within a nation. In Nigeria, a multiethnic country of almost 200 million, cultural distinctiveness is contested but relative. Even the vaunted African communalism that privileges the collective over the individual applies chiefly to the local ethnic group, which is often violently defended. On the other hand, for younger Africans, presumed cultural differences are insignificant because "life is more or less the same whatever the country" (Ugochukwu, 2013). In both cases, social class is a primary ingredient, if even through its absence in some indigenous egalitarian groups. A brief look at Nigeria should help summarize some of the claims this book has made about social class and transnationalism.

In the 1990s, neoliberalism and the structural adjustment programs implemented by the Nigerian government reduced funding for filmmaking. With few public theaters, increased access to video players, unconstrained legal limits, and the opportunistic entrepreneurial production and sales of short videos, Nigeria's video film production (termed Nollywood) became a global media phenomenon. According to the United Nations, more than a million people work in media production in Nigeria (UNESCO, 2009). Although touted as the second biggest movie producer after India, using common international standards for what constitute films, only a handful of movies are produced in Nigeria each year (Haynes, 2018, p. 21). In fact, for decades, the one million media workers in Nigeria produced films grossing only $12 million a year. More notably, early Nollywood production consisted almost entirely of short, inexpensive, poorly-produced videotaped films expressing culturally diverse but often stereotypical representations of Nigerian indigenous communities based on colonialist tropes, displaying "witchcraft, ritual killing, and crass immorality" (Tobechukwu, 2009, p. 76). Production was based in Lagos; most films were in Yoruba. At first, lacking access to studio production, thousands of VHS tapes and DVDs replete with voodoo and witchcraft were filmed quickly in the street (Okeowo, 2016)—about 50 per week—and sold informally at kiosks, shops, and along the streets. The more recent appearance of Hausa videos in the Islamic north of Nigeria have also spread to Niger and Chad. Ironically, Yoruba and Igbo producers make almost 50% of the Hausa films. Although charges of Yoruba imperialism have yet to be uttered, for at least one scholar there is a "cultural neo-colonialism of the African continent by Nollywood films" (Ugochukwu, 2013).

Given the mass response to Nollywood films, in the last 15 years, the Nigerian government, the World Bank, transnational co-productions, and foreign investment has provided more resources, bigger budgets, and more access to international distribution, especially through film festivals. Now, those same 1 million media workers produce films that generate almost $1 billion in yearly revenue (Olaoluwa, 2019). Unsurprisingly, Nigerian movie producers "are emulating Western lives" while simultaneously tweaking and complementing the hegemony of the capitalist culture industry (Onuzulike, 2009, p. 184) using African inflections. Many early Nigerian films used the myths of the colonizers, along with pop music hits in popular film genres that displayed an excess of love and singing in Hausa and an excess of blood and witchcraft in English and Yoruba to present and also escape the current social conditions of instability and suffering (Zajc, 2009, pp. 69, 83). Yet, despite the richness of cultural diversity within Nigeria, in fact, Nigerian video film production articulates a cultural heritage that is synthetic and also conducive to consumerism, individualism, and neoliberal market norms.

With new media technologies, the production and sale of videotapes and DVDs was replaced by television networks, internet access, smartphones, and streaming platforms. The political economy of transnational media entertainment has supplanted previous informal structures and practices. As Jonathon Haynes (2018) would have it: Nollywood has been corporatized as a new capitalist sector (p. 5). Nollywood producers have formed partnerships with media in South Africa, France, Britain, and the US. No longer, if ever, are Nigerian videos the "real voice of the people" (Haynes, 2018, p. 4). Yet, we should also note that Nigerian culture was never completely distinct or representative of the cultural diversity of the country, rather Nollywood was always commercial—albeit sharply critical from a popular perspective.

Haynes (2018) identified several interlocked developments of this new political economy of Nigerian entertainment. First, transnational partnerships with Nollywood producers dominate film and television production. Two, distribution forms have changed from video to television, cable, pay-TV, and internet streaming platforms. Three, due to transnational partnerships that insist on low costs and high returns, television series predominate because they are cheaper than films. Fourth, multiplexes have reappeared in Nigerian cities, especially in upscale malls that cater to the new professional middle classes that prospered under neoliberal privatization. Additionally, production to scale has increased smartphone use and lowered costs, changing the means of entertainment exhibition and access. Moreover, the market-driven Nigerian media industry now "transcends nation-state boundaries" (Arewa, 2015, p. 373).

US media has limited presence in Nigeria. The largest TNMC presence in Nigeria is Naspers, the South African media company with media investments and joint ventures around the world. Naspers has a 30% stake in China's Tencent; 28% in Russian internet giant Mail.ru; investments in Amazon's Middle East Souq.com; and shares in the videogame maker Zynga. Naspers operates the African satellite network DStv; the pay-TV MultiChoice; the production company M-Net and its satellite bouquet of channels under Africa Magic—broadcasts to 53 countries. Africa Magic includes stations for Angola, Mozambique, Uganda, Botswana, Zimbabwe, and Ghana, all which broadcast in local languages. Most content for Africa Magic comes from its partnerships with national media, especially Nigerian producers. Africa Magic channels express "corporate cultural politics" (Haynes, 2018, p. 16) even with their "hastily-prepared and poorly-edited subtitles" (Ugochukwu, 2013). Africa Magic Epic is the most popular channel with its traditional, pre-colonial village settings—videos coming from Eastern Nigeria where the low end of Nollywood productions are centered. These are not films that reflect contemporary popular culture, but films feeding nostalgia for a fictional, yet comforting prior world. Africa Magic has other channels for urban youth and elite viewers that prefer premium content. M-Net adjusts each channel to best exploit each audience. Through M-Net, a South African TNMC relies on multiple transnational partners in Nigeria to co-produce profitable content distributed across the continent.

Naspers has only a couple of competitors. The most challenging is probably Chinese StarTimes, a broadcast, satellite, and internet company serving 30 African countries with 13 million subscribers. StarTimes has media joint ventures in Tanzania and Zambia. The other major provider has less effect on production. iROKO, a British-Nigerian internet subscription company, with Swedish and American investors, delivers on-demand Nigerian videos to subscribers in Africa, North America, and Europe. iROKO also offers two channels on Britian's Sky TV. iROKO has distribution deals with YouTube, Amazon, iTunes, and several international airlines. iROKO claims to be one of the "largest funders, co-producers, and commissioners of content in Nollywood" (Okeowo, 2016). It has content partnerships with media in UK, Zimbabwe, Nigeria, and Latin America, but none rival the co-production output of Africa Magic. In 2012, Vivendi's Canal launched Nollywood TV with French dubbing. Meanwhile, iROKO and smaller Nigerian studios and individual producers develop skits and clips for YouTube, including "brand-infused content" that blurs distinctions between fiction and commercials—underscoring the primary commercial motives for Nollywood video production.

Further evidence of the pre-existing commercialism of Nigerian media comes from the smash hit films *The Wedding Party* (2016, 2017). Not only did the films display celebrity stars, slick high-production values, and multiple plots and characters, they also featured expensive, glamorous clothing, autos, and settings. The two films grossed $4 million in an impoverished country. Netflix picked up both films.

One of the co-producers, the vertically-consolidated studio Film One signed a 2019 co-production deal with China's HuaHua to make the first major Nigerian-Chinese movie. Film One also won distribution rights for Disney films in West Africa. Meanwhile, ROK Studio merged with Canal+ to create more movies in French. Of course, transnational partners provide things Nigerian filmmakers have always needed: "bigger budgets from stable sources, superior equipment, good access to international distribution, a chance to feel like a full professional and practice one's craft..." (Haynes, 2018, p. 13). Yet, in Nigeria, as elsewhere, only a few studios reached the top, creating something of an oligopoly where before there were myriad small producers (See Table 7.1).

TABLE 7.1 Top Five Nigerian Films (2016–2020)

Title	Year	Gross	Languages	Distributor
Omo Ghetto: Saga	2020	$2.7 M	English	FilmOne
Wedding Party	2016	$1.7 M	Yoruba, Igbo, English	FilmOne
Wedding Party 2	2017	$1.65 M	Yoruba, Igbo, English	FilmOne
Chief Daddy	2018	$1.5 M	Yoruba, English	FilmOne
Sugar Rush	2019	$1.1 M	Yoruba, English	FilmOne

NOTE: All are comedies. All stress wealth and consumption as key to happiness and success in romance, business, and relations.

Also, as elsewhere, "corporate neoliberalization of Nollywood distribution introduced inequalities" (Haynes, 2018, p. 10) determined by social class. Even exhibition is social class informed: from luxury flights, film festivals, and theater premiers for the conspicuous rich to local Nigerian cinema in exclusive gated neighborhoods and then to pay-TV subscription services. Perhaps in a couple years, affordable DVDs will be available to the general population. Internet streaming and the massive digital divide is also social class determined. In Nigeria, two-thirds of the population lives on less than $2 a day. The neoliberal consumer boom missed the overwhelming majority in all its cultural diversity. In short, Nollywood's transnational development has been gated by technology and subscriptions available only to capitalists and their managers, just as solidly as the gated communities in Lekki, Ikoyi, Alausa, and elsewhere in Nigeria (Haynes, 2018, p. 12). In West Africa, colonialism sucked and skimmed local economies for profit rather than imposing mines and plantations. Cultural imperialism certainly exuded class culture, but did not disrupt the post-colonialist national culture.

Today, transnationalism propels and consolidates social class inequality, as co-productions shift away from traditional cultural identities and austerity continues to crunch filmmakers lacking transnational connections. Nollywood's direction is being set by a new class of capitalist overlords, as Nigerian media owners profit from "a kind of cultural strip mining: profiting from a cadre of personnel, a star system, a way of working, a style, a set of genres, an assembled audience—that they did nothing to create" (Haynes, 2018, p. 15). Nigeria is one of the most linguistically and culturally diverse countries in Africa, and we must avoid essentializing Nigerian and African identities. The search for "authenticity" is not useful in the 21st century—unless we want to accept the "cultural references, colloquialisms, mythologies, and the designed look" of Disney's *Black Panther* (2018) as evidence of an "unprecedented commitment to authenticity," as Imruh Bakari (2018, p. 11) enthused. Rather than appearing as a disruption to the status quo, the spectacle of *Black Panther* constructs an effective hegemonic overture to cultural diversity and individualism within neoliberal capitalism. The cultural autonomy that Bakari sees in the hero T'Challa is essentially an ideological spokesmodel for hierarchy and accommodation to global capital.

More to the point, as journalist Emily Witt (2017) concluded in her book on Nollywood, "globalization did not produce a single cultural capital, but several of them," whereby "humanity now has a visual vernacular: in Hollywood, Bollywood, Nollywood, Korean drama, and the Latin American telenovela the symbols of material wealth are imported bottles of liquor, big watches, sleek cars, and carefully styled hair... Nollywood marks this phase of self-writing, where the assertion of Nigerian identity is not conducted in opposition to the forces of globalization and multiculturalism, but within them" (Witt, 2017, pp. 112–113).

In other words, in structure and content, media transnationalism uses class-constructed Nigerian identities to applaud cosmopolitan styles based on self-interest and private profits at the expense of humanity. Transnational media production will expand, as will its content "selling a neoliberal consumer and professional lifestyle of the kind displayed in many of iROKO's web series" (Haynes, 2018, p. 16). Historically South African movies catered to the country's Afrikaans white minority. Immediately after apartheid was overturned, films featured poverty and political struggle. Now, as neoliberalism benefitted professional managerial class and heightened economic inequalities, a flood of transnationally co-produced South African films emphasize wealth—"mansion parties with bouncers, infinity pools soaked in neon lights... a trendy art gallery" with "chicly dressed glamorous housewives and high-powered lawyers" (Goldbaum, 2021). Netflix partners, as does China's StarTimes, Vivendi's Nollywood TV, and South Africa's ShowMax streaming service, among others. This is not Western imperialism. It is the skimming of profits from rising middle-class audiences and consumers by collaborating consolidated national media owners in Nigeria, Ghana, South Africa, and across the continent working with other transnational producers.

The Hegemony of Transnational Content, Production, and Distribution

Each chapter in this book is thick with multiple examples of regional and trans-regional co-productions, joint ventures, and partnerships. Perhaps too much information distracted from the primary concern—national media have built alliances with other national media to produce and distribute culturally diverse entertainment that nonetheless carries messages beneficial to neoliberal capitalism and its capitalist classes both nationally and globally. One very important conclusion from this dense overview of regional transnational media activities in India, China, Latin America, and Europe must be that cultural imperialism no longer dominates media or culture in any geographic region. While Hollywood and US television programming continues to appear in theaters and on screens everywhere, they no longer overwhelm because new transnational and national productions have adopted and adapted the lessons of privatization, deregulation, and competition. Crucially, this is not because national media have defended the interests of some authentic, democratic culture on behalf of the public. Rather, the owners of media companies making regional transnational entertainment products enthusiastically consented to the protocols of privatization, consolidation, austerity, and market norms.

The top grossing films in Korea demonstrate how posing an opposition between national culture and US cultural imperialism misses the cross-pollination of neoliberal capitalism. The top grossing films in Korea include US blockbusters, but since 2015 Korean co-productions had the largest

TABLE 7.2 Top Grossing Films in Korea Since 2015

Title	Year	Admissions	Distributor
Extreme Job	2019	16.3 Million	CJ Entertainment
Along with the Gods	2017	14.4 Million	CJ Entertainment
Avengers Endgame	2019	13.9 Million	Disney
Frozen II	2019	13.7 Million	Disney
Veteran	2015	13.4 Million	CJ Entertainment
Aladdin	2019	12.5 Million	Disney

audiences, while the 2014 Korean war action film, *The Admiral*, remains the leading box office film with 17.6 million viewers (See Table 7.2).

Notably, CJ Entertainment is a leading South Korean transnational producing videogames, films, television, and internet services, with multiple regional joint ventures with Chinese, Thai, Vietnamese and Indonesian media, as well as partnerships with North American media, including Warner Bros. Thus, a regional mid-major transnational media company produces and distributes films as appealing as Hollywood superhero and fantasy films. The leading Korean movies are all action movies, with the same codes and conventions as action movies in India, China, and the US: spectacle, heroic action, and defense of hierarchy. Transnational media has effectively incorporated the values, beliefs, and ideologies of neoliberal capitalism—willingly—without imperialist imposition or subterfuge.

Coercion and Consent

Over the centuries, capitalists and their state powers have energetically used forces of violence and coercion to protect their wealth and their right to accumulate more. Global colonization, two world wars, recurring regional wars, continuing interventions, clandestine operations, and more recently economic sanctions have been used to defend the private property of the robber barons of each era. Still, for transnational corporations and their government allies, peaceful cooperation by other social classes, even reluctant acceptance, is preferable and more profitable. "Corporations and other establishment organizations co-opt almost unconsciously. They send ambitious young people powerful signals about what level of dissent will be tolerated while embracing dissident values as a form of marketing. By taking what was dangerous and anesthetizing it, they turn it into a product or a brand" (Brooks, 2021).

Thus, political campaigns, news media, and above all, mass entertainment and popular culture teach, persuade, and socialize populations toward consent to beliefs, values, and norms acceptable and essential to capitalist social relations. Undoubtedly consent begins at home, in school, and at work. In our other eight plus hours of each day, media entertainment provides some escape from drudgery, some distraction from social problems, and some visceral pleasure. At the same time, messages within entertainment trumpet values useful to neoliberalism—self-interest, consumerism, individual responsibility, and deference to authority—while downplaying democracy and social justice.

These transnational messages are nothing new. A markedly anti-democratic emphasis has characterized Hollywood films for decades. In an extended review of democracy in the movies, the *New York Times* film critic, A. O. Scott (2021), provided several examples of popular films that portrayed the "contradictions, inconsistencies, and outright delusions" about democracy exhibiting "reasons for faith and grounds for skepticism in the same gesture." In other words, the media construct hegemonic appeals for audience consent. Referring to *Dawn of the Planet of the Apes* (2014), Scott noted that a "benevolent tyranny—the rule of the smart and sensitive in the name of progress and good sense—is the political ideal of 21st-century Hollywood. It defines the utopian horizon of the Marvel universe, where a politburo of super-empowered, unelected strongmen (and a few women) defend the interests of a passive and vulnerable public." Thus, Scott acknowledges the passive and incapable citizens of TNMC action movies. He also determined that the 1991 pseudo-feminist film *Thelma and Louise* distracted audiences from its fatalism, but ultimately, according to Hollywood, "the drive for freedom is strong, but the law of gravity—the inertia of propriety, patriarchy and state power—will win in the end." As also apparent in contemporary action movies, one may challenge, but none can overcome the system. Likewise, the edgy reincarnation of Batman in the *Dark Knight* (2007) as "a maverick, an anti-institutional player whose disregard for rules and procedures marks him as a rebel, an outlaw on the side of the good guys" (Scott, 2021) has become a standard trope in transnational action movies, where democracy is irrelevant to the vigilante defense of law and order for the elite. In *The Wolf of Wall Street* (2013), Hollywood does its best to reconcile capitalism and democracy as the film "oscillates between disgust at its selfish, obnoxious, amoral protagonist and giddy fascination with his exuberant, unabashed greed" (Scott, 2021) Thus, Scott concludes that any "indictment of the money culture, or at least of the shallow scammers who treat the serious business of capitalism like a casino" is embedded in a dazzling and distracting spectacle of drugs, cars, boats, fashion and Margot Robbie. These and other movies gleefully fulfill the ideological needs of capital by privileging consumer goods, condoning extralegal violence against purported enemies, and elevating authority and power—which helps win consent for existing social relations of power by pleasing viewers through spectacle and diversity. What Scott referenced as US movie messages have become central in transnational productions—without coercion, subterfuge, or financial pressures from any cultural imperialism. Equally important, as chapters in this book have shown, European, Indian, Chinese, Latin American, and African transnational entertainment contain similar content in form and theme. A non-nation specific, multilingual, and multicultural individualism, consumerism, and authoritarianism has become the global cultural norm.

The ideology of action movies and telenovelas are apparent on reflection, but at the time of delivery the spectacle, the drama, the framing, music, images, and vibrant scenes overwhelm viewers who often suspend their critical abilities during the excitement and seduction of the stories, images, and spectacles. In the process—a process repeated thousands of times in television programs and supplemented by feature films and mini-series—viewers discover which behaviors, which characters, and which values are most effective and beneficial. We learn what is good and just. We observe the proper response and behavior to adversity and opportunity. We discover that royalty, authority, vigilante violence, and self-interest are the means to happiness. This doesn't register as a list of claims and data, but occurs seamlessly through the magic of sound, motion, color, and narrative. Being pleased opens us to being persuaded. If it works for Salman Khan, Jackie Chan, Til Schweiger, and Dwayne Johnson or Li Bingbing, Nicole Kidman, Andhadhun Tabu, and Juliette Binoche, it should work for me… Inclusive of challenges and criticisms of a corrupt social order, as in all action movies with spectacles and diversity like those summarized in the chapters on India and China, entertainment narratives incorporate critiques to better win consent for the existing social order (that just needs a few personnel changes or modest reforms). Consent for the movie narratives all but previews consent for the political and economic relations of society. Identifying with protagonists and their actions in defense of the existing fictional order opens the possibility for viewers to accept hierarchies and authorities off the screen.

Global Media, Global Culture, Global Power

The strength of capitalist globalization is transnational production, assisted by national deregulation allowing for foreign direct investment, joint ventures, partnerships, mergers, and equity partners seeking profits—all based on local labor that been constrained from developing transnational relations with labor elsewhere. Moreover, the relations between structures of transnational partnerships and content of transnational productions reveals how entertainment produced by TNMCs large and small expresses values, norms, beliefs, and ideologies favorable to consumerism, social hierarchy, and deference to authority—practices necessary for both transnational media and for market dominance over social decisions. Media are more than just institutions and corporations; they are producers of global culture, which includes the culture of self, consumption, individualism, and consent to authority. The prevalence of cultural diversity in most TNMC film and television is the logical outcome of the political economy of TNMCs which need enthusiastic audiences and fans from multiple cultures, including those within most countries. Villains, superheroes, and sensational special-effects help attract paying audiences while reproducing the social relations of production and consumption necessary for the success of TNMCs and neoliberal globalization.

Spectacle and Diversity

As noted in the Introduction and demonstrated in each chapter, spectacular actions and culturally diverse characters and settings attract and please mass audiences. Delightful visceral responses thrill and tingle, as constructed narratives and ideologies nurture and socialize. We don't often recognize the social and political cultivation of acquiescence that occur amid explosions, chases, and the conflicts. With transnational media producing and broadcasting similar codes and conventions for entertainment to audiences everywhere, a hearty applause for cultural diversity arises. Yet, the appearance of more national and regional entertainment has not overcome the concerns about cultural imperialism—which noted the lack of democracy with the dominance of US media entertainment and advertising.

Transnational media owned and organized by companies and investors from multiple nations has elbowed aside US dominance. Transnational media has not opened communication and entertainment to public access and participation by working classes, indigenous groups, and their allies. Rather, transnational media create entertainment that narratively dismisses democracy in favor of hierarchy and protagonist self-interest clothed in crude representations of commodified conceptions of cultural identities that smooth the rough edges of stereotypical archetypes: Women are independent, but must be fashionably attractive; Chinese, Indian, Brazilian male heroes are sympathetic and ethical, but still powerfully masculine and capable of violence; Non-European actors take lead roles comforting audiences with barely disguised racial stereotypes, such as *The Intouchables* (2011) that attracted almost 20 million viewers.

Thus, although transnational media has displaced cultural imperialism, the dominance of neoliberal capitalism has become even stronger in media structures and content. Culturally accessible entertainment validates constructed national and cultural identities based on nostalgic beliefs, familiar images, and undemocratic social values useful to national and international capitalist classes. One of the dangers of cultural imperialism critiques was always that nationalist appeals by commercial media, film studios, and television owners would direct opposition to US or Western influence toward support for self-serving national media. Under the guise of advocating for cultural independence against foreign interference, the ideology of individualism and support for hierarchies was popularized. Transnational media has improved the hegemonic appeal of capitalism by replacing foreign dominance and influence with home-grown entertainment that more effectively wins consent for the social norms of accepting the authority of elites, managers, and other authorities while reducing social problems to individual choices and responsibilities. Every drama and spectacle of fantasy action, comedy action, war action, and animation features rests on the premise that each individual through luck and pluck can achieve happiness and success while remaining in their proper social position—whether at the end of street in *Avendia Brasil* (2012), as a Gaul Soldier on the Silk Road in *Asterix* (2021), or the African immigrant caregiver in *Intouchables* (2011). When Disney and Warner Bros. movies made these hierarchical assertions, the cultural settings, language, and behaviors of characters could sometimes be recognized as contrary and disruptive to national cultural values. When those same messages are carried by regional transnational media telling geographically and linguistically familiar stories, the ideological assumptions and suggestions are less obvious.

What Nigerian producer Femi Odugbemi (who was quoted in the Introduction) recognized about Nigeria applies everywhere. Media are political. Media only work for those in charge. To entertain, to show, to tell, to communicate depends on access to producing and distributing media content. Transnational media demonstrates that Hollywood and other global media giants are not the only ones capable of providing news and entertainment.

It is necessary and urgent for citizens everywhere to recognize that transnational media are also not the only ones capable of providing news and entertainment. Public access to media must be championed, so that cultural diversity is voiced and acted in stories told by people from those cultures, however conceived. Fights for national self-determination and independence defeated colonialism. A similar consciousness of our collective interests is necessary now. We need our own international non-capitalist collective movement for human independence to overcome commercial media, consumer culture, and reigning neoliberal transnational and national capitalist dominance. Transnationalism of and by national capitalist classes was conceived and organized to further their own economic and political interests. The global working class, indigenous peoples, and their allies need to create and construct our own media and other social institutions to further the social interests of humanity. And it must be more than a radical mini-series on some screen.

References

Arewa, O. B. (2015). Nollywood and African cinema: Cultural diversity and the global entertainment industry. In I. Calboli, & S. Ragavan (Eds.), *Diversity in intellectual property: identities, interests, and intersections* (pp. 367–383). Cambridge: Cambridge University Press

Bakari, I. (2018). African film in the 21st century: Some notes to a provocation. *Communication Cultures in Africa* 1(1). https://communicationculturesinafrica.com/articles/abstract/10.21039/cca.8/v

Beech, H. (2021, April 30). "Now we are united": Myanmar's ethnic divisions soften after coup. *New York Times.* https://www.nytimes.com/2021/04/30/world/asia/myanmar-ethnic-minority-coup.html?action=click&module=RelatedLinks&pgtype=Article

Brooks, D. (2021, May 14). This is how wokeness ends. *New York Times*, A 22.

Goldbaum, C. (2021, May 11). Moving past the struggles of apartheid and poverty. *New York Times*, A7.

Gonzalez, U. (2021, April 8). Sony movies to stream on Netflix, not Starz, in new multiyear deal. *The Wrap*. https://www.thewrap.com/netflix-and-sony-pictures-ink-exclusive-multiyear-film-licensing-deal/

Haynes, J. (2018). Keeping up: The corporatization of Nollywood's economy and paradigms for studying African screen media. *Africa Today 64*(4), 3–29.

Hoyler, M., & Watson, A. (2017). Framing city networks through temporary projects: (Trans)national film production beyond 'Global Hollywood.' *Urban Studies 56*(5), 943–959.

Kraidy, M. (2006). *Hybridity: The cultural logic of globalization*. Philadelphia: Temple University Press.

Lee, E., & Hirsch, L. (2021, May 19). AT&T is returning to its roots after cutting off bad connection. *New York Times* B1, B1, B4.

Okeowo, A. (2016, February 22). The Netflix of Africa doesn't need Hollywood to win. *Bloomberg.com*. https://www.bloomberg.com/news/features/2016-02-22/the-netflix-of-africa-doesn-t-need-hollywood-to-win

Olaoluwa, J. (2019, October 7). Nigeria's movie industry, Nollywood generates about $1 billion yearly—Afreximbank. *Nairametrics.com*. https://nairametrics.com/2019/10/07/nigerias-movie-industry-nollywood-generates-about-1-billion-yearly-afreximbank/

Onuzulike, U. (2009). Nollywood: Nigerian videofilms as a cultural and technological hybridity. *Intercultural Communication Studies 18*(1), 176–188.

Scott, A. (2021, May 13). What I learned about democracy from the movies. *New York Times*. https://www.nytimes.com/2021/05/13/movies/democracy-dark-knight-wolf-wall-street.html

Tobechukwu, N. (2009). Nollywood, communication technologies and indigenous cultures in a globalized world: The Nigerian dilemma. (D-net communications, Norway). *International Journal of Science and Management Sciences 4*, 62–83. https://www.researchgate.net/publication/340428668_Nollywood_New_Communication_Technologies_and_Indigenous_Cultures_in_a_Globalized_World_The_Nigerian_Dilemma

Ugochukwu, F. (2013). Nollywood across languages—Issues in dubbing and subtitling. *Journal of Intercultural Communication 43*. https://www.academia.edu/2633390/Nollywood_across_languages_issues_in_dubbing_and_subtitling

UNESCO (United Nations Education, Social, and Cultural Organization). (2005). *The convention on the protection and promotion of the diversity of cultural expressions*. https://en.unesco.org/creativity/convention

UNESCO, Institute for Statistics (2009). *International survey on feature film statistics*. Montreal: UIS.

Witt, E. (2017). *Nollywood: The making of a film empire*. New York: Columbia Global Reports.

Zajc, M. (2009). Nigerian video film cultures. *Anthropological Notebooks 15*(1), 65–85.

INDEX

Note: Page numbers in *italics* indicate figures and **bold** indicate tables in the text.

9780367754174